Oil, Dollars, Debt, and (

The Global Curse of Black Gold

Oil, Dollars, Debt, and Crises studies the causes of the current oil and global financial crisis and shows how America's and the world's growing dependence on oil has created a repeating pattern of banking, currency, and energy-price crises. Unlike other books on the current financial crisis, which have focused on U.S. indebtedness and American trade and economic policy, *Oil, Dollars, Debt, and Crises* shows the reader a more complex picture in which transfers of wealth to and from the Middle East result in a perfect storm of global asset and financial market bubbles, increased unrest, terrorism and geopolitical conflicts, and eventually rising costs for energy. Only by addressing long-term energy policy challenges in the West, economic development challenges in the Middle East, and the investment horizons of financial market players can policy makers ameliorate the forces that have been causing repeating global economic crises.

Mahmoud A. El-Gamal, Ph.D, is Chair of the Department of Economics and Professor of Economics and Statistics at Rice University in Houston, Texas, where he also holds the endowed Chair in Islamic Economics, Finance, and Management. Before joining Rice in 1998, he was an Associate Professor of Economics at the University of Wisconsin in Madison. He has also worked as an Assistant Professor of Economics at the University of Rochester and the California Institute of Technology. During 1995–6, he worked as an Economist in the Middle East Department of the International Monetary Fund. During the second half of 2004, he served as scholar in residence on Islamic finance at the U.S. Department of Treasury. He has published extensively in the areas of econometrics, economic dynamics, financial economics, economics of the Middle East, and the economic analysis of Islamic law. His most recent book is *Islamic Finance: Law, Economics, and Practice* (Cambridge University Press, 2006).

Amy Myers Jaffe is the Wallace S. Wilson Fellow for Energy Studies at the James A. Baker III Institute for Public Policy and Associate Director of the Rice University Energy Program. Her research focuses on oil geopolitics, strategic energy policy, and energy economics. She is coeditor of *Natural Gas and Geopolitics: From 1970 to 2040* (Cambridge University Press, 2005, with David G. Victor and Mark W. Hayes) and *Energy in the Caspian Region: Present and Future* (2002). She has published widely in academic journals and edited collections, including the keynote article "Energy Security: Meeting the Growing Challenge of National Oil Companies" in the *Whitehead Journal of Diplomacy and International Relations* (Summer 2007) and "The Persian Gulf and the Geopolitics of Oil" in *Survival* (Spring 2006). Ms. Jaffe served as project director of the Council on Foreign Relations task force on strategic energy policy. She currently serves as a strategic advisor to the American Automobile Association on developing an AAA members' voice on U.S. energy policy debates.

Oil, Dollars, Debt, and Crises

The Global Curse of Black Gold

Mahmoud A. El-Gamal

Rice University

Amy Myers Jaffe

Rice University

Foreword by James A. Baker III

CAMBRIDGE UNIVERSITY PRESS
Cambridge, New York, Melbourne, Madrid, Cape Town, Singapore,
São Paulo, Delhi, Dubai, Tokyo

Cambridge University Press
32 Avenue of the Americas, New York, NY 10013-2473, USA

www.cambridge.org
Information on this title: www.cambridge.org/9780521720700

First published 2010

Printed in the United States of America

A catalog record for this publication is available from the British Library.

Library of Congress Cataloging in Publication data
El-Gamal, Mahmoud A., 1963–
Oil, dollars, debt, and crises : the global curse of black gold / Mahmoud A. El-Gamal,
Amy Myers Jaffe.
p. cm.
Includes bibliographical references and index.
ISBN 978-0-521-89614-6 (hardback)
1. Petroleum industry and trade.   2. Petroleum products – Prices.   3. Financial crises.
I. Jaffe, Amy.   II. Title.
HD9560.5.E42   2009
338.2′7282–dc22   2009038039

ISBN 978-0-521-89614-6 Hardback
ISBN 978-0-521-72070-0 Paperback

Contents

List of Illustrations

List of Tables

Foreword

The current economic and financial crisis – by all appearances, the worst since World War II – has already generated a vast amount of commentary. Some have been polemical. Some have been measured. Analysis has ranged from the well-informed to the superficial. But most have, understandably, focused on the immediate causes of the crisis. An unsustainable real estate bubble, shoddy credit standards, disastrous risk management by major banks, counterproductive incentives for managers, the rise of esoteric and unregulated financial instruments, and broad-scale failure by regulatory agencies are just a few of them. All are important. And all will need to be addressed by policy-makers and financial executives as they forge strategies to avoid similar crises in the future.

Yet there are even larger factors at work. A number of observers, for instance, have stressed the role of structural global imbalances in creating an environment conducive to the world-wide financial turmoil witnessed in 2008. Surely, the perverse Sino-American financial relationship – under which, essentially, relatively poor Chinese loan their savings to relatively affluent American consumers – played an important part in fostering the loose credit that helped precipitate the current crisis.

Oil, Dollars, Debt, and Crises by Mahmoud A. El-Gamal and Amy M. Jaffe addresses another structural global imbalance. Their subject is the huge transfer of resources from energy-importing to energy-exporting countries. This transfer, prompted by the rise in petroleum and natural gas prices that began in the late 1990s and sharply accelerated in the middle of the present decade, created giant reserves of petrodollars that, in turn, helped to overheat financial markets in the United States and elsewhere.

The book is remarkable on several counts. First is its timing. Begun in 2006, before today's financial turmoil exploded into public consciousness, *Oil, Dollars, Debt, and Crises* is impressively prescient in highlighting the risks associated with major imbalances in the global financial system.

Second, the book moves well beyond economic analysis to assess other factors that shape production decisions by major energy exporters. These factors include institutional weakness, domestic constituencies, internal opposition movements, and, not least, an often harsh geopolitical environment. The last is particularly salient. The world's most important energy producing region – the Middle East – is one long characterized by simmering animosities and outright conflict.

Third, El-Gamal and Jaffe detail the role of international energy markets – largely denominated in dollars – in sustaining the United States' unique role as supplier of the world's reserve currency. Ironically, the current crisis has seen a flight *to* the dollar, as international investors lower their exposure in riskier currencies. But the long-run viability of the dollar as the de facto reserve currency of the world (absent a sustained increase in our national savings rate) is for the first time beginning to be an open question.

Above all, the authors continually – and rightly – stress the *global* nature of the challenges confronting us. Even so large an economy as the United States can no longer be analyzed in isolation. Chinese fiscal policy matters. So do European interest rates. And so does military conflict in major energy producing regions such as the Persian Gulf. The integration of the world economy has led to substantial gains from increased trade and investment. But it has also raised the risk of financial contagion. And it has made international coordination all the more important *and* difficult. Such cooperation was hard enough when I was U.S. Secretary of the Treasury from 1985 to 1988. Today, with immensely greater capital flows, critical new players like China, and a plethora of opaque financial instruments, the task is even more daunting. The hard reality – rather than the easy rhetoric – of globalization infuses *Oil, Dollars, Debt, and Crises*.

I know and admire both the authors. Mahmoud is a brilliant scholar with an impressive background that includes work as the International Monetary Fund's desk economist for the West Bank and Gaza. Amy is one of the nation's top energy experts, with decades of experience with oil and gas markets. Together, they give *Oil, Dollars, Debt, and Crises* a richness of analytic texture rare in books of its kind. Both, I am proud to say, are affiliated with the James A. Baker III Institute for Public Policy at Rice University.

We may be certain that economists and historians will be assessing today's crisis for years to come. Indeed, the current turmoil has revealed the extent to which, seventy years after the event, informed observers still differ sharply on the causes of the Great Depression. In short, the debate about today's crisis has just begun. *Oil, Dollars, Debt, and Crises* will surely hold an early and estimable part in it.

James A. Baker, III, Honorary Chair
Baker Institute for Public Policy, Rice University

Preface

We began to work on this book in late 2006. At the time, we felt that the problem of petrodollars was not receiving sufficient attention, a short presentation by Saleh Nsouli of the International Monetary Fund (IMF) on "petrodollar recycling and global imbalances" in March 2006 notwithstanding. Discussion of global trade and financial imbalances and the sustainability of the Dollar-centered international financial system were still mainly concerned with accumulated reserves in Asia, especially China. As we show in this book, both groups who thought that the system was sustainable for another decade and those who thought that it wasn't seemed to ignore the role of petrodollars in accelerating systemic instability.

As we started to work on the book project, we discovered a bigger problem yet: the literatures on energy markets, financial markets, and Middle-East geopolitics were highly compartmentalized, with few notable exceptions that are cited in this book. Our focus therefore turned to integrating all three domains of investigation and showing that all three spheres integrate to perpetuate, and potentially to amplify, a cycle that we were witnessing for the second time in our own lifetimes. We were both struck by the remarkable similarities between the events that we were observing in 2006–7 and those that we had earlier witnessed in 1979–80, and reached the conclusion that we are likely to see a steep spike in oil prices followed by a crash and severe global recession.

We knew enough to know that history does not repeat itself exactly. Therefore, we spent considerable effort trying to understand the cycle and its consequences, in part to address skepticism in 2007, including by Cambridge University Press referees, regarding our claims of fragility of the financial system. The book in your hand contains some of the facts and analysis that we accumulated to justify the assertions that we made in our initial book proposal. However, in the interest of brevity, we deemed it best to tone down our lengthy arguments of why "Peak Oil" theories were overstated and we were in fact in the midst of a speculative bubble in oil futures. Fragility of the global financial system hardly requires much proof at this point in time, and indeed previous authors who have analyzed this fragility, such as Hyman Minsky, have become posthumous best sellers as their views have gained currency anew. We may, of course, have been simply lucky in making those assertions, but we leave it to the reader to decide.

If we are at least partially correct in our analysis, then the cycle is likely to repeat, with most of its characteristics intact, at least one more time. Global economic recovery from the financial meltdown in late 2008 and early 2009 may take a few years, but low interest rates, moderate oil prices, and probable avoidance of 1930s-style breakdown of international trade suggest that the recovery will be vigorous when it arrives. Our analysis, presented in the pages before you, suggests that even the best efforts in migrating to alternative fuels will not be sufficient to wean the world economies from dependence on fossil fuels during this phase of the cycle. The other forces that we discuss in this book, geopolitical and financial, are also likely to remain intact, therefore forcing the world through at least one more upswing and downswing of the cycle – the third such phase of the cycle since the early 1970s.

Many of the ways that the world has changed – especially globalization and proliferation of weapons of mass destruction – make the downswings of the cycle potentially catastrophic, especially in light of the geopolitical interactions with energy and financial markets that we analyze in this book. Consequently, we slowly converted this project to produce a "policy book" focused on those interconnections that have not been systematically analyzed by other authors. Policy books often focus on mechanics of solutions, but we explicitly aimed to show that there are cycles in such policy mechanics, for example in regulating various markets, which are themselves part of the bigger cycle. The book has therefore become what we may consider a meta-policy book, one that focuses on the general framework and urges policy makers and analysts alike to be cognizant of "unanticipated consequences" of their policy advice that may in fact be possible to anticipate.

We would like to thank the James A. Baker III Institute for Public Policy and the Institute for Energy Economics of Japan for their generous support for this research, which grew out of the Baker Institute's study: "The Global Energy Market: Comprehensive Strategies to Meet Geopolitical and Financial Risks – The G8, Energy Security, and Global Climate Issues." We would also like to acknowledge the following Baker Institute research staff, research assistants, and interns who assisted us in this project: Basil Awad, Jareer Elass, Ibrahim Ergen, Lauren Smulcer, Adnan Poonawala, Devin Glick, Julie Chao, and Matthew Schumann.

Mahmoud A. El-Gamal and Amy M. Jaffe
Houston, March 2009

I

The Challenges of Resource Curses and Globalization

The coincidence of oil and financial crises can be traced back historically to the time of the industrial revolution. Our story begins, more modestly, with the dramatic increase in crude-oil prices in 1973 – an episode that continues to live as a vivid memory in Western and Middle-Eastern imaginations alike. For the former, this memory serves as a constant reminder of Western economies' vulnerability to market and geopolitical forces, especially in the Middle East. For the latter, it feeds nostalgic yearning for the moment when the Organization of Petroleum Exporting Countries (OPEC) cartel's market and political power reached its zenith.

As the world continues to struggle with the task of containing the economic, financial, and geopolitical ramifications of the financial crisis of 2007–9, it is important to recognize this and the previous 1970s crisis, as well as a number of others, as phases of a larger ongoing cycle. To paraphrase Mark Twain, rumors of the death of the business cycle – as well as the energy-price cycle, the financial boom-and-bust cycle, and the cycle of Middle-East geopolitical turmoil – have all been greatly exaggerated. In this book, we study the interaction of the global business cycle with these closely related energy-price, financial, and geopolitical cycles. We show that this super cycle is endogenous and self-perpetuating.

Like the human ego, this cycle is most dangerous when we assume that we have tamed or killed it.[1] Prolonged periods of stability and prosperity become grounds for hubris, which in turn breeds unrealistic levels of confidence and greed and compels policy makers to relax counter-cyclical regulations and policies. We argue in this book that financial and energy-sector investment cycles, as well as income distribution within and across countries, play pivotal roles in perpetuating the cycle, which can be attenuated only with proper understanding and vigilance.

We write this book to gain a better understanding of the perennial cycle and its driving forces. This is especially important for informing policies today, as globalized financial contagion and the spread of weapons of mass destruction make the cyclical swings increasingly, and potentially catastrophically, more dangerous.

1

Over the past four decades, the alternating ebb and flow of petrodollars have been key forces influencing financial markets. Petrodollar recycling has amplified as well as perpetuated recurring global financial and currency crises. These crises have, at times, reached severe proportions in "perfect storms" driven by three forces:

(i) The first force is the Dollar-centered and debt-driven global finance that has emerged since the early 1970s. Thus, our story of petrodollars and financial crises is as much about the U.S. Dollar, and its role in global finance, as it is about gyrating energy prices and Middle-East geopolitics.

(ii) The second force, to which we have already alluded, is the volatile market for oil and gas, which is governed not only by the real-economic business cycle, but also by investment cycles and financial-market speculation.

(iii) The third factor is the continuation of Middle-East geopolitical conflicts, which are driven by self-perpetuating arms races funded by petrodollars and serving as one of the main tools for the West to recycle the latter.

1973–80 vs. 2001–8 – Déjà Vu?

With perfect hindsight, we may notice many striking similarities between the two crises of 1973 and 2008, which highlight the importance of understanding the cyclical nature of such perfect storms. The oil crisis of 1973 was very much the product of the three factors that we have listed: (i) sustained global economic growth accelerated the growing demand for oil and other commodities, (ii) U.S. deficit spending had just recently forced the United States to abandon the quasi-gold standard of the Bretton Woods Accord in 1971, thus ushering in a new era of inflation, and (iii) the Arab-Israeli war of 1973 served as a catalyst for OPEC to restrict supply, thus forcing oil prices to rise tenfold. Higher oil prices (1973–80), in turn, resulted in a flood of recycled petrodollars that led to an international debt crisis.

Those same forces were again coinciding and reinforcing one another in 2001–8: (i) global economic growth that started in the 1980s and continued through the millennium mark – with the briefest of interruptions by historical standards – had resulted in accelerating demand for oil; (ii) United States indebtedness was growing unchecked, putting pressure on the Dollar and jeopardizing its dominance and anchoring effect in global finance; and (iii) terrorist attacks on the United States and military invasions by the latter of Afghanistan and then Iraq in 2001 and 2003, respectively, served as catalysts to inflate oil prices fivefold. Now, as then, the higher oil prices drove a new wave of Middle-East petrodollar outflows that contributed substantially to an international credit bubble. In turn, that bubble eventually caused an international financial meltdown the economic ramifications of which are not yet fully understood or recognized.

Left unchecked, U.S. dependence on oil in the coming years will continue to contribute to her precarious level of national debt, especially if oil prices recover their upward path with global economic recovery. In the meantime, the latest round of petrodollar inflows to the Middle East is unlikely to bring lasting economic growth and political stability to the region. Now, as in the 1970s, Middle-East economies exhibit limited absorptive capacities, and petrodollar flows have fueled real estate, stock market, and credit bubbles regionally and globally. The façade of political and social stability in some Middle-East countries, made possible in part by rising government spending on security, masks significant threats throughout the region. The latter include a potential nuclear arms race, conventional armed conflicts, sectarian strife, increasing income inequality, and continued failure to diversify regional economies. The recent rise in global terrorism is but one of the consequences of fermenting forces of regional discontent.

Progressively Increasing Financial Contagion

The forces that made globalized financial contagion possible in the new millennium will continue to influence international finance for the foreseeable future. In this regard, advances in communication and financial technology have led to financial integration at a scale that dwarfs other forms of globalization. In the 1970s, recycling of Middle-East petrodollars fueled a credit bubble of bank and sovereign loans to developing countries, especially in Latin America. That bubble crashed in the early 1980s following the rise in United States interest rates, with substantial repercussions for global finance and economics. Later crises in Asia, Latin America, and Eastern Europe in the late 1990s illustrated that similar financial shocks today would have significantly greater impact on the international financial system and economic conditions worldwide.

It is against this backdrop of today's precarious geopolitics and global finance that we seek to revisit the history of boom-and-bust petrodollar cycles that have influenced economic and political development in the Middle East, and financial conditions worldwide, since 1973. Until very recently, oil exporters have recycled petrodollar trade surpluses by investing mainly in Dollar-denominated assets. Investment in United States debt instruments has helped simultaneously to keep interest rates low and the Dollar from depreciating precipitously. This has allowed spending in the United States, financed by debt, to serve as an engine for domestic as well as global economic growth. However, continued strength of the U.S. economy and Dollar is predicated on other countries' continued willingness to hold their investments and reserves in Dollars, even in the face of mounting U.S. debts. Most observers agree today that the status quo is not sustainable.[2]

History, of course, does not repeat itself, and the circumstances of today's energy and financial markets are very different from those of the early 1970s. However, there is today, more than ever, a need to anticipate potential future crises and to understand the means to avoid them by managing various risk components. Toward that end, understanding the anatomy of previous crises, especially those of 1973 and 1979, is the most logical starting point. In the process, our story will focus on the three risk components that we have identified, which are likely to interact again to create the next perfect storm: Dollar-centered and debt-driven global finance, volatile energy prices, and Middle-East geopolitics.

The Dollar, Gold, and Black Gold

The story of the 1973 oil crisis began on August 13, 1971 in Camp David, where President Richard Nixon met with his economic advisers, including Secretary of the Treasury John Connally, Federal Reserve Board Chairman Arthur Burns, and Undersecretary of the Treasury Paul Volcker. The Dollar had already come under pressure by market speculators. Under the Bretton Woods monetary system that had prevailed following the end of World War II, countries aimed to keep their exchange rates fixed, with balance-of-payments support and supervision from the International Monetary Fund (IMF). However, the United States, as the world's largest economy, did not have the option of devaluing its currency or getting help from the IMF. As a remnant of the gold standard that had prevailed before World War II and had made the earlier waves of globalization at the turn of the twentieth century and between the two world wars possible, the U.S. maintained convertibility of the Dollar to gold at a fixed price.

Leading up to 1971, the U.S. started to run deficits that raised doubts regarding her ability to maintain the long-standing price of gold at $35 an ounce, and international financial speculators were already challenging that price (by selling Dollars and buying gold). In August 1971, Britain demanded that all of its Dollar reserves, $3 billion in total, be paid in gold. Two days later, on August 15, 1971, President Nixon dropped the gold-Dollar link. The Dollar then depreciated multiple times, allowing U.S. exporters to become more competitive once again in international markets. By 1973, the Bretton-Woods monetary system was dead.

If we think of oil priced in gold, which was effectively the case under the gold standard and the Bretton-Woods monetary system, we would have expected Dollar-denominated oil prices to increase steadily after 1971. In fact, however, as the Dollar depreciated and monetary policies allowed inflation in the prices of most commodities, Dollar prices of oil remained remarkably stable, as we can see in Figure 1.1. The resulting decline in oil prices relative to gold between 1971 and 1973 is illustrated more clearly in Figure 1.2. Between 1970 and 1973, the gold price of oil (gold ounces per barrel) had been cut in half. In fall 1973, the dramatic rise in the Dollar price of oil allowed the gold price to quadruple, overshooting the 1971 level, to which it returned briefly in 1975.

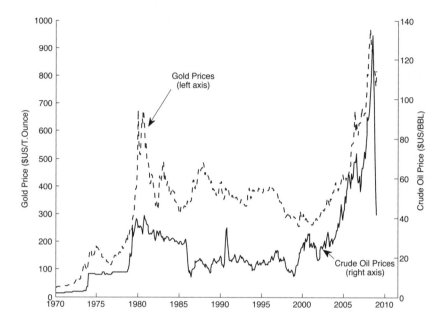

Figure 1.1. Dollar prices of gold and oil 1970–2009. *Source*: IMF – International Financial Statistics.

It is instructive to note that the same pattern was repeated before the oil shock of 1979. Inflation in the mid-1970s allowed gold prices to rise faster than oil prices, again cutting the gold price of oil in half between 1976 and 1979, leading to a major correction in oil prices following the Iranian revolution in 1979. The inflation of the 1970s was finally brought to an end when Paul Volcker, appointed as Chairman of the Federal Reserve Board by President Carter in August 1979, began a series of dramatic increases in United States interest rates, doubling them from 10 percent to 20 percent, and held them at those extremely high levels until 1982. This drove the United States and world economies into recession, which brought down gold from price levels that it did not revisit until the spike in commodity prices post 2003. It is clear from this simple narrative that the dynamics of the Dollar price of oil and the resulting petrodollar flows are governed in large part by United States economic policies that influence the real value of the Dollar.

Using gold prices to measure the real value of the Dollar, we can see in Figure 1.1 that the dramatic increase in Dollar prices of oil since 2003 is overstated by the declining real value of the Dollar. Indeed, Figure 1.2 clearly illustrates that the gold price of oil has remained below its high in 1979 throughout this latest phase of the cycle. Countries with currencies that appreciated relative to the Dollar, for instance in the Euro zone, were thus insulated to some extent from the higher Dollar prices of oil. The declining real value of the Dollar has prompted Kuwait to dismantle the long-standing peg of the Kuwaiti Dinar to the Dollar. The possibility that other countries may shift their exchange rate pegs, and possibly their foreign reserves, away from the Dollar will be discussed in Chapters 6 and 7.

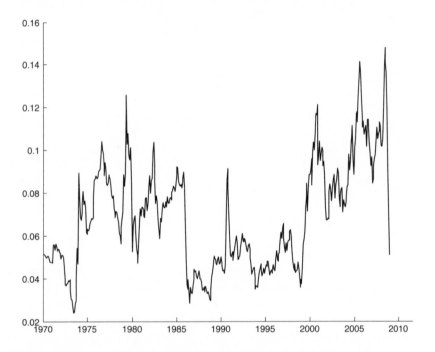

Figure 1.2. Gold price of crude oil 1970–2009 (troy ounces/barrel). *Source*: IMF – International Financial Statistics.

Oil Supply and Demand

The second set of factors that must be considered in our story of Middle-East petrodollars are the forces of energy supply and demand. The seemingly sudden ability of OPEC to exercise power in 1973 cannot be explained on the basis of Arab nationalism alone, nationalistic rhetoric of an "oil weapon" notwithstanding. The forces of global supply and demand for oil were very important contributing factors. In the background, there was the secular increase in demand for energy as the world economy reintegrated and enjoyed one of its longest periods of economic growth after World War II.

This increase in demand initially prompted the United States' regulators, such as the Texas Railway Commission, to eliminate all restrictions on production. This meant that because Texas was producing the maximum that it possibly could from its fields, no excess capacity remained as backup to be brought to the market in case of supply-shortage emergency. The resulting loss of excess capacity, in turn, eliminated a long-standing stabilizing force in global oil markets.

Another set of stabilizing forces in the global oil market, the oligopoly of large multinational oil companies, known generally as the "seven sisters," were losing market power due to the advent of independent oil companies and a trend toward nationalization of oil resources. As we shall show in Chapter 2, those forces of supply and demand coincided to give OPEC an incredible oligopolistic power to determine crude oil prices directly.

There was, of course, a nationalistic aspect to the Arab OPEC members' strategy to put pressure on the United States and the West more generally by using "the oil weapon." However, it is not clear whether these political considerations could have dominated the oil-exporting countries' economic self-interest. As early as 1974, Secretary of State Henry Kissinger announced after a series of discussions with oil-exporting Arab countries that the use of petroleum as a weapon to influence the outcome of the Arab-Israeli conflict had little merit in reality.[3]

In fact, some supply disruptions unrelated to the conflict appear to have contributed significantly to the oil shock of 1973–4.[4] Meanwhile, Saudi Arabia was secretly selling oil to the U.S. military to help fuel America's operations for the Vietnam War, even as it was publicly announcing its oil-sale boycott of America in solidarity to the Arab cause.[5]

Nonetheless, those other considerations did not undermine the significance of the oil-weapon rhetoric. As we shall discuss in Chapter 3, there is ample evidence that oil prices have been often influenced significantly by fear of supply disruptions, which expectations may be based mainly on political rhetoric. Therefore, our analysis of oil-price fluctuations, petrodollar flows, and the possibility of financial crises must take into account not only physical supply-and-demand considerations, but also market sentiments. The importance of the Middle East in the global supply of oil and gas thus makes its geopolitics an important component of our analysis.

Middle-East Sociopolitics

Every oil-exporting country makes its supply decisions based on multiple economic, political, and social considerations. Different factors dominate at different times, but a baseline economic model may help to predict supply decisions. In this regard, the seminal work of Hotelling can be used to explain the basic economic dynamics of oil extraction.[6] Hotelling argued that the owner of a nonrenewable mineral such as oil makes a decision whether to extract the resource and sell it based on a simple investment calculus: The owner has to choose between extracting the oil and selling it at the current price, or keeping it in the ground for extraction at a later date. It must therefore compare the expected present value of future prices of oil to the current price that it can fetch on the market. The analysis is thus reduced to comparison of the rate of return that the resource owner can expect to make by investing the potential oil-sale proceeds with the implicit expected rate of return that it would make were it to keep the oil in the ground for future extraction.

Keeping this economic analysis in mind, we can explain the fact that the price of oil depends not only on actual supply disruptions, but also on expectations of potential future disruptions, as discussed in Chapters 3 and 4. Expectations of turmoil, even in the distant future, mean not only higher oil prices in the future, when supplies may be disrupted, but also higher prices immediately, as the opportunity cost of extracting oil increases, other things being constant. Of course, other things are far from constant. When oil prices increase significantly, that gives incentive for energy consumers to seek other sources of energy, thus bringing prices back to sustainable levels. In this manner, the global recession starting in 2008, brought about in part by high energy prices and the associated petrodollar-flow contribution to the credit bubble, brought the latest wave of petrodollar flows to an abrupt end.

Starting with their dramatically increased revenues in 1973, however, OPEC members did not react as predicted by economic models. Instead of planning long-term strategies for optimal investment of their limited mineral wealth, those countries behaved as if their resources were inexhaustible and high prices were going to continue indefinitely. Jahangir Amuzegar, who observed the behavior of OPEC countries firsthand, described how those countries essentially consumed their mineral wealth instead of investing it:

When oil prices were on the rise, the assumption ordinarily was that they would continue uninterrupted. ...

Unrequited oil receipts tended to introduce a new politics of rising expectations, social welfare largesse and greater state paternalism. Fiscal policy in the form of reduced taxes, increased subsidies, enhanced welfare payments or expanded public employment encouraged profligate consumerism, relaxation of fiscal discipline and living beyond one's means. ...

Exchange-rate policy, as the kingpin of other macro policies, not only influenced the sectoral composition of the domestic development model but (and more importantly) invited and reinforced an insidious rent-seeking behavior. The latter helped create a new class of social parasites, i.e. wheeler-dealers or apparatchiks – which often sabotaged needed timely adjustments. . . .

The absence of foresight and prudence in the selection of policy alternatives during oil booms made it doubly difficult to shift gear, correct mistaken policies or adopt counteracting adjustment measures once booms turned inevitably into busts.[7]

Despite this largesse on the part of their ruling elites, the limited absorptive capacities of the oil-exporting countries left them with large petrodollar surpluses. The trade surpluses of OPEC countries during the 1970s corresponded to massive trade deficits for oil importers. Dealing with this financial imbalance required the development of a massive petrodollar recycling scheme, which eventually fueled a debt crisis in Latin America, as we shall discuss in Chapter 2. The latest wave of petrodollar flows and the credit bubble that it helped to inflate, with mounting U.S. debt and a weakening Dollar at the center of the financial storm, will be discussed in Chapter 5.

As we shall discuss in Chapter 3, the Middle-East oil-exporting countries' reaction to the most recent wave of petrodollar flows was very reminiscent of their response in the 1970s. The lessons of that earlier episode of the cycle have not been learned. The failed economic policies of the 1970s and 1980s, in both oil and capital-exporting countries, as well as their labor-exporting neighbors, meant that high economic expectations of the middle class – driven by boom-year euphoria – were dashed in the 1980s. Denied economic aspirations of middle-class youths, together with built-up anger at the insulated rent-seeking elites and their Western patrons, were significant contributors to the region's security problems.

The resulting geopolitical disturbances had the unintended consequence of bringing oil prices to new highs. This, in turn, allowed the ruling elites in those countries to use the new wave of petrodollars to pacify their populations with a combination of security heavy-handedness and economic relief. However, recent stock-market and real-estate bubbles in the region suggest that economic absorptive capacity continues to be relatively low, and the long-term economic prospects for the region remain dim. Most recently, the global recession – brought about because of the high energy prices, and in the aftermath of the financial crisis caused by the deflating credit bubble – has brought this wave of petrodollar flows to an abrupt end. With limited excess capacity in oil production, the region's geopolitical turmoil is thus intricately connected to global financial conditions. The region's economic and political problems are typical of regions that suffer from a resource curse, which has now been globalized, as we discuss in Chapter 7.

Volatilities: Financial, Economic, and Geopolitical

We have identified three main factors that interact to perpetuate, and potentially to amplify, cyclical movements in petrodollar flows: financial conditions, energy supply and demand, and Middle-East geopolitics. The manner in which petrodollars are used domestically in oil-exporting countries and recycled internationally, in turn, feeds back into the cycle through those three channels. As we have seen in our brief description of the circumstances surrounding the 1973 spike in oil prices, extreme events are more likely when multiple factors coincide. (In 1973, the factors were high energy demand, a deteriorating Dollar, and technical and geopolitical disruptions of Middle-East oil supply). Consequently, to understand past volatilities and to anticipate the nature and extent of potential future crises, we need to understand the relationships between those three factors. We now review pairwise interaction mechanisms briefly, further detailed historical analysis occupying the bulk of Chapters 2 through 7.

The Dollar and Energy Economics

The current energy markets blossomed during the golden age of the Dollar post World War II. Hence, despite occasional attempts to trade oil for currencies other than the Dollar, the fortunes of oil-exporting countries have been intimately intertwined with the strength of the Dollar. In May 2007, Kuwait decided to revalue its currency relative to the Dollar, abandoning a long-standing peg. Perhaps this was done in preparation for the Gulf Cooperation Council's (GCC) common currency. However, the explanation that accompanied the announcement of abandoning the Dollar peg cited the falling dollar and its effect on domestic inflation.[8] Some part of inflation in the GCC may be, indeed, attributed to the falling Dollar. However, the main driving force behind inflation, for example in real estate, is simply the increased liquidity due to petrodollar inflows and limited absorptive capacities of the oil-exporting countries' economies.

There is no doubt, historically, that the denomination of energy prices in Dollars has been a complicated issue, as we shall discuss in Chapter 6. Shortly after the first oil shock of 1973, National Security Advisor Henry Kissinger helped to orchestrate a system for petrodollar recycling, which featured most prominently the agreement that oil would continue to be priced in Dollars. Major OPEC countries, especially Saudi Arabia, were also given incentives to continue extracting oil and selling it for Dollars, by providing investment opportunities for their petrodollars in Dollar-denominated assets and debt instruments such as federal bonds and FNMA (Fannie Mae) mortgage-backed securities.[9]

As long as big portions of oil-exporting countries' assets remain invested in Dollar-denominated instruments, those countries will have every incentive to continue supporting the Dollar by pricing their exports in the currency. Therefore, despite short episodes when some countries such as Russia, Iran, Venezuela, and Iraq preferred to sell their oil for Euros or in barter, the Dollar-denomination has continued. With the growth of U.S. debt, not only to oil-exporting countries, but also most prominently to Japan, China, and Korea, the U.S. creditors are now engaged in a financial game of chicken: In the event of a Dollar crisis, no country wants to be the last left standing with large amounts of severely depreciated Dollar-denominated assets.

Figure 1.3. Crude prices and U.S. trade deficit. *Source*: IMF, IFS.

The 2003 to mid-2008 high oil price put pressure on the Dollar, through mounting trade deficits and debts, as shown in Figure 1.3. The ideal solution for creditors would be for the United States to reduce the growth of its debt levels by reducing its twin fiscal and trade deficits. As a reminder of terrible things that could happen if debt levels are not checked, creditors occasionally signal their intention, and sometimes act on a small scale, to diversify their assets away from the Dollar. However, some trigger event, for instance if one of the major exporters of energy announces with credibility its intention to sell oil and gas for Euros or a basket of currencies, can start a flood of diversification away from Dollar-denominated investments. A disorganized Dollar selloff would spell catastrophe not only for the American economy, but also for the world economy of which it is the largest part. In this regard, the world has been extremely fortunate, indeed, that the latest financial crisis was not accompanied by a Dollar-centered currency crisis.

If the transition away from the Dollar going forward is gradual, then there may be sufficient time for the American economy to diversify its energy consumption away from imported oil and gas, reinforcing the current recession's trend toward reducing the U.S. trade gap. Advances in biofuels, coal-to-liquid fuels, and utilization of renewable energy, such as solar and wind power, have been underway for some time. With financial risks better understood by policy makers and the public alike, the political will for greater self-sufficiency in energy may finally provide the incentive to make those alternative sources of energy viable. Of course, the threat of developing those alternative energy sources, especially ones that are environmentally friendly, could reduce the expected future value of oil reserves and increase the incentive for extraction, thus increasing supply and reducing the prices of oil and gas further. This, in turn, may relieve the pressure on the Dollar and thus reduce the incentive to develop alternative energy sources, as we witnessed in the 1980s. This issue will be revisited in detail in Chapter 8.

The Dollar and Middle-East Geopolitics

Over recent years, the level of dislike for American foreign policy in the Middle East has reached unprecedented levels. It is not coincidental that Ossama bin Laden's tirades against the U.S. included accusations of artificially low oil prices that – he claimed – robbed the Arab and Muslim nations of trillions of Dollars.[10] In this respect, the September 11, 2001, attack on the World Trade Center towers in New York City, as well as earlier attempted attacks at the same towers, targeted the symbolism of American capitalist hegemony. A year earlier, Saddam Hussein had announced his intention to sell Iraqi oil for Euros instead of Dollars. In recent years, Iran has shifted much of its foreign reserves into Euros and has announced most recently the establishment of a Euro-denominated oil exchange in Tehran. Those efforts are in large part viewed as direct attacks on the United States by attacking the Dollar's dominance.[11]

The dominance of the U.S. Dollar as the global reserve currency, especially after it was delinked from gold in 1971, was built on two pillars. The first was international political and economic goodwill acquired over the first half of the twentieth century, as European colonialism came to an end, and the second was the absence of a viable alternative to the Dollar. As we shall discuss in Chapters 4 and 6, the U.S. has consumed its stock of goodwill in the Middle East, with a few exceptions. In the meantime, a viable competitor for the Dollar may have emerged over the past decade. The expanding European Union's economy has now exceeded the size of the United States of America's, and its relatively young currency has appreciated significantly against the Dollar over the past few years.

The European Union is also an increasingly dominant trading partner with the oil-exporting countries of the Middle East, suggesting that a shift to pricing their exports in Euros would insulate them from the effects of Dollar depreciation.

Of course, this does not necessarily establish the viability of the Euro as the central piece of a new monetary order to replace the Dollar-centered Bretton-Woods and post-Bretton-Woods systems. However, it does provide a better alternative than the returning to the gold standard and other anachronistic proposals. We study various alternatives to the Dollar-centered international financial system in Chapter 7.

The United States could have resorted, and may still choose to resort, to heavy-handed strategies to prevent Middle-East exporters from forging bilateral agreements with China or pricing their exports in Euros. However, that would result in further overstretching of American military and financial limits, thus weakening the Dollar further and adding economic as well as geopolitical incentives to switch away from the Dollar. The trend to abandon Dollar pegs by very different Middle-East countries – most recently by Kuwait and Syria in mid-2007, and earlier by Egypt – suggests that a combination of economic and political forces is already at work.

As it turned out, the United States chose to use carrots instead of sticks, offering GCC countries a $20 billion arms deal that helps simultaneously to appease high-ranking officials who benefit from such deals and to recycle some of the accumulated petrodollars. In the meantime, beggar-thy-neighbor policies among European countries, each of which opted to guarantee only the deposits at its own banks, letting Iceland suffer a complete meltdown of its banking system, prevented massive flight away from the Dollar and toward the Euro. Indeed, it is likely that Euro-zone countries, especially Germany, are averse to having their currency supplant the Dollar as the primary reserve currency, in large part because serving the latter role may require the European Central Bank (ECB) to accept higher levels of inflation than it would otherwise.

Energy Economics and Middle-East Geopolitics

The dramatic rise of oil-based rentier states in the Middle East accelerated during the 1970s. The new economics of the region were built, directly or indirectly, on the oil and gas industry. Traditional business elites and middle-classes were replaced by new elites with ties to oil-rent-collecting states. This stifled the possibility of balanced economic growth and encouraged rent-seeking behavior that continues to this day – with occasional scandals of massive "commissions" for white-elephant public projects and procurements by the oil-rich states.[12]

During the early boom years, a quasi–welfare state system of subsidies and transfers emerged to appease the population of the region, which began growing at unprecedented rates. Increased religiosity was encouraged by official actions to counter the tide of secular socialism and communist parties in the region and in the process to curb the influence of the Soviet Union, which was backing such political forces in the region. In addition, religiosity was spread through the cultural influence on and of migrant workers from labor-exporting Arab and Islamic countries, as many first discovered religion during their working yeas in the Gulf.

As Islamism rose in popularity in the region, it effectively ended the decades-long rise in Arab nationalism, which was closely associated with secular socialism and equal rights for non-Muslim minorities. Arab nationalism was replaced during the 1970s, in both the Arab consciousness and rhetoric, by its twin-sibling: Islamist nationalism. This rise in Islamist identity politics is also evident in the economic sphere, with the mergence of Islamic finance and the creation of a well-capitalized and high-profile Islamic (not Arab) Development Bank.

The boom years of the 1970s increased the Middle-East population and raised their economic expectations. Those new expectations relied on rent-seeking behavior and welfare-state dependency, which de-emphasized education and human-capital building in the various fields that would support the regional economy when oil rents dried up.[13] During the lean years of the 1980s and 1990s, the increased economic and political frustration of middle-class Arabs, who were slowly sinking into poverty, turned portions of their youth to violent interpretations of political Islam that have only continued to grow. The vowed enemies of this movement are the region's ruling elites and their ostensible American patrons.

The ensuing sporadic and organized-military violence in the region, ironically, contributed to the dramatic rise in energy prices (2003–8), which strengthened the hands of the very states and state-related business elites whom the militants had identified as their targets. The relative period of calm in many countries of the region since 2003, with obvious notable exceptions, is in large part caused by the increased resources of those states and their affiliated business elites. New petrodollar flows have allowed the ruling elites simultaneously to disarm the militant groups through tightened security and to reduce their grassroots support through financial transfers to the general population. Of course, security crackdowns drive dissident networks underground and support their claims that there are no alternatives to violent strategies. They wait for the next phase of the cycle when the state is weakened and the population is sufficiently disgruntled to support their approach, and the vicious cycle continues.

Petro-States, Hydrocarbon Dependence, and Resource Curses

Despite three decades of intermittent oil wealth, the resource-rich Middle-East countries have failed to invest in relevant human capital or to develop a diversified economic base. Those countries have thus been the consummate contemporary examples of the "resource curse" at work. The resource curse for oil-exporting countries emanates in part from the political economy of oil rents, which discourages investment in sectors conducive for long-term growth, increases patterns of corruption and patronage, and provides irresistible incentives to consume beyond long-term means and invest in rent-seeking "white-elephant" projects.[14]

Books with titles such as Karl's *The Paradox of Plenty* and Chaudhry's *The Price of Wealth* have discussed in detail the social, political, and economic dimensions of the resource curse in oil-rich GCC countries.[15] Just as the resource-curse economic theory has suggested, resource-rich, especially oil-and-gas-rich, countries have in fact generally exhibited lower levels of sustainable economic growth, less diversified economies, less democratic governments, and more potential for political turmoil, all in part driven by the volatile nature of energy markets, and long-term movement of terms of trade against exporters of raw materials.[16]

While some resource-rich countries have been able to escape the resource curse, for example Scandinavian countries and the United States of America, the resource curse has plagued the Middle East for decades. It has not only afflicted the GCC countries with massive oil and gas resources, but also their neighboring labor-exporting countries such as Egypt, Lebanon, and Jordan. Those countries have suffered from the Dutch-disease scenario wherein large inflows of foreign exchange – through workers' remittances from exported labor – created asset-market and real-estate bubbles and conspicuous-consumption patterns that crowded out potentially export-oriented growth sectors of the economy.

Like their richer GCC neighbors, the only thriving non-hydrocarbon sectors in Middle-East labor-exporting countries are construction and consumables (including consumer-oriented information technology and telecommunications). The entire region continues to spend beyond its long-term means, essentially consuming the region's nonrenewable capital, instead of finding smooth paths for sustainable consumption and investment. This consumerist culture amplifies the social and economic effects of volatility of oil and gas rents, and the resulting stark inequalities in income and wealth, thus perpetuating the cycle through geopolitical turmoil during its downswings.

The political, economic, and technical means for *Escaping the Resource Curse*, as the recent volume edited by Humphreys, Sachs, and Stiglitz is titled, are relatively well understood based on well-established research in economics and political science.[17] They involve some degree of privatization of the energy sector, more equitable distribution of income, better transparency and governance in extraction and spending, and resistance of the urge to overspend on the wrong projects. The editors admit that, well-understood as those measures may be, implementation may prove difficult politically:

We assume in particular that governments are willing to take sometimes bold and difficult steps to try to succeed where most states have failed. If states are unable or unwilling to take such steps, then the best solution may well be to leave the oil and gas in the ground.[18]

This conclusion is predicated on the assumption that leaving the oil and gas in the ground only results in the loss of accrued interest had the resources been extracted and invested. However, if oil is indeed left in the ground for future generations that can manage it more effectively, then oil prices will be higher in the short term. This increases the incentive to extract immediately for two reasons: the ability to sell at the higher current price, and the expected lower future price due to the buyers' incentive to develop alternative sources of energy. Therefore, as difficult as it is to find partial solutions to various components of the problem (while holding other factors constant), the overall understanding of system dynamics requires studying the system at substantially higher levels of complexity. Needless to say, different strategies will be viable and effective under different circumstances. The fundamental economic, political, and social tradeoffs between short-term and long-term goals is at the core of policy problems addressed in Chapter 8.

Geopolitical Conflicts and the Politics of Discontent

National oil companies in the Middle East are a relatively recent phenomenon. The first major attempt to nationalize Middle-East oil resources, carried out by Iran's Mossadeq in 1951, was thwarted by a British- and American-supported coup. Only a few decades later, the situation has been totally reversed, with international oil companies currently denied any direct access to the oil and gas resources in many oil-rich countries. The historical rise and the performance records of national oil companies are discussed in Chapter 2.

The 2007 *Strategic Economic Trends Report* by the Ahram Center for Political and Strategic Studies (ACPSS), the premier think-tank in the Arab Middle East, stated that the United States "uses its political influence and financial aid to enhance foreign demand for its civilian-use goods and services, and sometimes uses its military power directly and violently, as currently witnessed in Iraq, with the intention of opening the oil sector of this large Arab country to American oil companies, and also to provide other American companies access to reconstruction efforts in that country, if colonial American rule of Iraq continues."[19] Kevin Phillips has also argued that a three-pronged partnership of military, financial, and energy sectors has shaped American foreign policy for decades.[20] Such impressions have perpetuated the geopolitical component of the cycle, by stoking the fires of nationalist (and by implication anti-American) discontent.

Well into the 1960s, with the memory of European colonialism vivid in their minds, most people in the Middle East favored United States hegemony over any other. Four decades later, the United States is widely viewed in the region as a direct military occupier, an enabler of Israeli occupation and settlement expansion in Palestinian lands, and the primary supporter of oppressive totalitarian regimes in various Arab countries. Fairly or otherwise, this view has led an increasing majority in the region to attribute many of the economic and political failures of their countries to American involvement. Quite recently, for instance, celebration of the fall of the Iraqi dictator Saddam Hussein lasted only very briefly, giving way not only to sectarian violence, but also to blaming the United States ultimately for its role in overthrowing the government of Abdul-Karim Qassim and enabling the rise of Hassan Al-Bakr and Saddam Hussein to power in the 1960s, as well as supporting the latter through the devastating war with Iran 1980–8.[21]

In this regard, it is important to note that regime change, or the danger thereof, poses a number of threats for oil-exporting countries. One is the financial risk of freezing the *ancien régime*'s Dollar-denominated assets, thus robbing the new regime of a primary source of investment financing. Another, as evidenced in the cases of Iran circa 1979, Iraq circa 2003, as well as in Libya and Venezuela at the time of ascendance of radical leaders, is the potential for technocratic brain drain, which in turn results in lower long-term productivity. Generally speaking, regime change is associated with reduced oil production for roughly five to ten years.

Anti-Americanism and the Dollar

Rising anti-Americanism, generally associated with the rise of radical regimes, provides a strong political incentive to undermine the Dollar, which adds to the incentive to diversify away from potentially freezable assets. The scope of politically motivated attacks on the Dollar depends on the likelihood of regime change in various Middle-East countries and the smoothness of transition in policies. The establishment of a new regime with declared animosity to the U.S., or the armed struggle to establish one, could restrict production and transportation of oil and gas from the region, increasing energy prices and enhancing the economic incentive to abandon the Dollar, as U.S. trade deficits and debt continue to mount.

The lack of transparency of political processes in the region creates substantial uncertainty. As a result, the slightest disturbance (such as a small band of terrorists attacking a residential compound) can lead to massive oil-price volatility. Western involvement to reduce that uncertainty can aim to establish regional political transparency and stability in the long term, but that leads almost certainly to nationalist discontent and short-term turmoil. This short-term turmoil, in turn, increases uncertainty even in the long term.

Conversely, Western military and political involvement may continue to favor maintaining short-term stability. This reduces the chances of small-to-moderate changes, but increases the chance of massive turmoil and drastic regime change. This probability may remain small in the short run, but it becomes significant in the medium to long run, especially during downswings of the energy-price cycle. In Chapter 7, we discuss the risk for Middle-East turmoil interaction with energy-market and financial factors to perpetuate and amplify the cycle.

Mounting Debt and Fragility of the Global Financial System

Perfect storms are very low-probability but very high-impact events. At the center of worst-case possibilities lies the greatest fiction in our economy: money. Chapter 5 covers the historical evolution of our current financial system, the crises that this system has produced in the past, and the ones that it may likely produce in the future. Most financial crises are driven by debt. The most recent crisis driven by mounting U.S. debt has not – thus far – undermined the Dollar and the post-Bretton-Woods international financial system built around it.

However, the question is no longer if, but when and how, the system that has come to be known as Bretton Woods II, with surplus trading partners of the U.S. supporting the U.S. Dollar, will be replaced. In this regard, although the current recession (2008–9) has allowed the U.S. deficit, the latter is likely to resume its upward trajectory once the global economy recovers and oil prices return to higher plateaus. The link between mounting U.S. debt and energy prices under Bretton-Woods II is summarized in Figure 1.4, which shows the phenomenal growth of the U.S. trade deficit since the early 1980s, and its direct relationship to crude oil prices over the past decade.

Under the Bretton-Woods system, or under the gold standard that preceded it, a country that ran trade deficits consistently – as the United States has now done for more than a quarter of a century – would have suffered a net outflow of gold or gold-pegged Dollars or, more realistically, would be required to raise interest rates to prevent this outflow.[22] Money supply would thus decline in the trade-deficit country and increase in the trade-surplus country. This would have a deflationary effect in the deficit country and an inflationary effect in the surplus country, thus adjusting international competitiveness and terms of trade to restore balance.

Under the current flexible exchange rate regime, following the collapse of the Bretton-Woods system, the Dollar retained its unique status as reserve currency of choice – in no small part due to being the numeraire for energy trading. This means that the United States enjoys the unique ability to pay for its trade deficit with its own debt, seemingly indefinitely. This debt financing may be accomplished directly by selling government debt instruments, or indirectly by allowing the inflation of asset prices – such as stocks, real estate, and commodities – purchased with Dollars. By January 2009, the gross national debt of the United States had exceeded $10.5 trillion.

An alternative to debt accumulation would be simply to allow the Dollar to depreciate against other currencies. A large depreciation of the Dollar would cause a U.S. recession in the short term. The cheaper Dollar eventually increases American competitiveness – reducing imports and increasing exports, until balance is achieved. Of course, domestic political considerations in the United States would prevent this recession-inducing policy from being embraced.[23]

Moreover, two major blocs of United States creditors have no incentive to allow the Dollar to depreciate too quickly. Asian economies have grown in large part by exporting to the American market. The current U.S. recession works to reduce relative competitiveness of Asian exports and stunt the growth of those economies. Perilous as it may be, the earlier trend of debt financing of American spending seems less risky. The continued demand for long-term United States bonds kept long-term interest rates low, thus allowing the U.S. economy, and its consumption of imported goods, to remain strong. The second group of United States creditors are Middle-East oil-exporting countries, whose petrodollar fortunes are likewise tied to American and global economic growth.

We have argued that the 1973 and 1979 crises were precipitated by the end of the Bretton-Woods system and the resulting U.S.-debt-driven global inflation. Mounting American deficit spending and debt compromised the Dollar's role as a quasi–gold standard after World War II. However, the world's continued willingness – to date – to accumulate American debt has allowed the Dollar to continue playing a central role in the international financial system. During the 1970s, as now, the attempts – explicit and implicit – to recycle Middle-East petrodollars have eventually caused debt crises and threatened the global financial system. If the world can muster another period of multinational cooperation for smooth transition away from the current – obviously fragile and outdated – financial system, then the current episode of economic globalization and growth may be sustainable beyond the near future.

Constants and Variables in the Cycle: 1970s to the Present

The secular cycle that governs oil prices, which we described earlier, has continued for more than a century. As we can see in Figure 1.4, prices similar to the ones observed in mid-2008 – extremely high as they may be – are not uncommon. Although constant-Dollar prices may not be as effective in making our point as gold prices, it is clear that similar oil-price spikes had been observed before, most

notably during the periods 1860–80 and 1970–85, which were similarly characterized by massive banking and financial crises.

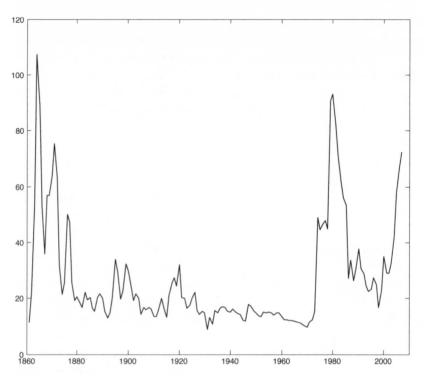

Figure 1.4. Brent oil prices 1860–2008, constant 2007 Dollars. *Source*: BP Statistical
Review Database.

Recap of the Main Energy-Price-Cycle Story Lines

Our story has been quite simple, and it may be instructive to compare the current
episode not only to our starting point around 1973, but also to the previous
period of extremely high prices in the late nineteenth century. One dimension of
the story is purely about the physical aspects of energy supply and demand: High
rates of economic growth increase demand for oil significantly faster than capacity
for extraction and refining can respond. In addition, fast growth can – in its early
stages – allow the fast-growing countries to continue increasing their demand for
energy even in the face of higher prices. In other words, short-term supply and
demand are both highly inelastic, and increased demand thus drives prices up
very significantly. In the long term, however, higher prices reduce demand, as

higher costs lead to economic recession, and increased supply further contributes to falling energy prices.

The nature of the recession in the 1980s, and the inflationary episode that preceded it in the 1970s, were different from the inflation of 2003–8 and ensuing recession. As many economists have pointed out, the inflation of the 1970s was driven by wage increases as well as higher prices, each feeding the other in a seemingly endless spiral. In contrast, the latest inflationary spiral lacked a wage component.

The mechanics of the current inflation in energy prices more closely resembled commodity bubbles of earlier times.[24] As economists Hyman Minsky and Charles Kindelberger have shown, a financial cycle of bubbles, panics, and crashes seems to be as perpetual as the energy-price cycle that we are studying. In the latest episode, the two cycles have reinforced one another. The initial increase in oil prices was driven by the standard story of rising demand due to economic growth (in Asia) and inelastic supply (in part due to OPEC coordination, but mainly due to the physical constraints discussed previously).

Like other manias before it, the rise in prices attracted trend-following speculative traders, who bought oil futures because oil prices were rising, and of course oil prices were rising because they were buying. We identified this mania, and predicted the crash in oil prices, in early 2008.[25] Suffice it to say in this introduction that oil exporters themselves were baffled by the price levels reached by mid-2008, which they attributed to speculative trading. This interpretation of the higher prices further delayed oil exporters' efforts to increase supply, since they saw the higher prices as a passing phase, which was the case, and feared that increased capacity would lead to lower prices not only because of the eventual recession, but also because of the same speculative traders who have accelerated the positive trend in prices later accelerating their negative trend.

The Role of Petrodollars

The latest bubble in commodity prices was fed by excess liquidity due to low interest rates on Dollar-denominated assets, which were in large part caused by the growing U.S. debt. This lax monetary environment created serial bubbles in recent years: first in technology stocks, then in real estate and mortgage-backed securities, and finally in commodity prices. The standard financial story has been focused on China and other major creditors of the United States. Continued trade imbalances have allowed those countries to accumulate trillions of Dollars in funds that they had traditionally invested in U.S. treasuries. This high demand for treasuries helped to depress interest rates, contributing to real estate inflation as mortgages became deceptively affordable. It would therefore seem that the story is different in the first decade of the 21st century from the story of the 1970s, let alone previous high-energy-price episodes. Those differences, the argument implies, suggest that lessons from the 1970s and earlier crises are not instructive for understanding the latest crisis. However, as we have already suggested, more similarities between the current and earlier episodes can be detected upon closer inspection.

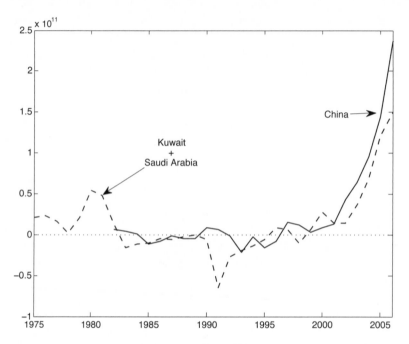

Figure 1.5. Chinese vs. Middle-East capital and financial outflows, in U.S. Dollars. *Source*: IMF, BOP.

We need to emphasize that recycled petrodollars played an extremely, if not equally, important role in the latest financial crisis. In this regard, Figure 1.5 shows that net capital outflows from Kuwait and Saudi Arabia alone had been of the same magnitude as the flow from China leading into the crisis. Needless to say, the Chinese economy has seemingly unlimited absorptive capacity relative to those Middle-East countries, in terms of increased domestic investment as well as consumption. In this regard, the periodic reemergence of petrodollar flows should no longer surprise anyone, and the next international financial system has to accommodate those periodic floods through appropriate mechanisms. It is for this reason that we focus on Middle-East geopolitics to understand not only the oil-supply side of the cycle, but also the financial side. In this regard, understanding what happened during the 1970s and 1980s, and what happened a century earlier in the 1870s and 1880s, will be important for understanding the latest and potential future crises.

The Role of Financial Crises

Returning to Figure 1.4, we note again that the three episodes during which real oil prices reached all-time highs were all periods of financial distress, with currency and/or banking crises. The first period toward the end of the nineteenth century was also a period of fast-increasing globalization, which ended with World War I, and the ensuing protectionist policies between the two world wars. It was also a period of relative financial anarchy, with mania in various asset markets, including real estate and railroads, leading to multiple financial crises. The frequency of such financial crises during times of economic growth was markedly lower following the increased financial regulation after the Great Depression and the Bretton-Woods fixed-exchange-rate regime after World War II.

Delinking the Dollar from gold and bringing about a new era of flexible exchange rates after 1971 has contributed greatly to the current phase of globalization, a century after the previous. As ex–Fed Chairman Paul Volcker pointed out with puzzlement, foreigners were more willing to hold Dollars backed only by the strength of the U.S. economy than they were to hold Dollars backed by and convertible to gold.[26] The virtual uni-currency world that emerged made it much easier especially for developing countries to increase their trade and competitiveness in global markets, as currency risk was eliminated for trade denominated in Dollars. In due course, increased levels of debt, and the speculative activities that accompany cheap credit and fast economic growth, have led to a number of financial crises during the 1980s (including sovereign debt crises in Latin America), 1990s (including currency crises in Asia, sovereign debt crises in Latin America and Russia), and early 2000s (including in the U.S. stock market, real estate market, and commodity markets).

When the latest bubble in commodity prices crashed, as all bubbles do, it caused a financial crisis as most crashes do. Every financial bubble is fed by fiction that suggests why this particular run-up in prices is different and justified by market forces. The latest speculative bubble in oil prices was in part fed by the commonly held belief that economic growth in China and India would continue unabated, even if high energy prices were to drive the United States and other Western countries into deep recession. Those countries' continued demand for oil and other fuels was therefore expected to continue, rather than follow the same cyclical pattern. Moreover, on the supply side, many believed that shortages in fuel would not only continue in the short term, but also in the medium and long term, as peak oil and other hypotheses (which we discuss in Chapter 5) gained traction.

Forecasts of continued uninterrupted high growth of Asian countries, especially China, were very reminiscent of beliefs about the continued growth of Japan circa 1980. The story that supports the latest bubble missed those obvious parallels with the Japanese export-oriented growth model. When the United States and other importers from China fell into a recession, Chinese growth naturally had to decelerate. As this scenario is currently unfolding, a large number of bad loans in the Chinese banking system will become increasingly difficult to mask with new loans, as assets that were previously used to justify such loans fall in price. In the case of Japan, the resulting banking crisis, despite aggressive financial and political resource dedication from the Japanese government and central bank, drove Japan into a deflationary spiral and anemic economic performance for a full decade.

Plan of the Book

We have now summarized the three interacting factors that contribute to the on-going cycle. The first factor is the secular cycle in oil prices, which is driven by the global business cycle and may be amplified by geopolitical factors as well as financial mania and crises. The second factor is Middle-East geopolitics, which is shaped for better and worse by the periodic floods and droughts in petrodollar flows, as oil prices rise and fall, in part driven by financial-market conditions. The third factor is financial market dynamics, which have been characterized by numerous cycles of mania and crashes, especially in periods of lax regulation following prolonged periods of prosperity and relative stability, during which prudential regulations seem unnecessary.

In the remainder of this book, we investigate all three risk factors and their interactions, focusing mainly on historical, geopolitical, financial, and economic developments since the 1970s. Chapters 2–4 are focused on the historical path that energy markets, Middle-East geopolitics, and financial markets have traversed during those four decades. Chapters 5 and 6 are focused on the international financial system in the post-Bretton-Woods era, and the near end of the U.S. Dollar–based international financial system. Chapter 7 combines the historical evidence and analyses of earlier chapters to suggest that the cycle will continue and may be amplified significantly if appropriate policy measures are not taken. The final chapter provides some policy suggestions to ameliorate the cycle by managing all three risk factors in a mutually coherent framework. It is tempting to think of ending the cycle once and for all, but that may only lead to extreme amplification thereof. The prudent, and more modest, approach is to learn the cycle's dynamics and try to manage it.

2

New Middle East: Childhood 1973–84 and Adolescence 1985–95

Without a doubt, oil was the most important commodity in the twentieth century. Oil was literally the fuel of the previous round of globalization at the end of the nineteenth century and lasting until World War I. Its importance continued to increase as the main fuel for war machinery, and then to fuel the global growth between the two world wars and following World War II. The roots of increased demand and dependence on oil, which continue to shape current and future demand, were set in the mid-to-late nineteenth century.

Trends in oil demand are highly correlated with rates of economic growth, modes of transportation and production, and wealth accumulation. It is on the supply side that strategic behavior becomes more interesting. Following very high prices in the U.S. in 1860, during the Civil War, a classical case of "tragedy of the commons" emerged. The law of capture in the United States, which was then the fastest growing region for demand and economic growth, encouraged excessively fast oil extraction and reduced prices precipitously.[1]

Excessive extraction and lower prices are, of course, the economic outcomes theoretically predicted in a competitive environment. Rockefeller's Standard Oil restored higher prices by monopolizing production in the United States. Antitrust law eventually broke Standard Oil's monopoly, but the idea of strategic control of supply never died. Starting in the 1920s, an international oligopoly of large oil companies emerged. The "Big Sisters" originally consisted of Anglo-Persian (later, British Petroleum), Royal Dutch Shell, and Jersey Standard (the New Jersey part Standard Oil after division, later named Exxon). Other global oil companies soon joined, forming a group of "Seven Sisters" at the end of World War II. In the United States, production was regulated by local state entities such as the Railroad Commission of Texas and the Oklahoma Commerce Commission, which were commissioned to regulate oil production to match market demand.

During the 1950s, the international oligopoly of international oil companies, and the various responsible commissions in the United States, regulated supply through a series of geographical market-sharing agreements. The most famous international division was known as the Red-Line Agreement. It allowed five American firms to share ownership of oil assets in Iraq. It also included a cooperation clause that forced companies to act in concert in Middle-East oil development, thus preventing them each from acting unilaterally by honoring "red-line" boundaries demarcated on a map of the former Ottoman Empire.

Oligopoly of International Oil Companies and the Origin of OPEC

The majority of oil-exporting countries in the Middle East, Asia, and Latin America – for example, Saudi Arabia, Indonesia, and Venezuela, respectively – were not industrialized. Therefore, they were forced to rely on foreign oil companies to mine and develop their resources. The companies controlled all aspects of the industry, including production, distribution, and processing. In return, they paid the producing countries royalties based on a somewhat arbitrarily set price for crude oil, known as the "posted price."

As nationalist sentiments continued to grow during the late 1940s and early 1950s, oil-producing countries began to agitate for greater control and a larger share of oil revenues. Their demands for larger shares coincided with and were eventually aggravated by worsening market conditions. At the time, the multinationals' profitability was hampered by import quotas imposed in the United States in 1958, as well as the USSR's eagerness to strike bilateral deals to sell cheap oil to European countries as part of the greater Cold-War strategy.

The multinational oil companies tried to pass some of the financial pain due to weakening markets to the oil-exporting countries. A group of those latter countries – Iran, Iraq, Kuwait, Saudi Arabia, and Venezuela – countered that pressure by creating the Organization of Petroleum Exporting Countries (OPEC) in 1960, as an attempt to balance the market power of the international oil companies' oligopoly with their own. The new cartel was, in fact, immediately successful in frustrating the international companies' attempts to reduce the posted price of oil. Leading up to 1973, six more countries – Algeria, Indonesia, Libya, Nigeria, Qatar, and the United Arab Emirates – joined OPEC, bringing the total number of members to eleven. Throughout the 1960s, OPEC's role was focused mainly on providing bargaining power over extraction taxes. The cartel's mode of operation changed substantially in the early 1970s.

OPEC's Market Power: Economics, Politics, and Volatility

A series of events transformed OPEC's role from an oligopolistic negotiator of the oil majors' posted price, the latter still controlling world production and distribution, to a direct oligopolistic player in the international oil market. OPEC owed its change of fortune to several developments. First and foremost, in the late 1960s and early 1970s, oil demand – most notably in the United States – was growing faster than new supply sources could be developed.[2] Initially, surplus capacity of about three million b/d remained in the Middle East. However, that margin was cut by half by 1973, thus reaching what was considered a dangerously low level equal roughly to 3 percent of total world demand.[3] At the same time, President Nixon imposed price controls in the United States, which ironically discouraged domestic exploration and simultaneously encouraged the continued growth of demand.

During the late 1960s, the United States started realizing significant trade deficits, which continued to grow into the 1970s, in part because of the Vietnam War adventure. The Dollar was still convertible to gold under the Bretton-Woods regime, but private speculators and governments around the world were doubtful that the United States could continue to run deficits and still support the Dollar's convertibility. They traded their Dollars for gold and other currencies or assets, causing gradual inflation in the Dollar-price of gold, as shown in Figure 1.1. Convertibility of the Dollar to gold was eventually dropped in 1971, and the Dollar-inflation of most prices continued unchecked.

As the oil market tightened and the Dollar weakened, OPEC sought an increase in the posted Dollar-denominated price of crude oil, to compensate for the Dollar-driven real depreciation. Some countries, such as Libya, also sought the participation of emerging independent American companies such as Occidental Petroleum, who were willing to outbid the majors on exploration terms and posted prices, in an attempt to gain a larger market share. Both of those factors put upward pressure on oil prices.

At the same time, oil-exporting countries used newfound market leverage to gain partial ownership of the oil resources within their borders. Nationalization presented countries with the challenge of trying to sell their oil directly, which thus sparked competition for access to the majors' distribution channels. Despite those difficulties, a number of countries proceeded to create their own national oil companies and gradually to nationalize their oil assets. A new system emerged, wherein countries negotiated posted prices with the oil majors. The posted price of oil thus began to rise. However, as we can see in Figure 1.1, the Dollar-price inflation of oil did not keep pace with that of gold. In Figure 1.2, we can see that the gold-price of crude oil rose slightly in 1971, as the monopoly of the oil majors was compromised, but then it continued to fall until October 1973.

Despite the strides that the cartel and its members made, the market power of OPEC was still limited during the 1970s. In the short term, the cartel's power was still balanced by the collective buying power of the oil majors and the independent oil companies. By the 1980s, it was even more circumspect as the oil majors and independents, also benefiting from rising oil prices, made new oil discoveries outside of OPEC countries, notably in Alaska and the North Sea. By 1984, OPEC's market power became severely limited by the ability of some non-OPEC oil exporters to increase capacity and production, and the ability of oil importers to diversify their sources of energy. We can see in Figure 1.1 that – with the exception of two jumps in 1973 and 1979, corresponding to the Arab-Israeli war of 1973 and the Iranian revolution, respectively – inflation in the Dollar price of crude oil continued to lag behind inflation of the Dollar price of gold, which is a good measure of overall inflationary trends. We shall discuss the inflation of the 1970s and its relationship to the recycling of petrodollars, and the ensuing Latin American debt crisis, in Chapter 5.

Political Catalysts, Economic Cycles, and Oil-Price Volatility

For now, we focus on the catalytic role of political events in oil-price volatility, sometimes producing persistent effects. In this regard, it is important to notice that the underlying economics of the oil market themselves contain a fundamental economic cycle. Long lags are required to create sufficient capacity by building rigs, pipelines, and ships for the extraction and delivery of crude, and building refineries to deliver final products. Low prices of energy spur high growth rates, which create excess demand conditions that result in higher prices. The higher prices simultaneously spur activity in capacity building, exploration, extraction, refining, and development of alternative forms of fuel. At the same time, the higher energy prices increase costs and reduce competitiveness in the non-energy sector, reducing the rate of economic growth. Because of economies of scale, lumpy capacity building inevitably leads to excess capacity, which combines with slower growth to drive prices back down. The lower energy prices spur a new wave of economic growth, and the cycle repeats.

The multinational oil majors, like Standard Oil before them, understood this cyclical behavior. They used their large market shares, financial resources, and long-term investment goals to attenuate the cycle. Of course, in their attempt to attenuate the price cycle by keeping prices higher in the 1950s, they exacerbated the recession in Europe and created the ideal environment for independent oil companies and the Soviet Union to challenge their control of the global oil market.

After a series of failed attempts to gain market power during the 1960s, OPEC finally had a perfect opportunity to exercise power in 1973, proving that the organization – and especially Saudi Arabia as its biggest producer – had some control over oil prices, at least in the short run. In the medium to long run, however, the basic economic conditions of the global business and oil price cycles remained, and long-term price elasticity was clearly higher. Therefore, the challenge for

OPEC was to have the discipline and long-term planning horizon to attenuate, rather than amplify, the cycle.

By March 1982, Saudi Arabia had clearly established itself as the "swing producer" within OPEC and worldwide, in effect managing the oil price cycle by controlling its own output, and in the process attenuating the closely related global business cycle. The Saudi swing-producer status afforded the country tremendous geopolitical weight, especially in its growing relationship with the United States. However, the Kingdom had on occasion to pay a hefty price for assuming and retaining this status, for example reducing its oil exports drastically during the recession years between 1980 and 1984 in a futile attempt to support OPEC's target price of $34 per barrel, which was eventually abandoned for a new target of $29, despite those Herculean efforts.[4]

The Political Economy of Childhood 1973–84

The years 1973 to 1984 constituted the period of happy childhood for the new Middle East. Oil prices reached a high plateau between 1973 and 1979, and then an even higher plateau between 1980 and 1982. Massive Dollar receipts from the sale of oil resulted in a very predictable "resource-curse" pattern. The first effect was strengthening the central state, which was the primary recipient of oil revenues, and the oil sector that financed that state, at the expense of other sectors of the economy and society at large.

This effect is expected for two reasons. The obvious first reason is that the primary and secondary beneficiaries of the boom in oil receipts use their resources to solidify their control of the country and economy. The second reason is the euphoria that typically overtakes a society when it receives such a sustained windfall. The governments of the oil-exporting countries felt that they could make up for lost time and join the club of newly industrialized economies in record time. They attempted to achieve that goal by investing in mammoth infrastructure and industrial projects – with the view that they were converting the exhaustible underground mineral capital into productive physical capital that would support long-term industrialization. The windfall of oil-sale receipts also allowed the state to fight poverty and increase the well-being of the lower and middle classes, even as the wealth gap between them and the business and political elites grew vast.

Tremendous wealth poured into large industrial and infrastructure projects, attracting rent-seeking behavior – the tendency to pursue fast enrichment by gaining access to the oil rents. An entire class of rent seekers thus emerged among the new political and economic elites and their associates. Rent-seeking behavior was tolerated because the inflow of funds far exceeded the absorptive capacities of the oil-rent recipients. Eventually, the rent-seeking behavior became institutionalized and impossible to control, even when oil rents declined sharply.[5]

Resource Misallocation

The first result of this rent-seeking behavior was gross inefficiency in allocation of resources. Economic logic dictates that a country with exhaustible mineral wealth should first consider the baseline scenario of leaving the wealth in the ground. The rate of return on oil in the ground must then be compared to the rate of return on extracting the oil and investing the proceeds. A country should only consume out of the interest or return on that investment of proceeds. However, rent-seeking behavior encourages relatively unproductive investment and direct consumption of the proceeds by funneling large sums to the rent seekers. Thus, the temptation to consume rather than invest nonrenewable resources was overwhelming.

In addition to inappropriate consumption behavior, massive investments in the oil sector, infrastructure building, and high capital-intensive industries, crowded out private investment in the sectors that were most appropriate for those countries' levels of economic development. Thus, the investment and consumption behavior of the new government and business elites who benefited from growth in the oil and construction sectors drove resources away from traditional investment activities that could have provided sustainable and diversified long-term growth potential in those economies.

Inappropriate consumption behavior was encouraged further by excessive redistribution of wealth. In the GCC oil-exporting countries, this redistribution meant that the local population developed an antiwork ethic, relying on imported labor from other Arab countries and Asia to do most of the work. Conspicuous consumption behavior became habitual for the host country's population and the migrant workers alike. When the oil rents stopped flowing in the 1980s and 1990s, those populations continued to consume beyond their means, even as generous wealth transfers were no longer sustainable.

In other oil-exporting countries, high levels of consumption and spuriously grandiose investment were supported by irresponsible borrowing. The episode of recycling petrodollars in the 1970s is generally characterized as lending from trade-surplus oil-exporting countries to trade-deficit oil-importing countries. In reality, a significant portion of petrodollars were lent to other oil-exporting countries. The latter thought that they could leverage their underground oil, which the banks considered to be very good collateral, to accelerate their growth and industrialization using borrowed funds. As oil prices plummeted in the 1980s, many of those countries' debts became unpayable, posing a threat to the entire international financial system.

In the Middle East, the fast growth of oil-exporting countries convinced some of their neighbors – most notably Egypt, the most populous country in the region – to abandon the import-substitution route to industrialization and to adopt an export-oriented or open-door policy. Leading up to 1973, many import-substituting countries were facing a crisis of foreign exchange, because their needs for some imports persisted but their exports were insufficient to fund the purchase of those imports. Raising interest rates to attract foreign currency would drive those economies into recession, and printing money to finance their industrialization would drive them into inflation. The failure of import substitution policies was in stark contrast to the success of Asian economies that adopted an export-oriented approach.

Circa 1973, Korea and other Asian countries had shown the way out of import substitution through export of labor-intensive products, which eventually led the way to gradual industrialization and sustainable economic growth. For the labor-rich and oil-poor countries of the Middle East, export of labor itself proved to be a quicker path to economic growth. Egypt, Syria, and Lebanon had long traditions of excellent education systems, which quickly supplied teachers, doctors, engineers, and other professionals to resource-rich but labor-poor countries such as Saudi Arabia, Kuwait, Qatar, the United Arab Emirates, and Libya.

Middle-East Flows of Labor, Capital, and Cultural Norms

The oil-exporting countries of the Middle East became more dependent on imported labor to support their growing economies, as well as to compensate for the local populations' progressively increasing aversion to work. As the migrant workers built up their savings, they eventually returned to their home countries with the consumerist and antiwork ethic to which they had aspired during their working years, and which they had transferred to their families through regular workers' remittances. Thus, consumerism and rentier-class ethics were exported from the oil-rentier states to the rest of the Arab Middle East and beyond.

Rentier States and Leisure Classes

This emergence of a "leisure-class" ethic during periods of unprecedented economic growth is well understood as a social and economic phenomenon. The most prominent economic analysis of this phenomenon is in the work of Thorstein Veblen, published in 1899 as a stinging criticism of emerging American consumerism at the height of the previous round of globalization under the gold standard.[6] Economic and sociological elements of the same analysis are also evident in Ibn Khaldun's analysis of the rise and fall of nations. Ibn Khaldun's analysis starts with poor and industrious nomadic tribes invading cities populated with spoiled rich inhabitants. Eventually, the invaders begin to enjoy the fruits of their newfound riches, building palaces and emulating the lifestyles of their predecessors, which makes them an easy prey for a new wave of nomadic invasion.[7]

In Veblen's analysis, leisure is highlighted as the ultimate luxury good, coveted by all members of society. Little has changed over the past century. In many social circles, a person's status can still be determined by the number of degrees of separation from work. The lowest-level inhabitants of this hierarchy are farmers and blue-collar workers. Their managers have one degree of separation from work, and therefore occupy a higher status in society. The company's owners have two degrees of separation, and therefore occupy a higher level still. The penultimate levels are reserved for those who make decisions on major financial deals, corporate mergers and acquisitions, and so on. The highest levels are reserved for those who have people who supervise people who supervise people, with a seemingly endless number of buffers to separate them from actual physical or mental work.

Religion and Social Norms

A new cultural and political climate emerged in the Middle East during the 1970s. The region had turned to Arab nationalism, socialism, and import substitution following World War II. All three strategies had failed, culminating in a devastating military defeat of Arab armies in June 1967 by Israel, which had a tiny land and population base compared to its Arab neighbors. The shock drove the population of the region to seek an alternative to the failed nationalist paradigm. They found that alternative in religion. In Egypt, this natural reaction was accelerated by President Anwar Sadat's decision to strengthen Islamist groups, as a counterweight to the Nasserist and communist groups that threatened his grasp on power. External signs of traditional religiosity in society became much more manifest in modes of dress, attendance at religious lectures, and political rhetoric.

The coincidence of this increased religiosity with wealth windfall in the form of oil rents reinforced the pattern. God appeared to be rewarding the conservative societies of the Gulf with easy wealth. The role of traditional religious scholars in the populous Islamic countries, especially Egypt, began to shrink, as the religious paradigm of oil-rich countries of the Arabian peninsula became dominant. Financial sponsorship of like-minded Islamic scholars, as well as marketing of indigenous Arabian scholars' views, hastened the process. Financial support of the Muslim Brotherhood, the Jamat-i-Islami, and other similar groups throughout the Islamic world was generally tolerated by the host countries of those groups for a variety of political and economic reasons. The United States and Western European countries were also content to allow and encourage this spread of Islamism as insurance against the spread of Soviet influence in this region with increasing strategic value. Covert support for Islamist resistance in Afghanistan, in particular, was aimed to hasten the downfall of the Soviet Union.[8]

More subtle channels for exporting the Peninsula's brand of Islam throughout the Middle East worked through the migrant workers' family and social networks.

Migrant workers attributed some of the wealth windfall to their host countries' brand of religiosity. They adopted many of its traits and exported those social norms back to their families. Migrant workers' remittances allowed their female (and some male) family members to withdraw from the workforce, thus weakening the indigenous social norms and replacing them with the norms of the migrant workers' host countries. Those families' economic influence in the labor-exporting countries' societies eventually eclipsed the economic influence of the traditional economic, political, and social elites of those countries. Attempts to attract tourism from the oil-rich countries also supported the trend, which has continued to this day.

Oil Price Collapse and the Politics of Discontent

In the mid-1980s, a series of supply and demand-affecting events brought the oil-revenues party to an abrupt end. The high prices of the 1970s and early 1980s had driven the world into a terrible economic malaise, known as stagflation – a combination of economic stagnation and inflation. Higher oil prices meant higher cost of production, which was an impediment to economic growth.

Under the Bretton-Woods system, Dollar flows from the trade-deficit countries to trade-surplus countries would have driven the world into a severe recession or depression, reducing demand for fuel and bringing oil prices down at an earlier date. Alternatively, deficit countries would have raised their interest rate system to support the par values of their currencies and prevent Dollar outflows, with the same result.[9] However, after Bretton Woods was abandoned, industrial countries, including the United States, were able to float their exchange rates and accommodate the higher prices and inflationary expectations by simply printing cash.

Double-digit inflation ensued in most industrialized countries, but higher prices did not translate into demand for factors of production.[10] High inflation and massive petrodollar flows into and then out of countries with limited absorptive capacities drove real interest rates to very low, even negative, levels. Negative real interest rates contributed further to inflation and fueled a global credit bubble. Lack of economic growth eventually meant that debts were not repayable, resulting in high-profile bank failures and fear of a global financial meltdown.

In 1979, Paul Volcker was appointed Chairman of the Federal Reserve Board, and he took drastic measures to combat inflation, even if it meant tolerating high unemployment rates. United Kingdom Prime Minister Margaret Thatcher's government soon began adopting similar "monetarist" policies, which aimed to reduce the growth in money supply and raise interest rates to combat inflation. In due time, inflation was tamed, but the high American interest rates also meant that the global economy was driven into a severe recession.

Reduced demand for oil, because of the recession, and expanding availability of alternative fuels, such as nuclear power, initiated a series of price reductions. In addition, and contributing to this trend, Libya began discounting its oil prices to counter a ban on its exports imposed by President Reagan. The spot market for oil, once selling at a premium to OPEC's official posted prices, started moving to a sharp discount, forcing other producers such as Norway and the United Kingdom to cut their posted prices. OPEC itself reduced its target price, and many countries began offering secret discounts through nontransparent systems such as barter deals, extended credit terms and shipping subsidies.

Economic Consequences

Saudi Arabia valiantly tried to stave off the inevitable by continuing to reduce its own production. Despite those efforts, prices continued to fall, aided by the creation of a new oil futures market that made spot-market price movements far more transparent.[11] In an attempt to end expensive non-OPEC oil production and alternative energy development, Saudi Arabia started a price war to regain its market share, aiming to return to its earlier production level of 6 million barrels per day. Instead of selling at the market price, Saudi Arabia began linking its crude export prices to the "netback value of its oil" – the market price of refined products less a fixed refining profit margin of $2–3 per barrel.

The result was instantaneous. Saudi production recovered dramatically but prices slid to under $8 a barrel as supply from the United States and the North Sea continued. It had been expected that rising Saudi production, aimed to create a price war and thereby falling prices, would force high-cost oil production from the United States and the UK North Sea to shut down. This did not happen, and the Middle East's economic fortunes collapsed with the price of oil.

By 1986, the nominal Dollar price of oil (without adjusting for the annual double-digit inflation of the previous decade) was back to its pre-1979 levels. The reality of a new era of oil prices had become undeniable.[12] The precipitous decline in regional economic welfare during this period is illustrated in Figure 2.1, which shows the dramatic decline in real Saudi Arabian per capita GDP. It is clear from Figure 2.2 that Saudi Arabia again bore the brunt of the 1985–6 post-price-war strategy. OPEC had announced production cuts designed to induce a recovery in oil prices, but other OPEC producers cheated, producing well above their quotas, in an attempt to maximize short-term revenues.

In 1990, Iraq invaded Kuwait, and the ensuing sanctions removed 5 million b/d of their production from the market. OPEC increased official production quotas to acknowledge production increases by key members such as Saudi Arabia, Venezuela, and Nigeria. Eventually, oil supply was restored from Kuwait, and from Iraq under the United Nations' oil-for-food program. This recovery

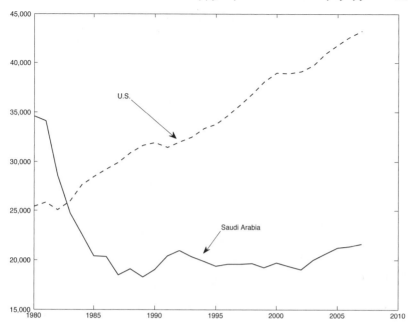

Figure 2.1. Real per capita GDP (PPP constant 2005 international Dollars) for Saudi Arabia and the United States. *Source*: World Bank, World Development Indicators.

of Middle-East oil supply renewed OPEC's difficulties in regulating production. Those difficulties were exacerbated further by capacity expansion in Venezuela. Oil prices plummeted again to $8 a barrel. Prices remained at that level until OPEC's meeting of March 1998, which ushered a new regime that we discuss in Chapter 3.[13]

The decline in the Saudi economy during the 1980s and 1990s meant fewer jobs for immigrant workers from neighboring countries, as well as lower wages and worker remittances for those who secured jobs there. Figure 2.3 shows the dramatic rise and then collapse of real (constant 1992 Dollars) workers' remittances per capita for Egypt, the Arab world's most populous country. The notable exception to the decline starting in the mid-1980s is the brief period following the first Gulf War after Iraq's invasion of Kuwait. However, by 1995, per capita real remittances had fallen back to their level in the mid-1970s, and they continued to decline further until the recent increase in oil prices during 2003–8.

By the late 1990s, the problem had reached such a level that Saudi Arabia recognized its high levels of unemployment and emerging problem of poverty. A programs known as "Saudization," which gives preference to Saudi nationals in

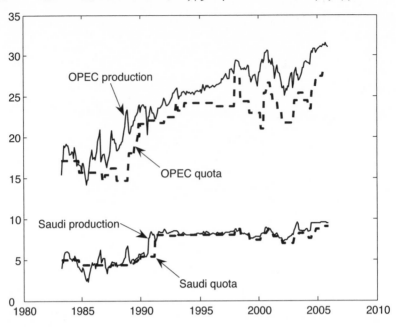

Figure 2.2. OPEC and Saudi Arabian quotas and production, millions of barrels per day. *Source:* OPEC and EIA.

employment, did not resolve those domestic economic problems. Only the recent rebound in oil prices during 2003–8 finally provided economic relief.

Credit Bubbles

The mania of the late 1970s sparked credit bubbles everywhere in the Middle East, inviting middle-class participation in highly speculative financial markets. One of the most volatile episodes in the region was the irresponsible credit-driven speculative bubble in Kuwait's *Suq Al-Manakh*. During the late 1970s, a number of prominent Kuwaiti family businesses thrived, driving stocks higher and encouraging numerous small investors to acquire credit from local banks with which they further inflated the stock market's speculative bubble. Starting in 1981, a sharp decline in oil prices and oil production drove the Kuwaiti government's balance sheet into deficit for the first time. In 1982, the bubble market crashed. Investors could not repay their debts to the banks, and the banks faced insolvency in the face of potential depositor runs on the banking system.[14]

A different crisis emerged in Egypt during the mid-1980s, as migrant workers sought investment vehicles for their accumulated savings over the previous decade. A group of unregulated financial intermediaries emerged, and came to be

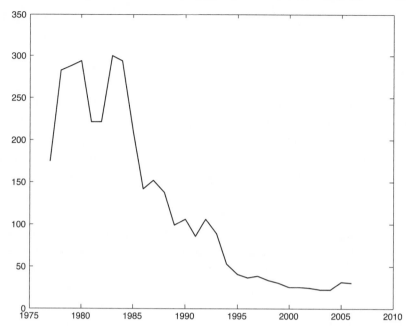

Figure 2.3. Real per capita workers' remittance receipts for Egypt (in constant 1992 Dollars). *Source*: World Bank, World Development Indicators.

known as "fund-mobilization companies." They promised higher rates of return than banks and used the rhetoric of "Islamic finance," which argued that variable rates of return from sharing the profits and losses of industry and trade were permissible, but that bank interest was forbidden *riba* (usury). A number of trading and manufacturing companies with connections to the Muslim Brotherhood and to Saudi Arabian investment companies began to attract the savings of migrant workers, paying very handsome rates of return even as conventional banks were paying negative interest rates.

The companies claimed to be investing in industry and trade of real assets such as appliances and automobiles. By the late 1980s, many of the companies were unable to meet their liabilities to investors, and the Egyptian government stepped in. It was then revealed that the companies' successes were based on two strategies. The first was a pyramid scheme, which allowed them to pay above-market rates of return as long as new investments were forthcoming. The decline in worker-remittances flow in the mid-1980s meant that the pyramid scheme could not survive any longer. The other revelation was that most of the funds were in fact invested in foreign currency, commodity, and stock markets. The stock market crash of fall 1987 coincided with the declining base of new investments, thus making those fund mobilization companies insolvent. The government and Central Bank of Egypt eventually intervened to repossess the companies' assets and repay some of the investors' funds over the following two decades.[15]

Sadly, the lessons of credit bubbles in the 1980s were not learned. Credit-enhanced stock-market bubbles reappeared throughout the region, including in Kuwait, following the resurgence of petrodollar flows after 2003. The new wave of petrodollars also sparked inflation in all asset and commodity prices. By 2007, Egyptian real interest rates were negative, again, and a number of small scandals suggested the return of "fund-mobilization" companies to the market.

Political Discontent

Accurate data on unemployment and poverty rates in the Middle East are generally unavailable. Fortunately, other reliable figures are available, and they tell the story of what happened during the 1980s and 1990s. Figure 2.1 illustrated the fall of Saudi real per capita income from a level higher than that of the United States to much lower levels, with the commensurate gap in standards of living growing similarly. As Figure 2.4 shows, there are two components in this problem. The first is great volatility in oil revenues, which are tied directly to real GDP growth. The second is an incredibly high rate of population growth that was sustained for nearly two decades.

Fueled by higher oil prices, phenomenal economic growth of the 1970s, in turn, caused an equally phenomenal rate of population growth. This has created a tremendous dependency ratio, not only in Saudi Arabia, but throughout the region. According to the United Nations Development Program's Human Development Report, roughly one-third of the region's population was under the age of 15 in 2004.[16]

We have already referred to the 1970s as the region's carefree childhood. Oil-exporting countries were flooded with petrodollars. The middle classes throughout the region benefited from appreciation in their property values, as well as increasing opportunities to accumulate wealth directly or indirectly through work in the oil-supporting sectors, investment in stock markets, and so on. Income inequality was certainly rising, but opportunities for upward social mobility were also substantial. The inflationary effects of petrodollar inflows did lead to some disruptive social activities, such as the bread riots in Cairo in January 1977, and emerging violent-Islamist groups became increasingly visible. However, the middle classes of the Middle East were generally content during that period, even as the value of their professional degrees and expertise lost ground to the new merchant class.

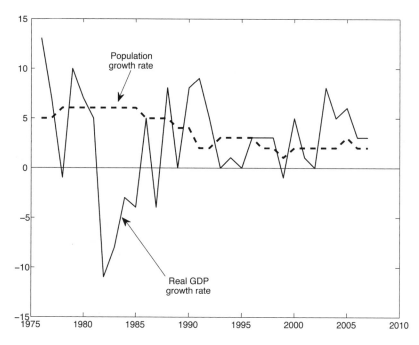

Figure 2.4. Saudi Arabian population and real GDP (constant 2000 Dollars) % growth rates. *Source*: World Bank, World Development Indicators.

That contentment began to evaporate in the 1980s. The precipitous decline in oil prices seemed temporary at first. By the mid-1980s, it was clear that the ambitions of middle-class Arabs were generally out of alignment with the economic reality. A trend of political Shiʿism – revolt against greedy and corrupt secular elites – began to take shape. Alarmist Arab discourse since the 1979 Iranian revolution tends to focus on theological Shiʿism. The more dangerous trend to Arab rulers, however, was success of political Shiʿism, which challenged the authority of monarchs and autocratic rulers. It is not a coincidence that a street in Tehran was named after Kahled El-Islambulli, one of the leading assassins of Egyptian President Anwar Sadat in 1981. This spread of political Shiʿism is still evident today in the similarity of tactics and general affinity between groups such as Lebanon's Shiʿite Hizbullah and the Palestinian Sunni-Islamist Hamas.

The seeds of militant Islamism were already in place in the 1970s. However, they did not gain momentum and larger grassroots support until the 1980s. It is often said that poverty cannot be blamed for militant and terrorist activities, citing the fact that leaders and significant contributors to militant-Islamist movements tend to be middle-class and university educated. This argument misses the mark entirely. Participants in militant and terrorist groups may not be poor themselves, but the fear of poverty must be recognized as one of the contributing factors to their enlisting in those movements.[17]

Increasing inequality in income distribution during the 1970s did not deny intelligent middle-class Arabs their dreams of upward social mobility. However, continually increasing inequality during the 1980s was coupled with increasing poverty, and hence increased likelihood of downward rather than upward social mobility for the middle classes. The poor are generally too busy trying to feed their families. Those who have the means to strike against the system are the middle-class individuals who see their cultural influence dwindling and their economic dreams dashed. Fear of poverty, rather than poverty itself, was the primary catalyst in converting the increasing religiosity of the 1970s into a political, and ultimately militant, religiosity. This militancy started within the region in the 1970s, and it was later directed toward the Soviet Union, but ultimately turned around against the United States and local Middle-East regimes.

The Rise of National Oil Companies

The 1956 Egyptian nationalization of the Suez canal, and the ensuing crisis, brought about major disruption in oil supplies. This prompted countries such as India and Brazil to seek self-sufficiency in oil resources through creation of national oil companies (NOCs). On the supply side, oil-producing countries created national oil companies as part of their planned industrialization and import-substitution policies. At the time, seizing control of their own oil resources was seen as a nationalist policy against foreign oil companies who were not serving the host countries' national interests. National oil companies were thus envisioned as state-run vehicles for quick industrialization through control and investment of oil rents.

Different Nationalization Models: Instantaneous and Gradual

In many cases, the process of nationalization of oil resources was gradual, due to lack of funds and technical expertise. Iran's early experience with nationalization was not successful for multiple reasons. Elected to office on a nationalist platform, Iranian Prime Minister Mohammed Mossadeq moved to nationalize Iranian oil resources in 1951. The move to nationalize, authorized by a parliamentary resolution, followed in the aftermath of failed attempts to press the Anglo-Iranian Oil Company to increase production and revenue.

The Mossadeq attempt was not successful for a number of reasons, one of which may be the lack of a successful precedent to emulate. The nationalization attempt prompted Britain to boycott Iranian oil, putting tremendous pressure on the Iranian economy. The United Kingdom and the United States covertly supported a coup that overthrew the Mossadeq government in 1953. Subsequently, a foreign consortium was installed in 1954 to run the Iranian oil industry for many years to follow.

A second wave of nationalization started in the 1960s, adopting a more gradualist approach. Iraq established the Iraqi National Oil Company (INOC) in 1964 to develop oil-concession areas previously controlled by the international oil majors that comprised the Iraq Petroleum Consortium (IPC). During its first decade, INOC was given exclusive rights to develop Iraq's undeveloped oil reserves, allowing international companies to continue managing the country's existing oil production.[18]

INOC started taking full control of Iraqi oil fields only in the mid-1970s. With Soviet financial and technical assistance, INOC began in 1970 to drill and extract oil from Rumaila in commercial quantities. Full nationalization of Iraqi oil fields took place finally in 1975, eleven years after the establishment of INOC. The Soviet Union backed Iraq's socialist-inspired nationalization by the ruling Ba'th party and offered the Iraqi government a protection treaty against foreign powers.

Saudi Arabia nationalized Aramco, the international consortium that owned concessions to Saudi oil, even more gradually. The Kingdom took a minority stake in Aramco's ownership, and then increased its stake gradually and began to place Saudi nationals in key management positions. Aramco executives recognized that a negotiated settlement would be preferable to outright nationalization. Aramco's parent companies thus began the first round of participation negotiations with Saudi Arabia in 1972.

Saudi Arabia agreed to pay $500 million in compensation for the initial 25 percent share, which entitled the Kingdom to crude-oil rights proportional to its share of Aramco. Saudi participation in early years focused on training and development of Saudi-national employees, especially at the management level, to create a cadre of future executives. The General Agreement of 1972 stipulated that Saudi participation, starting at 25 percent, would increase 5 percent per annum until it reached 51 percent in 1983. No date for full ownership transfer was set initially.

Later negotiations with American-consortium partners led to an agreement in June 1974 that gave Saudi Arabia the right to acquire 60 percent of Aramco. Agreement on Saudi nationalization of management and control of Aramco's assets was reached in 1976. Four years later, on September 5, 1980, Saudi Arabia announced its completed purchase of Aramco's assets from American partners. During most of the 1980s, Aramco accounted for approximately 90 percent of the Kingdom's oil production. Americans still administered Aramco on a daily basis, as Saudi nationals gradually took control of management positions. Ownership-transfer papers were eventually signed in 1990, following the establishment of Saudi Aramco as the Kingdom's state oil monopoly in 1988.

Effects on OPEC Production

Oil rents during the boom years of the 1970s were used, in part, to build local human resources and technical capabilities. However, by the time that human capital was reaching critical mass, oil prices collapsed in the 1980s. The national firms' budgets were severely strained, as governments extracted greater shares of the companies' operating cash flows to fund state expenditures. OPEC national companies were thus prevented from investing sufficiently in their core oil business, as governments used dwindling oil revenues to support their growing populations. In addition, regional wars, first between Iraq and Iran, and later between Iraq and Kuwait, resulted in massive damage to regional oil infrastructure, as well as saddling some regional governments with substantial financial burdens.

OPEC's oil-and-gas investments were also hampered by international and American economic sanctions, which discouraged investment in key oil-producing countries such as Iraq, Iran, and Libya for nearly three decades.[19] Those countries have never recovered from the sanctions imposed on them at various times. Their outputs continue to fall well below their respective levels during the 1970s.

As a result, many of OPEC countries' NOCs have suffered capacity deterioration since 1979.[20] Without a doubt, regional geopolitics and related boycotts have therefore played an important part in this failure to maintain capacity levels. A second critical factor in this failure has been the internal structures of many NOCs. Reserves were generally discovered and developed by international oil companies, not by the national oil companies that came to dominate the crude-oil sector in the 1980s. With the exception of Saudi Aramco, few NOCs inside OPEC have had good track records in exploration and development. This was caused, in part, by lack of fiscal discipline. With falling oil prices, the incentive was too great for states to divert oil revenues from investment toward social programs designed to maintain public order.

Neglect of core investment in resource development and exploration by many Middle-East countries' NOCs has combined with continued regional turmoil to hamper the region's productive capacity. Lack of proper maintenance of oil fields can be harmful in the long run, by causing geological damage to existing fields, for example in Iraq and Iran. Causes for alarm abound. For instance, Kuwait has recently downgraded its national reserve estimate, and Saudi Arabia has been criticized for field mismanagement.[21] Saudi Arabia's oil sector may be sounder than critics assert. However, experts agree that the existing reservoirs throughout the Gulf region decline by approximately 8 percent annually. Thus, billions of

Dollars in new investment are needed to maintain, let alone expand, production capacity.

Vertical Integration

The oil sector is generally divided into an "upstream" segment focused on exploration, development, and extraction of crude oil, and a "downstream" segment focused on refining and marketing of final products. During the oil demand and price collapse of the 1980s, Middle-East NOCs recognized that their lack of direct access to the downstream segment prevented them from smoothing revenues, as international oil companies had done in past cycles. As a result, several major NOCs focused their investment in the 1980s on expanding refining and marketing businesses.

Saudi Arabia, Kuwait, and Iran built export refineries and petrochemical plants, in an attempt to capture higher rents by selling higher-value refined petroleum products. In order to survive in the ultracompetitive market of the mid-1980s, Kuwait's national oil monopoly, Kuwait Petroleum Corporation, purchased Gulf Oil's operations in Europe, including 3,000 gasoline service stations in 1983. Shortly thereafter, Libya purchased refining assets in Italy from Amoco, and Saudi Arabia later purchased a stake in three U.S. refineries from Texaco in 1988.

Despite those efforts, NOCs remained less efficient than the international majors. One major factor has been governments' use of the NOCs as employment engines, and another is those governments' domestic sale of refined products at heavily subsidized prices. The most important factor, however, has been the NOCs' tendency to underinvest in developing reserves and to exploit existing fields excessively, shifting resource extraction to the present at rates that hamper long-term capacity. Refined-product subsidies, in turn, siphoned resources away from the NOCs and thus reduced their efficiency.[22]

Government subsidies of oil products led further to economic inefficiency by encouraging excessive energy consumption, smuggling, and corruption. Subsidies in Iran, for example, allow gasoline to be sold for $0.10 a liter. This has created an economic drain on the National Iranian Oil Company (NIOC) and forced Iran to use scarce hard currency to import gasoline in order to meet rising demand. Therefore, NOCs, once envisioned as engines of national wealth creation, seem in fact to have become drains on their countries' resources because of subsidies and mismanagement.

Countries that wish to use their oil revenues to pursue social and economic programs may be well justified in doing so. However, the form of wealth transfer through subsidies, as adopted in many Middle Eastern countries, is distortionary in the sense that subsidies encourage excessive energy consumption and other misallocation of those countries' scarce resources. Those countries would be well advised to seek more efficient means of monetizing their natural resources and to use other less distortionary mechanisms to achieve their social and economic goals.

Renewed global economic growth in later decades increased oil demand substantially relative to the 1980s. However, OPEC investment and capacity expansion have lagged, reducing the level of spare capacity in oil markets to dangerously thin margins.[23] By 2000, OPEC's spare capacity had declined to 2 percent of world demand, with 90 percent of the spare capacity being held in Saudi Arabia.

Continued decline in spare capacity and the continued threat of further supply-disrupting turmoil in the Middle East were the main supply-side reasons for the initial increase in oil prices after the 2003 invasion of Iraq. In this regard, it is instructive to note that from 1970 to 2000, more than 40 percent of the increase in world energy supply came from within the industrialized countries – mainly from Alaska, the U.S. Gulf of Mexico, and the United Kingdom's and Norway's North Sea. Productions in these regions was under the control of the international majors and independents.

In contrast, the International Energy Agency (IEA) projects that over the next quarter century, more than 90 percent of new oil supplies will come from the developing world, where NOCs control the development of reserves. The IEA estimates that rising demand would require 20 to 30 million b/d more than today's production level of 86 million b/d. It estimates that more than $2.2 trillion of new investments will be needed to raise production by this margin. It is not clear whether market conditions, national agendas, and geopolitical factors will allow this level of investment to take place.

Militarism, Debts, and Global Finance

Myopic government policies, military conflicts, and financial crises are common features of the resource curse that prevents resource-rich countries from following optimal investment and growth paths. In this regard, three factors coincided during the 1980s and early 1990s to globalize the resource curse of the Middle East. The first factor was increased incidence of war, which increased militarism and the associated diversion of funds from investment in productive capital to counterproductive arms races. This was nowhere as evident as in the cases of Iraq and Iran, which were positioned in the late 1970s as the only two countries in the region with sufficient absorptive capacity to make good use of the oil-receipts windfall. The second factor, which we study in Chapter 5, was the acceleration of lending to developing countries, as a major component of the strategy to recycle petrodollars in the 1970s. The increasing flow of funds to developing countries eventually diversified from debt to portfolio and foreign direct investment, resulting in renewed growth of globalization, unseen since the gold-standard era.

Military Conflicts

The Middle East has been no stranger to wars and smaller-scale military conflicts throughout its history. During the period 1973–95, there were many wars related to the Israeli-Palestinian conflict, including the main war in October 1973, but also smaller wars between Syria and Palestinian forces in Lebanon, as well as skirmishes throughout the region. However, wars during the period of the 1980s and 1990s were catastrophic in the sense of preventing the region from enjoying the economic fruits of petrodollar inflows. Wars and threats of war in the oil-rich area of Iraq and its neighbors were particularly devastating.

During the 1970s, the Ba'thist team of Hasan Al-Bakr and Saddam Hussein navigated a series of challenges from without: Syria to the West and Iran to the East, as well as from within: Kurdish independence movements in the North and Shi'ite political dissent in the South. Those challenges were navigated through a series of diplomatic moves (such as the treaty with Iran in 1975), military threats (such as amassing troops on the Syrian border), and direct persecution of Kurds in the North and Shi'ites in the South. According to one report, Iraq spent 40 percent of its massive petrodollar inflows during that period on weaponry.[24]

The greatest challenge to the Iraqi Ba'thist regime was posed by the success of the Iranian revolution in establishing a religious Shi'ite state to its east. Direct and inspirational support from the Iranian revolution emboldened the Iraqi Shi'ites, which prompted Saddam Hussein, who assumed the presidency in 1979, to expel tens of thousands of Iraqi Shi'ites that were identified by the regime as "Iranian Shi'ites." Shortly thereafter, in an attempt to assert Iraq's power in the region, Saddam Hussein started the first of two disastrous wars by invading Iran in 1980.

What Saddam Hussein had envisioned as a minor exercise of power turned into a devastating eight-year-long war, as Iran sought to reassert its presence and to defend the success of its revolution. Repeated attacks between Iran and Iraq on each others' cities and oil resources eventually tipped the scales in Iraq's favor, as Western powers – especially the United States – moved into the region to protect oil supplies. Financial support from Saudi Arabia and Kuwait, and military support from both the Soviet Union and the United States, eventually forced a cease-fire on Iran in 1988. However, the Iraqi economy was devastated from the long war, which exhausted the bulk of its Dollar reserves accumulated during the 1970s, and shackled it with a debt repayment that consumed 50 percent of its oil revenues in 1990.[25]

The second disastrous gamble by Saddam Hussein took place in 1990. Iraq had tried repeatedly to appeal for economic help from Saudi Arabia and Kuwait, in the forms of forgiveness of Iraq's $40 billion debt, used to finance the war with Iran, and reduction in their oil supplies to boost Iraq's oil revenues and finance reconstruction. When those appeals were rebuffed repeatedly, Saddam Hussein decided to take by force what he considered to be his rightful claim for fighting an eight-year war on behalf of the other Gulf states, which were equally wary of Iran and potential regional Shi'ite revival. In August 1990, Iraq invaded Kuwait, in the belief that it could dictate its terms to Kuwait and Saudi Arabia, by force and through the threat of force, respectively. Saudi Arabia sought the help of the United States, which led an international coalition in a swift war to liberate Kuwait. For Saudi Arabia, the massive financial cost of the war combined with low oil prices to exacerbate the Kingdom's economic problems.

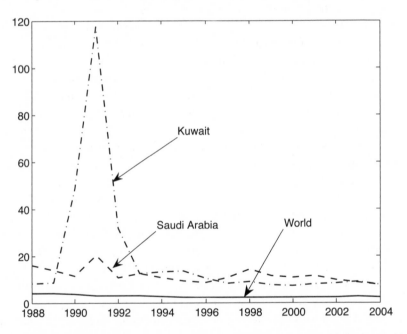

Figure 2.5. Military expenditure as a percentage of GDP. *Source*: World Bank, World Development Indicators.

Militarism and Unproductive Use of Capital and Labor

We have discussed previously the tendency of petrodollar inflows to redirect investment and expenditure away from productive capacity and toward areas that matter to the state. This is particularly true in the case of military expenditure, which protects the ruling elites from external threats (directly) as well as internal challenges (indirectly, by appeasing military leaders who could mount a coup). In

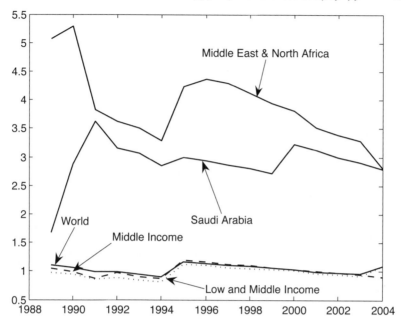

Figure 2.6. Military personnel as a percentage of total labor force. *Source*: World Bank, World Development Indicators.

the case of oil-rich Gulf states, the war between Iraq and Iran wasted a large portion of their oil revenues on both financing the war and financing reconstruction following war-related capital destruction.

As we can see in Figure 2.5, military expenditure in neighboring GCC countries – namely, Saudi Arabia and Kuwait – was also disproportionately high as a percentage of those countries' GDPs, even if we exclude the years 1990 and 1991. Perhaps even more importantly, Figure 2.6 shows the disproportionate allocation of human capital to the military throughout the region. This contributed further to the lack of long-term absorptive capacity in productive segments of the economy, by discouraging long-term investment, and thus ensured recurrence of the problem of recycling petrodollars when oil prices spiked again after 2003.

Debt and Global Finance

The roots of the current episode of globalization can be found in the early 1970s. As we can see in Figure 2.7, flows of debt financing in the 1970s set the stage for later waves of foreign direct investment and portfolio investment in developing countries, or emerging markets as they came to be known. When the Bretton-Woods system came to an end, the world started on an inflationary spiral that was enhanced by the sharp increases in oil prices in 1973 and 1979. Instead of raising interest rates to combat inflation, countries were allowed to print money to finance the purchase of various imports.

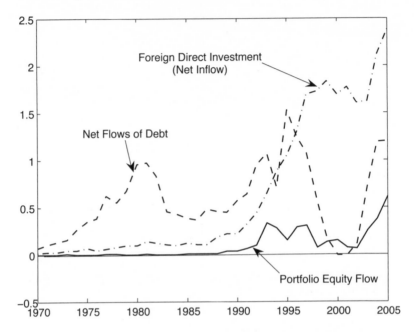

Figure 2.7. Foreign direct investment, portfolio, and debt flows to developing countries (US$ hundreds of billions). *Source*: World Bank, Global Development Finance.

As the United States' trade deficit with oil-exporting countries increased following October 1973, National Security Advisor Henry Kissinger and Secretary of the Treasury William Simon designed a system of recycling the petrodollars flowing into Saudi Arabia and other major oil exporters. A significant portion of those petrodollars were invested in Dollar-denominated assets or deposited in New York banks, which in turn lent them to other countries running trade deficits. High inflation and an accommodating monetary policy meant that real interest rates were very low, even negative, which encouraged many developing countries to seek more debt. As we can see in Figure 2.8, the bulk of this debt went to middle-income countries, many of which were themselves oil exporters that sought to accelerate their industrialization by borrowing against valuable oil reserves.[26]

This debt cycle did not end well for Mexico and other countries that accumulated large amounts of bank debt. When the Chairman of the Federal Reserve Board Paul Volcker raised interest rates during the period 1979–82, the Dollar-denominated debt servicing costs became prohibitive. In addition, the recession that ensued reduced demand for the exports of those indebted countries, and banks became reluctant to extend any more loans. The flow of credit to those countries thus slowed down during the early 1980s, as shown in Figure 2.7, but then recovered by the mid-1990s, leading into the Asian crisis of the late 1990s, which we discuss in Chapter 3.

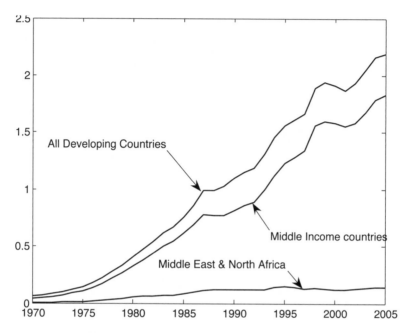

Figure 2.8. Long-term debt outstanding (in trillions of Dollars). *Source*: World Bank, Global Development Finance.

The credit boom of the 1970s led the way for other financial avenues of globalization. Prior to the 1970s, two world wars were followed by a wave of independence movements around the world. This put an end to the global economy of the late nineteenth and early twentieth centuries. Most developing countries were seeking to industrialize during the 1960s through import-substitution, and often socialist, policies. This made the developing world less hospitable to foreign direct investment by multinationals, let alone to portfolio investment.

On the other hand, moral hazard discouraged advanced economies from investing directly in countries that might nationalize their capital or prevent repatriation of profits. Loans to sovereign states were seen as safer means of investing in emerging markets, because, as Citicorp Chairman Walter Wriston put it: "Countries don't go out of business."[27]

In the long term, moral hazard was reduced as those countries abandoned import substitution policies and adopted legal and financial reforms as part of overcoming their debt problems. As a consequence, those emerging markets became more hospitable and attractive for foreign direct investment, which overtook debt financing as the main source of foreign financing by the mid-1990s. During the ensuing decade, globalization grew into its current form, allowing not only easier global transfer of goods, services, and finance, but also the global contagion of financial crises and resource curses, including the Middle East's curse of black gold.

3

Road to the Status Quo: 1996–2008

The mid-1990s ushered in new and fundamental transformations in the global landscape on all three dimensions of our analysis: energy economics, Middle-East geopolitics, and financial crises. Middle-East geopolitical transformations were perhaps the most obvious, with the globalization of militant Islamism and the direct United States military intervention in Iraq. Ongoing financial transformation became more obvious in the aftermath of the Asian financial crisis, as contagion spread from Asia to Latin America and Eastern Europe at unprecedented speeds. We discuss the mechanics of globalized finance and their effect on petrodollar flows and economic cycles in Chapter 4. The current chapter is focused on the energy economics and Middle-East geopolitical components of the analysis.

A New Era of Higher Oil Prices

On the front of energy economics, the early 1990s witnessed the restoration of Kuwait's oil production and renewed Organization of Petroleum Exporting Countries (OPEC)-member infighting on market shares and production quotas, which culminated in a virtual price war. The lack of discipline in OPEC combined with the recessionary effects of the Asian financial crisis of the mid-1990s to bring about the collapse of oil prices in 1998. This collapse, in turn, taught noncooperative OPEC members a valuable lesson, and made it possible for OPEC to reorganize its production strategy in time for global economic recovery at the turn of the new millennium.

Renewed OPEC discipline combined with increasing demand for energy to shrink spare production capacity, resulting in substantial price increases and contributing to increased U.S. debt and a weakening Dollar. All of those patterns are very reminiscent of the 1970s. Moreover, as shown later, many of the global-energy, economic, and financial repercussions of renewed petrodollar flows also mirrored those of the earlier episode in 1973–85. In particular, dynamics of the

51

credit-bubble crisis of 2007–8 are quite similar to the debt crisis of the 1980s, with petrodollar flows playing an important part in both episodes.

However, as we seek to analyze the status quo and envision potential financial crises, we should not allow those similarities to distract from some fundamental differences in the geopolitical, energy, and financial landscapes. The past two decades have witnessed a number of new developments that make the current situation, and potential petrodollar-driven crises in the medium term, quite different from the previous episode that ended in the mid-1980s.

In this chapter and the next, we discuss the status quo, which we characterize by the globalization of energy economics, financial contagion, and Middle-East geopolitics. The two chapters thus advance our main thesis that the resource curse of the Middle East has been globalized, potentially amplifying the effects of petrodollar cycles. This sets the stage for Chapters 5–7, wherein we focus on the role of the U.S. Dollar as monetary anchor for the global financial system and consider the possibility and the mechanisms through which the globalized resource curse may require replacement of the post-Bretton-Woods international financial system. We now turn to the main focus of this chapter, which is understanding the energy-market and geopolitical mechanisms that have shaped the status quo over the past decade.

Changing OPEC Politics and Renewed Oil Revenues

Remarkable economic growth, especially in Asia, dramatically increased the demand for oil into the mid-1990s. In this regard, similarity of mid-1990s global economic conditions to the conditions leading into the 1970s are quite remarkable, especially in terms of increased oil demand.[1] Another stark similarity between the energy-economics conditions of both decades was the inability of production capacity to keep pace with demand growth.[2] By 2008, OPEC spare capacity barely covered 2 percent of total world demand, with hardly any spare production capacity outside of OPEC.

We have discussed the two main reasons for limited capacity in Chapter 2. The first was mismanagement of petrodollar revenues, through subsidies and other distortions, which prevented sufficient investment in maintaining existing fields and exploring for new ones. The second was OPEC's restraint in expanding production capacity in response to price increases and forecasts of higher demand. The lesson of the mid-1990s for OPEC appears to have been that spare capacity invites competition between the cartel's members, and therefore one way to instill discipline was to ensure limited production capacity expansion.

Continued Production Capacity Constraints

Production capacity growth can be attained by redirecting some of the petrodollar receipts to exploration and development, or by reopening some capital-poor markets to foreign investment by international oil companies. The latter approach was attempted with mixed results, for instance in Iran's July 2003 tender round, Venezuela's post-2001 tenders and 2006 contract negotiations, Saudi Arabia's gas initiative during the lean years of 1998–2003 (abandoned shortly thereafter as petrodollar flows resumed), and stalled 1990s programs in Indonesia.

Foreign direct investment flows to the oil sectors of OPEC countries slowed in this decade for two reasons. The first was domestic political opposition to foreign involvement in the oil sector, especially following the Iraq war in 2003. The second and closely related reason was that renewed petrodollar riches made OPEC countries financially self-sufficient, therefore discouraging further foreign direct investment in the oil sector. In the meantime, fear of another episode of low oil prices and a declining spirit of cooperation with the United States in light of Middle-East geopolitical developments have prompted OPEC to adopt a policy of defending higher oil prices by limiting capacity expansion. This policy has allowed OPEC countries to appease their local populations with transfers from higher petrodollar receipts, and through signs of declining cooperation with – or subservience to – the West, especially the United States.

The Politics of Production Capacity

The United States' official international oil policy during the 1980s and early 1990s was focused on protecting free access to Middle-East oil and its free flow to meet market demand worldwide. Special political and security relationships with key oil states in the Gulf were exchanged for an open commitment to maintain "stable" oil prices that would neither disrupt global economic growth nor fuel inflation. An assumption underlying this pact was that key producers, such as Saudi Arabia, would invest sufficiently to maintain a comfortable level of spare capacity.

Indeed, spare capacity has protected international oil markets from major disruptions in the past, including the eight-year-long Iraq-Iran war, in the aftermath of Iraq's invasion of Kuwait, and most recently when Saudi Arabia increased its production ahead of the 2003 U.S. invasion of Iraq. However, after returning to its earlier share of OPEC production following the 1990 Iraqi invasion of Kuwait, Saudi Arabia has been reluctant to resume its earlier role as a sole price stabilizer. In particular, the Kingdom no longer accepted disproportionate cuts of its output share within OPEC, insisting that all quota reductions must be pro rata.

Saudi Arabia thus refused to reduce its production disproportionately in order to defend prices during the early-1990s recession. In the meantime, Venezuela was aggressively attempting to increase its market share in 1992, through the aperture program that made its oil fields accessible to foreign investment by U.S. and European oil companies.[3] This capacity-expansion program could ultimately have equalized Venezuela's production levels with those of Saudi Arabia. In turn, this would have compromised the Kingdom's long-standing geopolitical and economic significance as a swing-producer-of-oil strategic partner of the United States.

Price War and a Global Recession

The confrontation between Saudi Arabia and Venezuela escalated as Iraqi oil began to reach markets in 1996, under the United Nations oil-for-food program. Venezuela continued to pursue higher revenues by increasing sales at declining prices, ignoring its production quota obligations under OPEC as well as Saudi warnings of initiating a price war. Both countries knew that lower prices favored Saudi Arabia and would discourage investment in expensive extraction of Venezuela's heavy oil.[4]

The main tool of the price war, increased production, had the advantage of preserving Saudi Arabia's relative share of sales to the United States and increasing its dwindling petrodollar revenues. Starting in September 1996, Saudi Arabia raised its production from 8 million b/d to 8.5 million b/d and kept it at that level throughout 1997.[5] The combined overproduction of the two countries created an excess oil inventory of 400 million barrels. The WTI barrel price fell from $27 in spring 1997 to $10 in winter 1998–9.

The Asian financial crisis in 1997 coincided with Saudi and Venezuelan overproduction to accelerate the collapse of oil prices. Leading into that crisis, Asian oil consumption had increased 274 percent, compared to an increase of 63 percent in the rest of the world.[6] A devastating series of Asian-currency crises started in 1997, leading to massive capital flights and negative rates of economic growth. The loss of economic growth, naturally, translated into an eventual decline in Asian demand for oil.[7] This decline in Asian demand, in turn, coincided with two consecutive warm winters in Organization for Economic Co-operation and Development (OECD) countries, as well as economic slowdown through the rest of the world, as financial crises spread to other emerging markets. Overall global oil demand thus rose only 0.5 percent during 1997–8, compared to earlier annual growth rates of 2-to-3 percent during the mid-1990s.

Oil Revenues: Collapse and Recovery

Increased oil supply and slowing growth of demand depressed prices so sharply that oil revenues declined significantly despite the expanded sales. Total export earnings for the OPEC countries was approximately $170 billion during 1996–7. The following year, oil price fell to $10, cutting revenues by almost 50 percent for some countries. Figure 3.1 illustrates the dramatic decline in oil revenues of OPEC and its largest members during 1997–8 and the subsequent rise in oil revenues following OPEC's revamping of its production strategy.

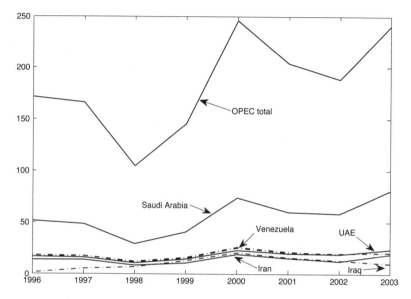

Figure 3.1. OPEC export revenues 1996–2003, in billions of U.S. Dollars. *Source*: US DOE and Estimates.

Following the price collapse of 1998, Venezuela and Mexico actively worked to reach a major agreement among oil producers to trim output and return oil prices at least to $22 a barrel. Losing the price war with Saudi Arabia, and suffering terrible economic pain from declining oil revenues, Venezuela turned to a new strategy under the newly elected Hugo Chavez. The long-term advantages of expanded capacity were shunned in favor of short-term boost in oil revenues through collective control of oil production. With capacity expansion and price wars behind them, OPEC countries reached a pivotal agreement in 1998.

The agreement in March 1998 mandated 1.485 million b/d reduction in output, with non-OPEC producers Mexico, Russia, and Oman vowing to cooperate.[8] Oil prices quickly recovered to the target price of $22 a barrel. Production cuts reversed the earlier excess-supply conditions, thus forcing market players to draw down inventories that they had accumulated in earlier years. By September, OPEC could boast 81 percent compliance with production quota allocations, which is uncharacteristically high for the cartel.[9] Success reinvigorated OPEC, paving the way for another set of agreements in March 1999, which triggered continued price rallies. In later years, as global economic growth recovered, OPEC has successfully defended dramatically higher price targets – first at $30 per barrel, and then subsequently to $50 per barrel and beyond.

Strategic Restraint of Capacity Expansion

The lesson of the Venezuelan experiment of the 1990s appeared to have been that expanded capacity led to irresistible incentives to cheat on production quotas. Restraining investment in new productive capacity would thus appear to be a natural precommitment and signaling mechanism indicating that members do not intend to cheat on their quotas. In order to undo the damage to OPEC's pricing power from the 1990s, OPEC's overall sustainable production capacity was kept virtually constant between 1998 and 2005, despite global economic recovery and rising demand for OPEC's crude oil. Investments in new productive capacity in Iran, Saudi Arabia, Kuwait, Algeria, Qatar, and Libya were carefully managed to offset declining productive capacity in Iraq, Venezuela, and Indonesia.

Table 3.1. *OPEC Production Capacity and Sales (in mm b/d)*

Member Country	1979	1983	1990	1997	1998	2000	2001	2005
K.S.A.	10.84	11.30	8.00	9.65	9.50	9.50	9.90	10.30
Iran	7.00	3.00	3.10	3.70	3.70	3.75	3.80	4.00
Iraq	4.00	1.50	3.60	2.30	2.8	2.90	3.05	1.80
Kuwait	3.34	2.80	2.40	2.40	2.40	2.40	2.40	2.60
UAE	2.50	2.90	2.20	2.40	2.40	2.40	2.45	2.40
Qatar	0.65	0.65	0.40	0.71	0.72	0.73	0.75	0.82
Venezuela	2.40	2.50	2.60	3.45	3.30	2.98	3.10	2.50
Nigeria	2.50	2.40	1.80	2.00	2.05	2.10	2.30	2.30
Indonesia	1.80	1.60	1.25	1.40	1.35	1.35	1.30	0.90
Libya	2.50	2.00	1.50	1.45	1.45	1.45	1.45	1.60
Algeria	1.23	1.10	0.75	0.88	0.88	0.88	0.88	1.35
Capacity	38.76	31.75	27.60	30.34	30.55	30.44	31.38	30.57
Sales	34.01	16.65	22.20	27.59	25.85	30.04	28.23	29.87
Spare cap	4.75	15.10	4.40	2.75	4.70	0.40	3.15	0.7

Source: Energy Intelligence Group and Baker Institute estimates

Table 3.1 illustrates the relatively stable total OPEC capacity, which resulted in reduction of spare capacity from 5 million b/d in 1998 to merely 0.7 million b/d in 2005. GCC countries, in particular Saudi Arabia, Kuwait, and the UAE, have been hesitant to expand productive capacity significantly in response to higher prices and rosy demand forecasts. In recent years, Saudi Arabia has invested $10-to-15 billion only to maintain spare capacity of 1 to 1.5 million b/d, in the face of declining output capacity at some of its mature fields. However, the Kingdom resisted calls from OECD countries to expand its output quickly to 15 million b/d in order to meet the expected rise in oil demand.

OPEC Switches to Offense

In 2000, OPEC's stance changed from protecting a target-price floor to active pursuit of the ceiling of a price range, namely, $22 to $28 per barrel.[10] Faith in global cooperation between OPEC countries and the West, to avoid recession and inflation worldwide, evaporated as Western countries failed to help the oil exporters circa 1998. The emerging relationship – driven by antagonisms between the United States and many OPEC countries – became competitive. As the Dollar began its slide in recent years, OPEC countries also felt that the fair Dollar price of crude must be increased to counter the Dollar's declining purchasing power.

Increasingly, oil-exporting countries were seen as competitors of oil-consuming OECD countries. When crude prices are high, the former prosper as the latter suffer slower growth rates because of high energy costs, and vice versa. Western commentators increased their calls for reduced dependence on Middle-East oil, as OPEC-country commentators increased their calls for fairer distribution of the oil rents. Moreover, high energy taxes in OECD countries became increasingly viewed as a direct transfer from the coffers of the oil-exporting countries' treasuries to those of their Western counterparts. OECD demands to boost production and reduce oil prices thus failed to resonate with OPEC countries as they had a decade earlier. Arguments about the tradeoff between short-term and long-term revenues, listing various alternatives to fossil-fuel sources of energy, were thus viewed as self-serving and disingenuous, and cooperative pursuit of price stability gave way to competitive bargaining.

Brief periods of cooperation were still possible, albeit less frequently. During spring 2000, Venezuela and Iran began pressing for an OPEC basket price between $22 and $28 per barrel. Behind the scenes, U.S. Secretary of Energy Bill Richardson pressed U.S.-friendly OPEC members to raise output and aim for a lower range of $20 to $25 per barrel. OPEC eventually endorsed the $25 target, but strikes in Venezuela and terrorist attacks in Saudi Arabia unnerved markets, creating a "terror premium." Saudi Arabia proved its continued willingness to cooperate by boosting production quietly in March 2003, during the buildup to the invasion of Iraq. However, those late episodes of cooperation with the West were short-lived.

In early 2004, despite prices above $35 per barrel, OPEC members, including Saudi Arabia, were endorsing production cuts. By October 2004, U.S. oil

prices had reached a record $55 per barrel as hurricanes pummeled oil produc-
tion platforms in the Gulf of Mexico. By year end, OPEC effectively redefined
its price target above $40, by agreeing to institute new counter-cyclical produc-
tion cuts during the high-demand winter period. OPEC explained that its new
policies were consistent with the earlier target of $22 to $28 in real terms, thus
attributing the rise in Dollar prices of oil to the Dollar's depreciation.[11] Despite
the claim that prices of oil have adjusted to reflect the declining purchasing power
of the Dollar, Kuwait cited the same decline in purchasing power as its reason for
abandoning the long-standing Dollar-peg of its currency in 2007.[12]

OPEC Objectives and Internal Politics

As the Dollar continued to depreciate in 2007, OPEC objectives continued to
favor an appreciating nominal price path, with $55 per barrel becoming a price
floor in mid-2007, rather than a price ceiling. OPEC countries were slow to respond to rising prices in 2007 with investments that would increase oil productive
capacity. Instead, most of those countries were satisfied to enjoy the internal political benefits from the windfall of renewed petrodollar inflows that were allowing
them to address the pressing social and economic pressures of their fast-growing
populations.[13]

This process of OPEC inaction in the face of rising oil prices continued unabated into 2008. During its regularly scheduled March meeting, OPEC refused
to increase its overall oil production in the face of rising prices, saying instead that
oil markets had enough oil and that the falling Dollar and market speculation
were to blame for market volatility.

Then, in mid-2008, Saudi Arabia in particular began to feel uncomfortable
with the continuing sharp rise in oil prices, which went well above $100 per
barrel, and the dampening ramifications of that rise on global economic growth.
Saudi Arabia was also concerned about high prices destroying long-term demand.

The Speculative Bubble in Oil Futures

As consumer protests against rising oil prices spread around the world to include
street riots and other violence, and the speculative bubble in oil futures continued
to inflate, Saudi Arabia's ruling cabinet of ministers called for a global summit of
oil producing and consumer nations to "look into the rise in prices and its reasons
and how to deal with it objectively."[14] In its statement calling for the summit,
the Saudi cabinet noted that high oil prices "could affect [adversely] the world
economy and especially the economies of developing countries." The meeting
was set for June 22, 2008, in Jeddah, Saudi Arabia.

In the meantime, a week ahead of the Jeddah session, Saudi Arabia leaked news
that it would increase its oil production in July by 500,000 barrels per day, in

an effort to slow down or reverse the inflating bubble, wherein markets had just witnessed a record one-day increase in prices of $10.75 a barrel during the second week of June. As it turns out, the Saudi production increase announcement did little to reduce oil prices, as oil traders dismissed the production increase as too little, too late.

During the Jeddah session, King Abdullah of Saudi Arabia referred to "selfish interests" of speculators as a key reason for the increase in oil prices. He also indicated that the Kingdom was angered by the Bush administration's continued insistence that there was no credible evidence that speculators were driving oil futures prices.[15]

Following the Jeddah summit, Saudi Arabia's concern about the high oil price did not last very long. Shortly thereafter, growing credit problems on Wall Street and a deteriorating global economic outlook drove speculators out of the New York oil futures market. Oil prices began falling precipitously after peaking at $147 in July 2008, as the speculative bubble burst. Prices continued to fall for the rest of the year, ending 2008 below $45 a barrel amid questions about what price OPEC was really willing to defend with aggressive production cuts.

Markets had expected OPEC to cut production to defend $80, but at its September 2008 meeting, divisions appeared between price-hawkish members Iran and Libya, who sought a pronouncement that OPEC would set $100 as a price floor, and Gulf Arab states who were unwilling to specify a preferred price. OPEC announced a supply cut of only 520,000 barrels per day at the September 9th meeting, not nearly enough to signal a firm commitment to stop the slide in prices.

At a later date, Saudi Arabia's minister paid lip service to the desirability of a $75 oil price and OPEC set targets for output cuts in early 2009 over 4.2 million b/d from the producer group's September production rates. However, questions still remained about OPEC's resolve to bring prices back to the $70 to $80 level.

At the September 2008 meeting, Saudi Arabia resisted pressure from Russia and Iran to make dramatic production cuts in order to stem the fall in international oil prices. Instead, the Kingdom focused on its own strategic concerns: (i) promoting the recovery in the value of its U.S. Dollar-denominated holdings, (ii) stimulating the global economy and thereby dampening the fall in global oil demand through lower energy costs, (iii) staving off new Western policies to promote alternative energy by offering competitive oil prices, and (iv) reducing the revenues of Iran and Russia to contain the geopolitical threat posed by their governments.[16]

Saudi Arabia had previously hinted that it might be tempted to use oil prices as a geopolitical lever against Iran. Saudi analyst Nawaf Al-Obaid, who was the Managing Director of the Saudi National Security Assessment Project, published an article entitled "Saudi Arabia's Strategic Energy Initiative," suggesting that Saudi

Arabia may be forced to use its oil policy as a means to restrain Iranian hegemony in the region:

Saudi Arabia not only has a strategic interest in reining in Iran, but it is well positioned to do so. With the price of oil at a high, the kingdom's influence as the world's central banker of energy is at its apex, making it the economic powerhouse of the Middle East.[17]

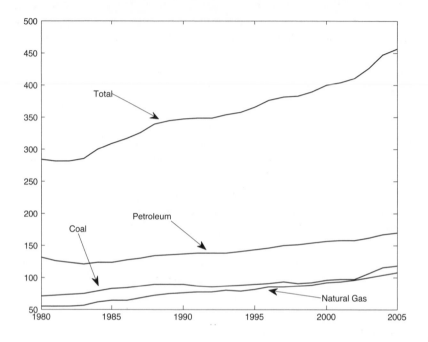

Figure 3.2. Primary energy by source (in quads). *Source*: IEA.

The Other Black Gold: Natural Gas

Natural gas has been steadily growing in importance as a primary source of energy, as shown in Figure 3.2. World gas consumption is projected to more than double over the next three decades, surpassing coal as the world's second largest source of energy and potentially overtaking oil as the primary fuel in many advanced economies. As the relative importance of natural gas increases, this can – in principle – alter the dynamics of global energy economics, Middle-East geopolitics, and global finance that we have outlined. We argue in this chapter and the next that any such effects will be short-lived. In particular, we argue in this section that natural-gas markets will be exposed to the same geopolitical risks that rattle oil markets. We also argue that the global economics of natural gas will be governed, eventually, by the same tension between competition for market shares and collusion to meet price targets that has shaped oil markets and OPEC. In Chapter 4, we argue that natural-gas liquefaction (refrigeration into liquid form) has made gas an equal partner to oil in globalizing the Middle-East resource curse.

Natural Gas as a Substitute for Oil

Starting in the 1980s, the rise of natural gas as an alternative fuel, especially for generating electricity, played an important role in protecting economies from oil-market disruptions. Geographic distribution of natural-gas reserves, and the fuel's environmental superiority to oil, also made it a welcome substitute for oil in some countries' residential and industrial sectors. However, despite preference for the cleaner-burning fuel, the use of natural gas was limited in some countries by availability of pipelines and clearance mechanisms to facilitate delivery to centers of demand. Advances in liquefaction of natural gas, which we discuss in Chapter 4, made it possible for the fuel to be transported on vessels and thus allowed its global market share to continue growing.

A significant part of the growth in the natural-gas market share was driven by replacement of oil in the power generation sectors of developed countries. This process of conversion has taken its course. As demand for electricity continues to grow, the role of natural gas may increase with it, albeit at a slower pace compared to the earlier period when it replaced existing demand for oil. The next major opportunity for natural gas to increase its energy-market share will most likely arise in the transportation sector. The technology for running automobiles directly on natural gas, or indirectly by using electricity generated by burning the fuel, has been available for some time. However, a number of economic factors have prevented natural-gas-run and plug-in-electric vehicles from gaining a substantial market share in transportation sectors worldwide.[18]

We discuss potential scenarios for use of natural gas as well as alternative fuels in Chapters 7 and 8. However, it is clear at this stage that the importance of the transportation sector in energy demand, and the slow rate at which the existing stock of oil-burning vehicles can be replaced by other modes of transportation, will guarantee a dominant role for oil in the short to medium term. This suggests that we must consider the interplay between the two energy sectors – oil and natural gas – in our analyses of Middle-East geopolitical and energy market economics.

Intertwined Geopolitics of Oil and Natural Gas

There are three main factors behind the importance of Middle-East geopolitics for the oil sector, and by inference for international economics and finance. The first factor is the world's continued dependence on oil to fuel economic growth. The second is the concentration of the world's reserves outside the largest consumers of energy. The third is disproportionate concentration of oil reserves in the Gulf region, which continues to be plagued with internal and external conflicts that threaten to disrupt production and shipping of the global economy's life blood.

All three factors are equally present in the gas sector. First, as natural gas becomes an important primary source of energy, its importance in fueling or stifling global economic growth increasingly mimics that of oil. Second, Table 3.2 shows that the bulk of natural gas reserves fall outside the world's largest economies in North America and Europe, and the fastest growing economies in East and South Asia. Third, with the notable exception of Russia and to a much lesser extent the United States, the table shows that the largest known reserves of natural gas are located in Middle-East Gulf countries.

Table 3.2. *Major Oil and Natural Gas Reserves by Country, 2003 (% shares)*

Country	Share of Oil Reserves	Share of Natural Gas Reserves
Saudi Arabia	25.3	4.1
Russia	5.7	30.5
Iran	9.7	14.8
Iraq	11.1	2.0
Qatar	1.9	9.2
UAE	6.1	3.9
Venezuela	5.1	2.7
Nigeria	3.1	2.3
Algeria	1.3	2.9
Kuwait	9.6	–
USA	–	3.4

Source: EIA. Oil reserves from World Oil. Gas reserves from *Oil and Gas Journal*.[19]

Thus, demand and supply factors that make oil markets dependent on Middle-East geopolitics are equally applicable for natural-gas markets. Russia plays an important role in arbitraging the difference between oil and gas distributions worldwide. Russia's share of gas reserves is approximately 30 percent, which is the difference between the Middle-East's share in global oil reserves, approximately 65 percent, and its share in gas reserves, which is approximately 35 percent. The Middle East only controlled approximately 10 percent of global natural-gas production circa 2007. However, this market share is expected to grow substantially over the next twenty years, as Qatar and Iran follow their ambitious expansion plans. Increased production capacity and focus on liquefied-natural-gas (LNG) exports in the Middle East is expected to give the region's supply of gas strategic importance similar to that of its oil supply.

For some Middle-East countries, most notably Qatar and Iran, natural-gas-export receipts rival traditional oil-export petrodollar flows. The limited absorptive capacities and economic mismanagement of large monetary inflows into gas-exporting countries of the Middle East are identical to the problems discussed in earlier chapters. In the remainder of this section, we argue that the inner dynamics and tensions of competition and collusion are also the same for oil and gas exporters, the important role of Russia in the gas sector notwithstanding. We show that competition for market share, similar to the Venezuelan experiment in the 1990s, is ongoing in the gas sector. As production capacity increases, an eventual global economic recession may cause the collapse of gas prices, similar to oil's collapse in 1998. This, in turn, would create an incentive for collusion to stabilize prices, which may take many temporary or permanent forms. Thus, we conclude, the Middle-East economics and geopolitics of natural gas are virtually indistinguishable from those of oil, and we may – for simplicity – include receipts from exports of both fuels within the expanded category of "petrodollars."

Competition: Market Shares and Geopolitics – Qatar, Iran, and Russia

Natural-gas markets are still at a nascent stage, wherein producers vie for market share, and supply is slow to respond to demand in certain regions – giving some well-positioned suppliers temporary monopolistic power. The development of LNG markets is widely assumed to make gas as fungible and transportable as oil, thus eliminating those regional monopolies in the medium to long term. In the meantime, market imperfections and competition for medium-term market share, together with relatively high and stable gas prices, have prevented collusion in the sector so far.

Qatar and Iran are competitively and massively investing in natural gas export capability, in a frantic race to establish themselves as dominant market players. Qatar, in particular, emphasized gas-sector development over oil, not only because of its limited oil endowment, but also to escape the sphere of influence of its giant neighbor, Saudi Arabia, in OPEC. The decision to focus on natural gas was reached in the mid-1980s, when oil prices plummeted, and the country's limited oil reserves, 3.3 billion barrels at the time, did not give it much ability to boost revenues.[20] The country's massive natural gas reserves, then estimated at three thousand cubic meters (TCM), provided a promising alternative to the oil sector.

Qatar's move toward gas was envisioned in the mid-1980s, but only materialized in the early 1990s, after the effects of the Iran-Iraq war and the economic slowdown in Japan had subsided.[21] The move enabled Qatar to move out of the Saudi regional sphere and forge its own security and economic ties. In 1991, Qatar signed a defense cooperation agreement with the United States, which subsequently ran its military operations in the region from massive air bases near

Doha. On the economic front, Mobil Oil joined the Qatargas project in August 1992, with plans to sell 6 million tons per year to Japanese utilities by 1997–8.[22] Subsequent investments gave Qatar the largest LNG liquefaction capability in the world, with multiple LNG projects in sight. Qatar has thus become the largest global LNG supplier, expected to control 30 percent of the LNG market by 2010. The only limit on Qatar's expansion to date has been fear of excessively rapid extraction that would compromise the productivity of its reservoir.[23]

Qatar's potential arch nemesis may not be Russia, with her massive proven reserves and easier access to Europe, but Iran, with which she shares her North Field. Iran's market share remains modest, but her plans for export to Europe and Asia are ambitious. The General Director of the National Iranian Gas Company (NIGC), has announced a goal to "achieve 8–10 percent of the world's gas trade and its by-products within 20 years."[24] While Qatar has pursued exports to the United States and elsewhere through gas liquefaction, Iran's export plans to Europe and Asia rely on pipeline projects. Pipelines to Western Europe may pass through Turkey or Ukraine, and pipelines to Asia would pass to India through Pakistan. Both sets of plans have, so far, been frustrated by internal dissent as well as external opposition.

In the meantime, South Pars, Iran's main gas field and a geologic extension of Qatar's North Field, has attracted $15 billion in investments. However, the project has been slow to develop due to technical, commercial, and geopolitical problems.[25] Out of 28 phases, the first five, finished in 2005, produced gas that was predominantly used for reinjection and domestic power generation. Phases 6 to 8 were finished in 2006, again with limited export potential. International involvement in gas liquefaction is slated for phases 11 to 14. Despite its ambitious hopes for capturing natural-gas market share, Iran's plans have been slow to materialize. Even then, competition for pipeline-gas market shares in Europe and Asia, and in the LNG market, put it in direct competition with market leaders Russia and Qatar.

Geopolitical considerations are particularly acute in this three-party competition, since Iranian pipelines may pass through ex-Soviet-sphere countries, and accusations of Qatari overextraction from the North Field are very reminiscent of Iraq's accusations toward Kuwait circa 1990. In April 2004, Iran's deputy Oil Minister Hadi Nejad-Hosseinian openly accused Qatar of overproducing gas at its North Field and warned that, absent an agreement on regulating offshore production, Iran will find "other ways and means of resolving the issue."[26] Iran has also been involved in disputes with Kuwait and Saudi Arabia over border demarcation in the northern-Gulf continental shelf, which contains the prolific Dorra gas field. Iran had begun drilling in the field in 2000, but stopped after a protest was lodged by Kuwait.

Collusion in Parallel or Jointly with OPEC?

As we have seen in the previous section, OPEC's politics have fluctuated between cooperation with oil-consuming countries to stabilize prices, on the one hand, and competition for explicit and implicit oil rents, on the other. It is natural to expect similar patterns to emerge as gas markets mature, especially when expanded capacity and an eventual global recession bring about a collapse in gas prices.

Qatar, the leader in capacity expansion, has been actively positioning itself as the United States' strategic partner in gas, mimicking Saudi Arabia's traditional role in oil markets. In this spirit, Qatar's Minister of Energy and Industry asserted in a speech in 2004 that his country will guarantee the impossibility of a Gas OPEC. He hinted that partnership with the United States is more valuable than cooperation with other gas exporters: "There are many uncertainties and challenges we have to deal with on a global scale, which makes the producer-consumer cooperation essential."[27]

This rhetoric notwithstanding, Qatar has, in fact, begun negotiating multi-year financial-swap agreements with Russia's Gazprom, allowing the two countries to coordinate arbitrage strategies in gas markets.[28] This is a first step toward cooperation. However, agreement on production quotas, target prices, and similar OPEC objectives are unlikely to emerge in the short term, as LNG markets continue to grow and the main exporters continue to compete for market share. The geopolitical isolation of and conflicts with Iran, potentially the second most important member of any cartel of gas exporters, also makes it difficult to envision scenarios under which an Organization of Natural-Gas-Exporting Countries, or an Organization of Fuel-Exporting Countries (both oil and gas) can emerge. However, cooperation between few of the gas exporters, perhaps sponsored by large and growing consumers such as China and India, may force other exporters to join an emerging virtual cartel. We study scenarios of this nature in Chapter 8.

The Economics and Geopolitics of Middle-East Discontent

Populations of oil-exporting countries suffered severe economic strain following the oil price collapse in 1985, and then in 1998. Policies that Western governments and commentators had viewed as internationally cooperative – to keep oil prices within a reasonable range – were increasingly viewed in countries as diverse as Venezuela, Nigeria, and Indonesia as unfair pricing of their national wealth to appease corrupt rulers' Western patrons.[29]

This political-economic grievance became central to the rhetoric of the most globalized militant-Islamist organization: Al-Qa'ida – "the base" or "the launching pad," established in 1988 to support the Afghani Mujahedeen in their fight against the Soviet Union, with the full blessings and support of the United States and Saudi Arabia.[30] Bin Laden returned to Saudi Arabia as a hero, but his relationship with the ruling family soon turned sour when he opposed the stationing of American troops on Saudi land in the aftermath of the Iraqi invasion of Kuwait.

Bin Laden's Summary of Islamists' Economic Grievances

In August 1995, bin Laden wrote a letter to King Fahd bin Abdulaziz of Saudi Arabia, enumerating his economic grievances against the governments of Saudi Arabia and the United States. He attributed the deterioration in education and health services in the Kingdom, growing foreign debts that reached 80 percent of Saudi GDP, and simultaneously high levels of inflation and unemployment, to the following list of Saudi and American policies:

- Political corruption and wasteful conspicuous consumption by the royal family, which depleted the Kingdom's dwindling resources.
- The direct role of King Fahd in establishing the servitude of the Kingdom's oil production and pricing policies to the United States' interests. Bin Laden interpreted increased Saudi production in the 1980s as being aimed at weakening Iran during its war with Iraq and keeping oil prices low, both of which served American objectives. Thus, he argued that those oil policies served the interests of Western consumers at the expense of the Saudi economy, which had to draw down its foreign reserves in the 1990s to support conspicuous consumption despite dwindling revenues.
- Failure to diversify the Saudi economy away from dependence on oil revenues.
- "Insane expenditure" on allied forces during the Gulf War, despite the country's dire financial position at the time. He estimated Saudi expenditures for the war to be $60 billion, of which $30 billion went to the United States, $15 billion went to other allied forces, and the balance was spent as overt and covert domestic bribes. In addition, he cited $40 billion in expenditures on "fictional military and civil deals with the Americans," and similar deals to buy British-made planes to appease [Prime Minister] John Major, when Saudi Arabia lacked the human capital to use the arms purchased from the United States and the United Kingdom.
- He accused King Fahd of squandering the Kingdom's reserves abroad, which he estimated to be $140 billion, within just seven years.
- Borrowing from usurious foreign banks to finance the growing debt, despite the explicit and most severe Qur'anic prohibition of that practice.[31]

Bin Laden also considered Saudi cooperation with the United States to keep oil prices low "the greatest theft in human history." In an interview with the Qatari satellite channel Al-Jazīra, he appears to have estimated the size of this transfer during the quarter-century 1973–98 as follows: The real price of oil should have been $36 per barrel (the high point of oil prices in the early 1980s). Since then, energy-intensive industrial products had increased in price fourfold. Hence, the nominal price of oil should have been $144. Since the price of oil at that time in 1998 was $9 per barrel, he computed a theft per barrel of $135. Multiplying this amount by the annual output of Islamic countries that he estimated at 30 million b/d yielded an estimated daily theft of $405 million. Over a quarter-century, that came to $36 trillion, or $30,000 for each of the world's 1.2 million Muslims.[32]

Bin Laden's view of the struggle with the Saudi royal family and the United States is thus economic in large part. It is, therefore, not surprising that much of his boasting after the attacks of September 11 focused on the decline of the Dow Jones Industrial Average, the loss of United States Gross Domestic Product, and so on. What started as a political-religious grievance with the Saudi government in 1991 became in August 1996 – in his Declaration of Jihad – a political-economic grievance with that "near enemy," as well as the "far enemy" (the United States and its allies) that supported it and benefited from artificially low oil prices.

The Globalization of Islamist Discontent

This vision was shared by other militant Islamist groups, including Egyptian Islamic Jihad, whose leader Ayman Al-Zawahiri joined Al-Qa'ida as the second in command, as well as others worldwide. Those groups' focus thus turned to tourist resorts, centers of finance, diplomatic missions, and other critical targets that can disrupt Western economics and finance. However, those groups thought that actual energy installations should be spared, as bin Laden argued, since they constitute the wealth of the "future Islamic state."[33]

By December 2004, however, with Al-Qa'ida still unable to mobilize popular support for the overthrow of the Saudi monarchy and in the face of sharp crackdowns on militants by the Saudi government, bin Laden reissued a call for attacks on oil facilities as part of his perceived Jihad. Bin Laden elaborated on his vision in a long anti-Saudi speech calling for the overthrow of the monarchy at the end of 2004:

Mujahidin, be patient and think of the hereafter, for this path in life requires sacrifices, maybe with your life . . . be sure to know that there is a rare and golden opportunity today to make America bleed in Iraq, in economic, human and psychological terms. . . . Remember, too, that the biggest reason for our enemies' control over our lands is to steal our oil, so give everything you can to stop the greatest theft of oil in history from the current and future generations in collusion with the agents and the foreigners. . . . Oil, which is the basis of all industry, has gone down in price many times. After it was going for $40 a barrel two decades ago, in the last decade it went for as little as $9, while its price today should be $100 at the very least. So, keep on struggling, do not make it easy for them, and focus your operations on it, especially in Iraq and the Gulf, for that will be the death of them.[34]

Al-Qaʿida subsequently tried, unsuccessfully, to attack the Saudi crude-oil processing facilities at Abqaiq, in February 2006. In a message claiming responsibility
for the attack, Al-Qaʿida of the Arabian Peninsula said the attack was part of the
war against "Christians and Jews to stop their pillage of Muslim riches."[35]

The 2006 failed attack at Abqaiq was followed by articles praising the attack
and providing the basis for its legitimacy even though it would destroy the oil
wealth. Bin Ladin's stance on the attack was detailed by Bassam al-Adib for *Sawt
al-Jihad*, in which it was portrayed as a success, based merely on adding uncertainty in energy markets and thereby hurting Western economies.[36]

Al-Qaʿida's 2006 attack on Abqaiq was met by intensified Saudi efforts to
tighten security in the Kingdom. Saudi police arrested 172 militants after the
Abqaiq incident and increased spending on security of oil facilities into the billions in an effort to ensure that oil-and-gas fields and installations would not become targets of a successful large-scale terrorist attack. Outside of Saudi Arabia,
however, foreign workers in the oil-and-gas industry, oil tankers, pipelines, and
other hard-to-protect infrastructure continued to be attacked.

Populist Sympathies

Bin Laden's calculation of the magnitude of perceived Western economic exploitation may not be shared by many. However, the general nature of his grievance is
widely shared by large segments of Middle-East populations, Muslim and Chris-
tian (the Egyptian-Orthodox Pope still forbids Christians from visiting Jerusalem
under Israeli control), be they militant, nationalist, democratically political, socially activist, mildly religious, or nonreligiously secularist. The vast majority may
also disagree with Al Qaʿida's tactics of suicide and terrorist attacks, but large
segments agree with the logic of using "economic weapons."

Calls for the use of oil pricing as a weapon, as Arab states ostensibly did during
the Arab-Israeli war of October 1973, remain alive as visions of an ideal solution.
Alternatives at the personal level have also been widely popular among Arabs and
Muslims. Lists of products made by American and Israeli companies are widely
circulated, with calls to boycott them to the extent possible. In a recent fatwa (response to a religious question), the moderate Professor Hussein Shihata of Egypt's
quasi-national Al-Azhar University compared the use of economic boycott today
to Gandhi's and the Egyptian nationalist Saʿd Zaghloul's boycott of English products during India's and Egypt's struggles for independence.[37]

Globalization of this phenomenon is best exemplified by a solicited fatwa on
how Muslims living in the United States can boycott American products, and
the permissibility of investing in U.S. assets or holding balances denominated
in U.S. Dollars.[38] Anti-Americanism at the state level has recently prompted
Islamist Iranian President Mahmoud Ahmadinejad, and had previously prompted

the nonreligious Iraqi President Saddam Hussein, to try to undermine the Dollar by selling their oil in Euros. We discuss those strategies, which were also similar in nature to suggestions to abandon the Dollar by the moderately Islamist ex-Prime Minister of Malaysia Mahathir Mohamad, in Chapter 6.

We conclude this section by recognizing that previously localized grievances, nationalist or religious, have been increasingly globalized and directed at United States and Western interests. Those grievances at once stem from the flow – or lack thereof – of petrodollars to various nations and groups therein, and help to shape energy policies in the oil-and-gas-rich world – through pressure on existing ruling elites, or replacement of the ruling class with one that would adopt stricter energy policies. We have already seen that popular pressure has transformed OPEC's strategies since 1998. It has also helped a movement toward anti-American socialism in Latin America and has even prompted gas-rich Russia's President Vladimir Putin, whose relationship with U.S. President Bush was generally characterized as friendly, to compare U.S. foreign policies to the Third Reich.[39] Those patterns, and potential disputes between emerging Asian economic giants and the West, suggest that geopolitics of oil and gas may change substantially in the short to medium term.

Taxonomy of Islamist Groups

Disruptions of energy supplies in the Middle East – as well as elsewhere such as in Indonesia – may result directly from militant Islamists' destructive attacks. However, this is not the only way in which rising Islamist sentiments in the region can affect energy economics. We have already noted that OPEC's movement toward competition with the West was partly in response to discontented populations, which the ruling elites in the region need to appease in order to maintain their legitimacy and stability. Therefore, we must consider not only the geopolitical impact of disruptive terrorism, but also geopolitical realignments that might result from Islamist moral influence, hard regime change such as in Iran in 1979, or soft regime change if Muslim-Brotherhood-inspired groups ascend to power – in a model similar to Turkey's mutation of Erbakan's hard-Islamist Virtue Party into the more successful softer Islamism of Erdogan's Justice and Development Party.

Toward that end, the taxonomy of Islamist movements formulated by the Ahram Center for Political and Strategic Studies in its *Directory of Islamist Movements Worldwide* is a very useful guide.[40] This taxonomy first classified Islamist movements into fundamentally religious movements on the one hand, and sociopolitical movements with an Islamist character on the other.

Religious-Islamist groups generally idolize the earliest few decades of Islamic history and view Islamic principles in absolute terms, with little historical flexibility. Some of those groups aim to Islamize societies through peaceful educational means, whereas others may adopt militant strategies. The militant religious Islamists, in turn, may be (i) domestically oriented, prioritizing struggle against "the close enemy," (ii) focused on secession of Islamic states, as in Kashmir and Chechnya, or (iii) globalized, struggling against both the "near enemy" and "the larger far enemy." The third category is a relatively new phenomenon that has emerged since 1996, as Western mobilization of militant Islamists against the Soviet Union during 1979–89 ultimately globalized a number of militant-Islamist groups.

Sociopolitical groups that adopt an Islamist program adopted a different view of Islamic teachings. Their understanding of Islamic texts is less literal and thus takes into consideration the evolution of Islamic thought over fourteen centuries. This category of Islamist groups may seek to ascend to power through peaceful, often democratic, means. When this avenue for ascension to power is not available, those groups are transformed into militant independence movements. Examples of the first subcategory include the Muslim Brotherhood and its factions throughout the Arab world, as well as the previously mentioned Islamist parties in Turkey. The latter category includes Algeria's Islamic Salvation Front (FIS), and the Palestinian Islamic-Resistance Movement (HAMAS), both of which won democratic elections but were politically marginalized and thus remilitarized by the international community. It also includes Lebanon's Hizbullah, which participates in the country's democratic political process while simultaneously maintaining its militant independence-movement characteristics.

Ruling elites in the Middle East purposefully lump all of those Islamist groups in a single category, since they all present threats to the continuation of their rulership. However, it must be noted that the geopolitical and economic consequences of the activities of the various Islamist groups are very different. It must also be noted that repression of the more peaceful groups has historically been a driving force in radicalizing and militarizing some of them.[41]

Regime Changes and Geopolitical Realignments

If forecasts of growing energy demand and constrained growth of energy-supply capacity are accurate, then competition for Middle-East energy resources between advanced countries and fast-growing Asian economies may become central pieces in global geopolitical chess. Already, China has famously accelerated its courting of Sudan's Islamist regimes – which started during Numeiri's rule in the 1970s and '80s – as the West sought to isolate them. Chinese-Sudanese economic cooperation allowed Chinese oil companies to move aggressively into Sudanese oil extraction and refining, starting in the mid-1990s, just when Malaysia's Petronas was also accelerating its oil-sector involvement in Sudan.

The Sudanese model can be a template for Chinese, and perhaps Indian or Russian, capitalization on anti-Western sentiments of rising Islamist groups, and anti-Islamist sentiments of Western nations that fail to distinguish between the different types of Islamism. In the global geopolitical game of energy chess, the current Western mentality of the "war on terror," which we discuss in Chapter 4, essentially surrenders increasing chunks of the energy-rich Middle East board to fast-growing economies that wish to check the continuing Western hegemony. Preferential energy-trade agreements with Islamist states, and with secular states that wish to appease their Islamists, can cause fundamental changes in global energy economics. We analyze various scenarios of Islamist-Eastern alliances and their effects on energy markets and global finance in Chapter 8.

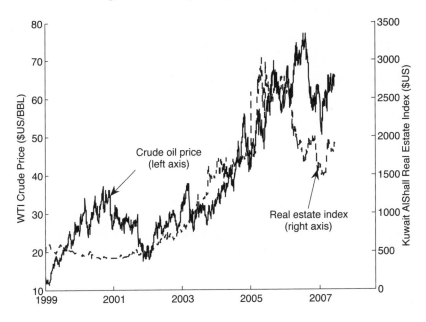

Figure 3.3. Kuwait Al-Shall Real Estate Index. *Source*: S&P/IFC.

Déjà Vu: Overgrown Children of the 1970s?

It was difficult to travel in the Middle East between 2003 and 2008 without noticing many of the similarities between 1970s social attitudes and political and economic trends and their recent counterparts. The return of white elephant projects was unmistakable, including university cities with mostly vacant buildings, and record numbers of rising skyscrapers in the middle of the desert. Real-estate bubbles deflated early in some countries, as shown in Figure 3.3. However, real-estate bubbles in other countries in the region have persisted even after the financial crash of mid-2008. In the long run, as the existence of a bubble becomes painfully obvious, and as the story supporting the bubble gets increasingly unten-able, speculators will begin to sell their properties and economically hurt owners of real estate will have to accept lower prices, eventually deflating the last bubbles.

Despite the collapse of real-estate bubbles in some countries as early as 2006, the construction boom continued unabated in Dubai, Qatar, Amman, Cairo, and many other cities well into 2008. This, in turn, fed a boom in the construction industry and its supporting sectors, especially steel and cement. Needless to say, banks in those countries had massive exposures to the real estate, construction, and supporting sectors. To the extent that the stock markets of those countries are also dominated by stocks of those three sectors (banking, construction and real estate, and steel and cement), the system is tightly coupled, in the sense described by Bookstaber in his description of other financial manias, panics, and crashes.[42]

Cheap credit, and renewed euphoria not unlike that which dominated the re-gion in the late 1970s, also fueled speculation in regional stock markets. Religious figures were enlisted to convince the public that it was not ethical or safe to shirk on the job in order to engage in day trading, which was reportedly the habit of school teachers and professionals in other fields.

With astronomical returns in the Saudi and other regional markets between 2003 and 2006, even star hedge-fund managers from Greenwich, CT, were find-ing it difficult to attract funds from the region, because they could not match the rates of return made on the bubble upswing. Market crashes in the region are not uncommon; we have already discussed the disastrous collapse of the Manakh market in Kuwait in 1982, when higher interest rates prevented the cheap-credit-driven bubble from continuing. This seemed a remote memory two decades later, as petrodollar inflows started positive trends in regional stock markets, inviting not only professional speculators, but also many middle-class professionals with-out prior investment experience to venture into those markets. The result, as shown in Figure 3.4, is that many of those latecomers to the market – many of whom acquired significant levels of debt to leverage their investment in the market – lost their life savings and more.

Absorptive Capacity and Sovereign Wealth Funds

In order to compare the roles of petrodollar flows in the 1970s and 2003–8, we need to investigate the fundamental question of the short-term as well as the medium to long-term absorptive capacities of regional economies, especially those of the oil-and-gas exporting countries. The record to-date is not promising. The three sectors that have been booming in the region continue to be petrochemical

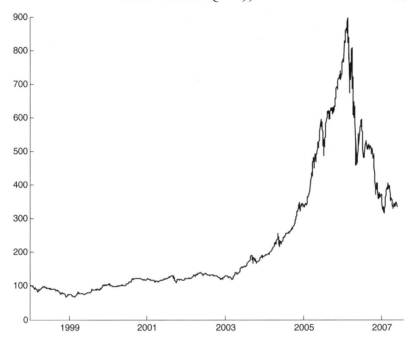

Figure 3.4. Saudi Arabia Stock Market Index. *Source*: S&P/IFC.

industries, construction, and consumables such as cellular phones and internet access. The third sector can be a catalyst for increased productivity and real-sector economic growth, but it can also be a pure consumable.

In the medium to long term, no phenomenon is more informative about the lack of regional absorptive capacity prospects than the growing role of regional sovereign wealth funds. It is estimated that only 22 percent of Gulf investments have been in Asia, the Middle East, or North Africa.[43] Therefore, the bulk of petrodollar investments have flown to North American and Europe, just as they did in the 1970s. More importantly, some of the larger investments in western banks, such as the Abu Dhabi Investment Authority's investment in Citicorp at the height of the credit crunch, have allowed credit markets to remain afloat, thus preventing financial meltdown and severe recession in the West, but also facilitating the continued hubris in credit markets, which continued to feed one financial bubble following another.

In this regard, the resource curse of the Middle-East oil and gas exporters gave rise to another – global – resource curse that afflicted many of the world's most advanced economies, especially the United States', through the vehicle of cheap credit. We now turn to this general phenomenon of globalization of the Middle-East resource curse, explaining the globalized resource curse later in Chapter 7.

4

Globalization of Middle-East Dynamics

With the start of the twenty-first century, all three factors in our story – financial markets, energy economics, and Middle-East geopolitics – have become major players on the global scene. In this chapter, we study how contagion and spillovers have grown substantially between different financial markets, markets for different sources of energy, and previously region-specific geopolitical conflicts. In the process, as each of the three factors has become more globalized, the interactions among the three factors – which constitute the core focus of this book – have also grown in importance, leading to what we have called the globalized curse of black gold.

We begin by reviewing some of the major developments that have led to this globalization of Middle-East dynamics. The first development has been the rise in structured finance, which facilitated the creation of derivative financial vehicles that have, in turn, allowed investment and fund-flow patterns that were not previously possible. The second closely related development has been the increasingly important role of hedge funds and sovereign wealth funds. The former are unregulated market participants that have been able to use derivative securities to play the role previously reserved for highly regulated banks, and the latter a new gargantuan phenomenon which continues to mystify much of the financial world.

Concurrent with those novel developments in the financial world, improvements in information technology have amplified the role, steadily increasing in importance, of developing countries both as sources of capital and as homes for inviting "emerging markets" for investment opportunities. The two developments combined to increase the level of contagion across financial markets, to the point that Mohamed El-Erian has argued that whereas previous contagious effects were sequential (e.g. between Mexico and then Columbia in the early 1980s, and later sequential episodes involving Mexico, Asia, Brazil, and Russia during the mid- and late 1990s), the current financial environment has made contagion between different markets simultaneous.[1]

On the energy-markets side, we revisit our discussion in Chapter 3 of the rising importance of natural gas as a substitute for oil. To the extent that natural gas markets were relatively insulated from oil markets, relying mainly on pipelines for delivery to markets in the geographic proximity of sources, the level of contagion between the two energy markets was relatively contained. In this chapter, we discuss the increasing effect of natural gas liquefaction, which allows the two markets for oil and gas to become increasingly integrated, thus enhancing contagion and reducing the effects of diversification across the two fuels.

Liquefaction also has significant geopolitical and economic consequences, because it allows Middle-East producers, mainly Qatar in the short term, but also potentially Iran, to become increasingly important players in the market. Thus, the financial, economic, and geopolitical aspects of oil markets are increasingly duplicated in natural-gas markets.

Finally, we turn to the most disruptive geopolitical factors of all: military and terrorist activities. To a great extent, the military buildup in the Middle East and the devastating wars during the 1980s and 1990s can be traced back to the effect of petrodollar inflows and the struggle to maintain or acquire local hegemony. The role of the United States and other Western powers was significant during this period, including in the aftermath of the Iraqi invasion of Kuwait in 1990, but minuscule compared to the occupation of Iraq following 2003. In this regard, the premeditated terrorist attacks on the United States on September 11, 2001, have been a spectacular success: they have elicited precisely the military response that has allowed regional geopolitics to become globalized.

No longer can foreign policy of Western powers toward the Middle East be restricted to ensuring the flow of oil and protecting the interests of Israel. The United States, the United Kingdom, and to a lesser extent other Western powers are now mired in regional minutiae such as Sunni-Shi'ite disputes in certain parts of Iraq and other Gulf Cooperation Council's (GCC) countries, the national aspirations of the Kurds, and so on. Those conflicts were fed with another wave of petrodollar inflows and arms acquisitions, which are likely to contribute to expectations of, if not actual, long-term regional instability and the concomitant effects on financial markets and energy prices. This entanglement of regional geopolitics in global energy economics and finance is central to our story of the continuing cycle and its potential amplification. We first turn to the financial dimensions of that story.

Hedge Funds and Sovereign Wealth Funds

At the turn of the century, advances in structured finance, which started in earnest during the 1970s and 1980s, had reached their peak. The development of markets for derivative securities started in the 1970s with foreign exchange and commodity futures markets, and the securitization revolution in the 1980s and 1990s allowed debt originators to rebundle their assets in a variety of forms that appealed to different market participants. This emergence of new financial products coincided with a surge in the number of large unregulated investors with high degrees of sophistication and corresponding appetite for risk.

The first group of such investors are a new breed of hedge funds, which have at various times mimicked the activities of private equity firms, banks, insurance companies, and other financial institutions. The other group of newcomers are sovereign wealth funds (SWFs), which invest portions of the accumulated trading surpluses of various countries. SWFs, for example, Government of Singapore's Investment Corporation (GIC) and the Abu Dhabi Investment Authority (ADIA), have been present for the past three decades. However, just as the hedge funds of the early twentieth century bear little resemblance to those of the twenty-first, the SWFs of today have assumed a very different posture, in terms of both size and investment philosophy.

Structured Finance

In recent years, the notional volume of over-the-counter (i.e. excluding trading at formal exchanges) derivative securities trading had increased a staggering 135 percent – from $220 trillion at the end of June 2004 to $516 trillion at the end of June 2007.[2] Two decades earlier, the development and utilization of seemingly ingenious derivative-based strategies, then known as "portfolio insurance," had led to the catastrophic market collapse in October 1987.[3] John Kenneth Galbraith had written a few months earlier, in January 1987 under the title "The 1929 Parallel" that "[a] second, rather stronger parallel with 1929 is the present commitment to seemingly imaginative, currently lucrative, and eventually disastrous innovation in financial structures."[4]

As we write, the world remains in the grips of a credit crunch that resulted from similarly "imaginative, lucrative, and eventually disastrous" series of innovations in credit derivatives, including credit default swaps, which had been the fastest growing segment. The series of market bubbles and crashes that have been witnessed over the past two decades were seen by George Soros, the legendary hedge-fund manager, as an unsustainable credit-driven super-bubble – a theme to which we shall return in later chapters.[5]

Structured financial products have allowed investors to assume risks that they want to carry while shunning risks that they do not. In the past, an investor who wanted exposure to the risk and return on an equity portfolio in a foreign country would have had to use her own capital and assume not only the risks that she desired, but also currency risk and political risks that may affect her ability to repatriate her funds, in addition to various costs associated with storage of purchased assets, dividend collection, and so on. Today, with the help of structured finance, that investor can simply engage in a total return swap, in effect leasing the assets from an investment bank, paying interest on the borrowed notional value, and gaining leveraged exposure to the risk that she wishes (capital losses on the portfolio), while avoiding other risks and costs.

This makes it extremely easy for large investors, especially hedge funds, to jump into and out of different markets at the speed of a telephone call to their primary brokers or other total-return-swap counterparties. Combined with advances in information technology, which allow investment firms to trade around the clock in multiple countries, and to observe price movements across markets nearly in real time, advances in structured finance have thus made it possible for investors to react to news from one market by adjusting their investment strategies in all markets simultaneously (as opposed to sequentially, as El-Erian has noted).

A secondary effect of the revolution in structured finance has been the encouragement of hubris on the part of investors who take too much comfort in their hedging strategies. Having forgotten the lessons of 1987, when "portfolio insurance" proved to be a good strategy if only one investor used it, but a disaster when everyone did, the collateralization of debt obligations, and the marketing of credit default swaps, in particular, encouraged irresponsible risk taking on a global scale. As early as 1998, Long Term Capital Management, the large hedge founded and staffed by star Ph.D.s trained by Nobel-laureate partners, collapsed in the aftermath of Russia's default because it had forgotten about something as simple as credit risk.[6]

A decade later, a slew of hedge funds and star financial institutions have failed because they did not recognize that rebundling pools of mortgages cannot create more assets that are worthy of AAA ratings *ex nihilo*, regardless of what credit-rating agencies say. Because of the other advances, such as total-return swaps, which allowed foreign investors to gain easy exposure to those pools of U.S. debt-based assets, the ramifications of the current credit crunch have extended well beyond the shores of the United States and were instrumental in the development of a debilitating global credit crunch.

Hedge Funds and Sovereign Wealth Funds

Advances in financial and information technology enabled the growth of hedge funds that utilize a variety of investment strategies into a multi-trillion-Dollar industry. Because hedge funds draw their capital from relatively wealthy, and thus presumably financially sophisticated, individuals and institutions, they are generally unregulated and unrestricted in their investment strategies. One of the main areas where hedge funds excel is the use of leverage to amplify small arbitrage opportunities, for instance between similar assets with divergent returns. This makes them primary players in cross-market rebalancing and speculation, which is one of the primary sources of financial contagion.[7]

In a recent article, Simon Johnson, Director of the Research Department and Economic Counsellor at the International Monetary Fund (IMF), likened today's hedge funds to the free-wheeling financial backers of the last episode of globalization at the turn of the previous century:

Hedge funds, while becoming more prominent in this century, are in some sense a throwback to the end of the 19th century, when large pools of private capital moved around the world with unregulated ease – and generally contributed to a long global boom, rapid productivity growth around the world, and a fair number of crises.[8]

A second class of gargantuan investors have begun to eclipse hedge funds in importance: sovereign wealth funds (SWFs), which are to investment vehicles what national oil companies are to the oil industry. Sovereign wealth funds have existed for a number of decades, primarily as vehicles for governments that rely financially on export receipts to smooth their investment and spending programs. With the recent surge in oil prices and sustained trade imbalances, most notably between the United States and China, sovereign wealth funds in Abu Dhabi, Norway, Saudi Arabia, China, and Singapore, among others, accumulated hundreds of billions of Dollars each and began to seek high rates of return on their investments.

With a total size of approximately $3 trillion, which was expected to triple within five years, SWFs have become major players in international markets. Their role to date has been assumed to be stabilizing, for example through cash infusion to banks that suffered during the mortgage-backed-security crunch of 2007–8. However, if claims by SWFs that they seek fair returns for their investments regardless of political objectives were to hold true in the long term, they are very likely to contribute further to market volatility and contagion.[9]

Like hedge funds, SWFs are generally unregulated, and they maintain a great deal of secrecy regarding not only their investments, but also their total funds under management. Efforts by the IMF and other bodies to pressure SWFs into adopting more transparent standards were met by cynical rejection; pointing out that unregulated and opaque hedge funds and other investment vehicles were the destabilizing forces in the recent collateralized-debt debacle, and SWFs were the stabilizing force that bailed out Western banks such as Citigroup and Merill Lynch.[10] Nonetheless, Western governments and regulators alike remain extremely concerned about the potential for SWFs to engage in destabilizing activities toward economic or political ends.

Over the next decade, SWFs were expected to control nearly $15 trillion, and hedge funds were expected to control a multiple of that sum, even with a conservative leverage ratio. Together, those huge investment pools will be employing thousands of skilled investment managers and traders who will continue to watch markets around the globe, constantly trying to exploit arbitrage opportunities or rebalance their portfolios to manage risks. This, in turn will contribute further to speeding the mechanics of financial contagion across markets, thus propagating real economic shocks at the speed of light (literally, using fiber-optic electronic networks).

Increased Financial Integration and Contagion

Mohamed El-Erian recounts (as a first lesson in market contagion) that as a young economist at the IMF in summer 1982, he and his colleagues were mystified by banks' unwillingness to lend to Chile and Columbia following the Mexican near-default.[11] In the late 1990s, currency crises spread much more quickly across Asian countries, and then traveled to other emerging markets in Latin America and Eastern Europe, with Mexico again playing a prominent role in raising worries about mismatches between a developing country's debts and its assets.

Today, it has become standard to use market performance in one country to forecast behavior in other countries where markets have not yet opened. Market contagion is particularly pronounced when multiple bubbles inflate and deflate simultaneously, as shown in Figure 4.1. With the renewed inflow of petrodollars, and repatriation of Saudi funds due to the tech bubble deflation in the United States and fears following the terrorist attacks of September 11, 2001, excess liquidity fueled multiple bubbles in the region. In early 2006, the standard dynamics of mania giving way to panic and then leading to a market crash spread across Middle-East stock exchanges.

Contagion across Geographic Regions

Contagion effects may not always be as obvious absent a major market crash as witnessed in March 2006 in Saudi Arabia. Absent such clear irrefutable evidence as seen in Figure 4.1, we need to decide what we mean by contagion. Following the observation that markets that appeared previously to be highly uncorrelated, for example emerging markets in Asia, Latin America, and Eastern Europe, have become victims of financial contagion, a variety of approaches for modeling and measuring contagion have been proposed.[12] One of the more promising methodologies focuses on extreme return shocks and their propagation across countries and regions.[13] The main finding is that extreme negative returns are more conducive to contagion than extreme positive returns.

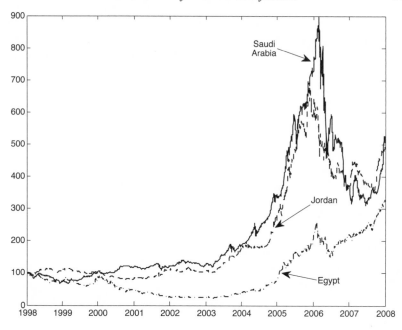

Figure 4.1. Stock indices of Saudi Arabia, Egypt, and Jordan. *Source*: S&P/IFC.

This result was confirmed in other studies, which also showed that simple correlation-based analysis of contagion may be misleading, in part because of the asymmetry between positive and negative returns, and in part because of different patterns of contagion for extreme events and average events, as measured by correlation.[14] To the extent that hedge funds, sovereign wealth funds, and other investors try to hedge their exposure to one market using instruments that track other emerging markets, or to the extent that they use diversified portfolios to reduce their risk of exposure to those markets, this difference between correlations and extreme comovements of stock indices in various emerging markets can play a very important role in crisis scenarios.

Consider three countries in Latin America, the Middle East, and Asia, in which a typical Middle-East sovereign wealth fund might be investing: Mexico, Turkey, and Malaysia.[15] Figures 4.2 and 4.3 show, respectively, the stock market indices and returns thereof for those three countries. It is interesting to note that days of extreme negative returns in one series do not necessarily coincide with extreme negative returns of similar magnitudes in the other two.

We investigated simultaneous extreme negative returns on the Mexican index and extreme negative returns on various portfolios of the other two indices, using standard measures of bivariate extreme codependence.[16] We performed this analysis on the raw negative returns of the three series, as well as on shocks to an estimated systematic model for returns and volatilities.[17] For both models, we found that a portfolio of 70 percent weight on the Turkish index and 30 percent weight on the Malaysian index exhibited significantly higher levels of extreme negative comovements with the Mexican index than either of the two indices alone.

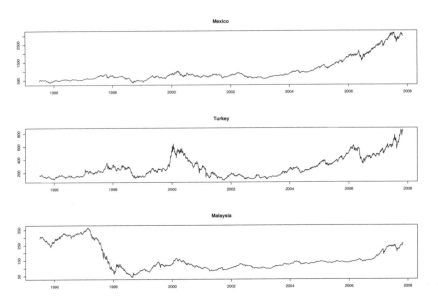

Figure 4.2. Stock market indices: Mexico, Turkey, and Malaysia. *Source*: S&P/IFC data.

Our analysis of simultaneous negative extreme comovements across emerging markets reconfirms the earlier results that correlation analysis may yield unreliable results, using a different methodology. Thus, we have mounting evidence that standard portfolio management, which focuses on correlations across asset returns for diversification and hedging, may encourage managers of large hedge and sovereign wealth funds to construct portfolios that they will need to unwind quickly once any of a number of assets in the portfolio experiences a large negative shock. In this sense, although the large funds cannot be faulted for starting a crisis, they contribute significantly to perpetuating the crisis and introducing correlations where none had existed previously, through their simultaneous rebalancing and trading patterns.

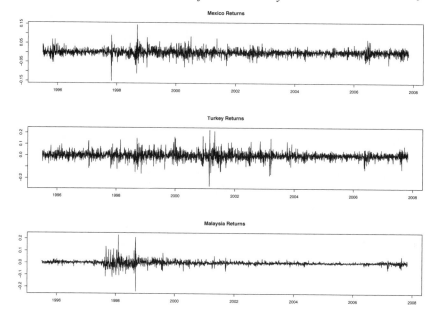

Figure 4.3. Stock market returns: Mexico, Turkey, and Malaysia. *Source*: S&P/IFC data.

Contribution to the Energy Cycle

This is a significant component of our story about the inherent secular cycle in energy prices. One counterargument to our story – which was championed during the high-oil-price episode 2007–8 by the International Energy Agency (IEA), among others – was the belief that Chinese and Indian economic growth will continue unabated, even if high energy prices lead to inflation and eventual recession in OECD countries. Part of the argument made by the IEA has already proven wrong. The IEA had argued that price subsidies would shield Asian consumers and producers from the effects of higher international energy prices. In fact, a number of Asian countries began to remove those subsidies, even before oil prices crashed in the second half of 2008, and the effects of high international prices were being felt in those emerging economies.[18]

Another popular argument during the period 2003–8 was based on the premise that this phase of the cycle was different and that high energy prices would continue for the foreseeable future, because it was argued that export-oriented Asian countries that have witnessed spectacular growth over the past decade can continue their contribution to global economic growth, and hence to energy demand, despite recession in the OECD. The argument suggested that those countries could very quickly develop their own domestic and regional markets to immunize themselves against a decline in exports to OECD countries.

There are three reasons why this counterargument should not have convinced anyone. First, real estate and other asset bubbles in those Asian countries had already demonstrated their limited scope for increased absorptive capacity in the short term. Second, Chinese banks, in particular, were able to mask bad loans (to finance the acquisition of overpriced assets) by continuing to extend credit – a pattern not unlike that witnessed in Japan during the 1970s and early '80s. As high energy prices and the declining Dollar lead to an economic slowdown in China, the volume of nonperforming loans may become increasingly difficult to mask, again in similarity to the earlier Japanese experience. Third, the inevitable financial panic was already known to have contagious effects across other emerging markets, thus resulting in a global slowdown in economic growth and oil consumption, putting downward pressure on oil prices as production capacity grows, and the cycle depicted in Figure 4.4 will continue.

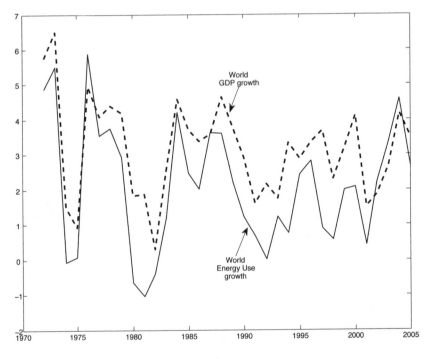

Figure 4.4. Growth in world GDP and energy demand. *Source*: World Bank, WDI.

Liquefied Natural Gas and Globalized Energy Markets

The past decade has seen an expansion in the contagion of price movements from one energy commodity to another with the rapid development of highly liquid futures and other derivatives markets in New York and London and more recently in Dubai and Asia. One of the more dramatic changes has been the commoditization of natural gas markets, which prior to the turn of the previous century had traditionally relied on slow-moving long-term bilateral contractual pricing agreements of 20 years or more.

Natural gas was initially viewed as a marginal fuel consumed in regionally disconnected markets. Advances in welding, metallurgy, and compression technologies in the late 1920s and early 1930s made it possible to transmit natural gas over long distance pipelines. This, in turn, helped to build a substantial U.S. market for natural gas after World War II. Before 1950, the development natural gas markets continued to be restricted mainly to the United States, with 90 percent of natural gas consumption occurring on U.S. soil. In stark contrast, one quarter of world gas consumption today is based on international trade. Seventy-eight percent of that international trade in natural gas in 2004 took place through pipeline transmission. Going forward, the role of liquefied natural gas is expanding rapidly.

As the share of natural gas in global energy supply increases, it has begun to create risk factors of its own. Like oil, gas markets are subject to many disruptive geopolitical forces, including attempts to exercise monopoly power by Russia. After the discontinuance of Russian gas supplies to the Ukraine in the winter of 2005–6, and again in 2008–9, consumer countries have begun to question the premise that natural gas imports will prove inherently more secure than oil. Moreover, the Russia-Ukraine disputes have prompted many consuming countries in Europe to seek diversification as means of mitigating the potential risks of being heavily reliant on any single supplier. As a result, several European LNG receiving terminals have been approved since the first Ukraine affair.

Liquefaction, Globalization, and Geopolitics

As more remote locations become crucial to meeting growing global natural gas demand, LNG will account for an increasing share of total natural gas exports.[19] By 2040, the internationally traded share of world natural gas demand is projected to rise to 48 percent, with LNG shipments responsible for the majority of this growth. Most of that growth, in turn, is expected to come from the Middle East.[20] In other words, as European countries seek reduced geopolitical risk by diversifying away from Russian natural gas, they expose their markets to Middle-East geopolitical risks, further contributing to the similarities with oil markets.

Disruptions in supply, such as unexpected delays of major gas export projects or the unexpected halting of production, create ripple effects throughout the global market, potentially amplifying any coinciding oil-market shocks. For example, disruptions of Indonesian LNG supplies to Japan during political upheaval in the producing area of Aceh in 2003 aggravated already tightening oil markets as Japanese utilities turned to burning oil instead of gas.

Competition and Cooperation in Natural Gas Markets

As the share of natural gas in total energy grows, it is likely to inspire the same geopolitical interventions as oil. The globalization and integration of natural gas markets makes each major consuming and producing region more vulnerable to events in other regions. Gas users in Japan, for instance, have a vested interest in the stability of South American gas flows to the west coast of the United States, and U.S. consumers are concerned about natural gas policy in Africa and Russia.[21] As natural-gas markets grapple with the same political and economic risks that currently influence the global oil market, it is conceivable that an international gas cartel – a Gas OPEC – could emerge to regulate supply and maintain prices in some target range.

At present, the development of a Gas OPEC is prevented by high levels of competition for first-mover market-share advantage. Although some well-positioned gas suppliers such as Algeria and Russia have been able to extract short-term rents in particular markets by manipulating supplies, such events have ultimately created openings for new suppliers to capture market share. Because of the diversity of supply and market competition, perceptions are that disruptions of supply from any particular exporter can be replaced by surplus capacity in LNG markets relatively quickly.

The existence of this diverse competitive fringe of alternative suppliers does not favor cartelization in the short run and has promoted the sense that natural gas markets are more immune to manipulation than are oil markets. However, a point will be reached, perhaps circa 2025, when alternative natural gas supplies in or near many markets would have peaked, and countries that possess large reserves – such as Russia, Iran, and GCC countries – will begin to exercise and coordinate their market power to serve economic and/or political objectives.

Historical Efforts to Control Gas Markets

Attempts to create a Gas OPEC have already been underway for nearly a decade. In May 2001, the Gas Exporting Countries Forum (GECF) held its first ministerial meeting in Tehran with the aim of enhancing coordination among gas producers. By the third session in Doha, Qatar, GECF had swelled to 14 members: Algeria, Brunei, Egypt, Indonesia, Iran, Libya, Malaysia, Nigeria, Oman, Qatar,

Russia, Trinidad and Tobago, the United Arab Emirates, and Venezuela (and one observer, Norway). Although most GECF ministers have maintained that they did not intend to manage production or set quotas, some vocal members have outlined the merits of market control.

The GECF has already tried, unsuccessfully, to exercise some collective influence in the European market. GECF helped the formation of a working group, headed by Russia and Algeria, that sought to defeat European Union's (EU) attempts to outlaw monopoly-enhancing destination clauses that prevent buyers from reselling gas. In another example, Egypt has sought a change in gas pricing systems that would end the link to crude-oil prices with the aim of easing the penetration of gas into European markets. Those and other efforts to date have generated little practical change, and an effective gas exporters' cartel remains unlikely in the near term. However, because the overall distribution of world natural gas reserves is more concentrated than the distribution of oil reserves, especially in Russia and Iran, the potential for cartelization remains a distinct possibility.[22]

Russia's Leadership Role

Gazprom, recognizing the potential for coordinated natural gas export policies, has been approaching alternative key suppliers to Europe over the past two years in order to lay the groundwork for building bridges to coordinate producer responses in the future. Moscow was nominated to host the GECF meeting in 2008 and has been pushing for more coordination inside the group through the formation of a high-level committee to study natural gas pricing mechanisms, including a move away from oil indexation.[23]

Russia initiated negotiations with Qatar and Algeria with the aim of protecting her control over European markets and insulating her gas-export revenues from supply-related price fluctuations.[24] During her years of plenty before the financial crash of 2008, Moscow had also sought to strengthen her grip on the European market by seeking larger investment and development roles in Libyan and Nigerian natural gas, promising debt relief for the former.[25]

Mechanics of a Potential Gas Cartel

Controlling capacity expansion will be more important to an effective gas cartel than it has been for OPEC. The very high cost of building infrastructure for a gas project puts great pressure on owners to fully utilize their capacity. However, capacity investments are difficult to coordinate, because higher capacity would translate into greater power within the cartel. In OPEC, Saudi Arabia's vast excess capacity advantage has allowed the Kingdom to play a dominant role as swing producer and enforcer against those who cheat on their quotas.

The higher cost of building excess capacity (in liquefaction, tanker-space, and pipeline capacity) makes that enforcer role significantly more difficult in natural gas markets. As one expert explained:

In the oil industry, it is estimated that a 1 percent capacity surplus in world-wide oil production (assuming an investment of $3,000 per daily barrel) would cost about $2.2 billion. By contrast, creating a 1 percent surplus in world-wide gas production, assuming that the entire 1 percent was brought to market as LNG, would have a price tag of about $13.8 billion (in field development, liquefaction and tankers).[26]

In theory, Qatar may be better placed than Russia to play the role of swing producer, even though her reserves are substantially smaller in absolute terms. This is because Qatar reserves are very high relative to her population, and the need to produce immediately to generate adequate revenue is not as urgent. Going forward, Qatar's exports will be primarily in liquefied form, which requires less dedicated transportation infrastructure than does pipeline transport, thus giving her access to multiple markets. Finally, given her first mover advantages and prolific reserves, Qatar "has the lowest exploration and development costs for gas of any region in the world."[27] Qatar is expected to control over 10 percent of global LNG exports by 2025, giving her sufficient leverage to influence world natural gas prices.[28]

By 2020, Russia, Algeria, Nigeria, Indonesia, Qatar, and Venezuela all together are expected to account for over 40 percent of world natural gas exports, potentially giving this group considerable market power. By 2030, this group plus Iran and Saudi Arabia will account for over half of world exports.[29] Russia's incentive to cooperate with these other producers, who are members of OPEC, is enhanced by the fact that oil and gas are close substitutes, and overall market power could be enhanced by cooperating on pricing for both fuels. Thus, it might be in Russian interests to collude with all OPEC members to coordinate and attempt to set prices for both oil and natural gas.

Iraqi and Saudi Gas

Geopolitical conflict in Iraq has thwarted the development of Iraq's massive natural gas reserves. Iraq remains a wild card for the future, especially because emerging national and regional governments have all indicated interest in inviting foreign investment in the country's natural gas sector.[30] Gas development has in the past taken a backseat to oil development, because oil markets and profits are more immediately tangible. It would require considerable institutional and financial reform in the gas sector for Iraq to pursue LNG and pipeline exports in the short to medium term. Other options, such as power plant use, though perhaps not as profitable financially, are easier to implement.

Saudi Arabia also has massive proven natural gas reserves.[31] In addition, Saudi Aramco has suggested that only 15 percent of the kingdom has been "adequately explored for gas." [32] Most new associated natural gas reserves discovered in the 1990s by the state firm have been in fields that contain light crude oil, especially in the Najd region south of Riyadh. The majority of Saudi Arabia's nonassociated gas reserves (Mazalij, Al-Manjoura, Shaden, Niban, Tinat, Al-Waar, etc.) are located in the deep Khuff reservoir, which underlies the Ghawar field. Natural gas also is located in the country's extreme northwest, at Midyan, and in the Empty Quarter, placing cost and logistical constraints on development.[33]

Another large undeveloped natural gas field in Saudi Arabia is the Dorra field, which is potentially a source of additional regional geopolitical conflicts.[34] Dorra development has been problematic because part of the field's resources is also claimed by Iran. The maritime border between Kuwait and Iran remains undemarcated, but Saudi Arabia reached an agreement with Kuwait in July 2000 to share Dorra equally. Iran, however, has objected to plans by Kuwait and Saudi Arabia to develop the field on their own.

Iran and the Role of Sanctions in Shaping Natural Gas Markets

Reza Kasaei Zadeh, Iran's deputy oil minister and General Director of the National Iranian Gas Company (NIGC), has stated that Iran's gas strategy is to obtain a market share of "8–10 percent of the world's gas trade and its by-products within 20 years."[35] This ambition notwithstanding, it must be noted that the first-mover advantage has been very important for natural gas producers in securing market access.

Iran, albeit potentially one of the largest players in natural gas markets, remains at a distinct disadvantage due to the continued threat of international sanctions. Other obstacles for Iran have included bureaucratic wrangling, heavy domestic political interference in the energy sector, and corruption.[36] In particular, export-oriented Iranian energy programs have been met by internal opposition, including strong political pressure to reinject natural gas to support oil exports and to use gas domestically as fuel for petrochemical plants.[37]

Iran has also relied increasingly on domestic use of its natural gas resources, as it has faced energy shortages due to a combination of domestic mismanagement and international sanctions. The construction of a planned nuclear power plant – which has contributed to continued and possibly escalating sanctions – would free up 200 million cubic feet a day of natural gas that could be directed to other uses outside the electricity sector, or exported to reap higher revenues.

In this regard, phasing out natural gas subsidies would be a more sensible policy approach to Iran's apparent natural gas shortages than building nuclear capacity.

In fact, it is estimated that removing the distortionary subsidies could free up as much as 2 billion cubic feet a day of Iranian natural gas for export.[38]

Conflicts, Economic Sanctions, and the "War on Terror"

As noted in Chapter 2, one of the unintended consequences of the petrodollar buildup of the 1970s was an arms race in the Middle East. Military expenditures for the major oil producers, Iraq, Iran, and Saudi Arabia, totaled over $100 billion between 1973 and 1981. Not surprisingly, this buildup of armaments in the region has led to an increase in regional tensions and distrust, which in turn has led to military confrontations and war, eventually contributing to higher oil prices in the long term. This oil-price-and-conflict petrodollar pattern has fed a perpetual cycle, whereby petrodollar flows create a military buildup that escalates the risk of conflict, which in turn increases the petrodollar flows and feeds more military buildups and potential conflict, and so on.

The Iran-Iraq War

Saddam Hussein was quick to utilize Iraq's oil wealth to expand military capabilities and pursue regional dominance. By 1980, Iraq had become one of OPEC's largest oil producers, and Baghdad was reaping oil export revenues in excess of $26 billion. Between 1973 and 1980, Iraq's annual military expenditures averaged 18.4 percent of GDP and the Iraq armed forces increased from 105,000 in 1971 to 430,000 in 1980.[39]

After the 1979 revolution, Iran's Islamist government backed Iraqi Shi'a that opposed the rule of Saddam Hussein and was linked to a plot to seize the Grand Mosque in Makkah. It was against this backdrop that Saddam Hussein made his tragic miscalculation that a military attack on Iran would quickly bring down the Iranian government and end the threat of the Iranian revolution toward Iraq and the Arab world. His foray to grab control of the important Shatt al-Arab waterway in September 1980 failed and led to a bloody eight-year war with Iran that resulted in over 1 million casualties and the destruction of much of the oil-export infrastructures of the two countries.

Oil prices oscillated significantly during the Iraq-Iran war, but the fluctuations were generally held in check by Saudi Arabia and Kuwait, who raised their oil production to replace war-disrupted exports and production from Iraq and Iran. In addition, Saudi Arabia and Kuwait provided loans to finance the Iraqi military, recognizing the threat of Iran to their own security. Saudi Arabia was particularly concerned following the 1981 disturbance in Madinah where a number of Iranian pilgrims were arrested and deported for distributing leaflets calling for the overthrow of the Saudi government.[40]

Heavier U.S. Military Presence and Iraq's Invasion of Kuwait

By 1987, the United States responded to escalating attacks on oil shipping through the Gulf with a military buildup of her own. The U.S. Navy began organizing a fleet of frigates, destroyers, and minesweepers in the region to combat the threat against shipping and protect the flow of oil from the region.[41] In March 1987, the U.S. government agreed to fly American flags on Kuwaiti oil and gas tankers. In July 1987, the U.S. Navy initiated Operation Earnest Will, which provided naval escorts to all tankers passing through the Gulf.[42] This was only the beginning of the direct military presence of the United States.

Starting in late 1987, Iraq began to expand its export capacity by pipeline through Turkey, as well as via the Gulf after the ceasefire with Iran in 1988. Despite low oil prices, Iraq refused to observe her production quota under OPEC. Instead, Iraq demanded that other OPEC countries reduce their quotas to accommodate her expanded exports and sought forgiveness of her debts to Kuwait and Saudi Arabia. Tensions escalated, ultimately resulting in Iraq's invasion of Kuwait in 1990. This invasion, in turn, escalated the buildup of U.S. troops in the region, first through operations Desert Shield and Desert Storm.

The Sanctions Game Continues

The initial international response to Iraq's invasion of Kuwait was to impose stringent economic sanctions against Iraq and to ban the export and use of Iraqi or Kuwaiti oil. Spot oil prices initially rose from $13 a barrel prior to the invasion to $40, eventually converging to the $20s as Saudi Arabia, Venezuela, and the United Arab Emirates increased their production. Oil prices rose again briefly after the U.S. military buildup in the Gulf and the subsequent military operations to remove Iraq by military force from Kuwait. In balance, the oil price shock from 1990, although short-lived and not as extreme as the 1970s, did contribute to the weakening U.S. economy in the early 1990s, again an example of the petrodollar/regional conflict cycle.

Throughout the 1980s and into the 1990s, economic sanctions became the hallmark of the United States and international response to the rise of military conflict and state-sponsored terrorism. This paradigm seemed to become a fixture of U.S. foreign policy in later years, as one author suggested: "Negative economic tools ... will be a crucial component of America's more activist foreign policy agenda. They will continue to play a key role in combating terrorism."[43] Thus, economic sanctions have become a multipurpose tool for containing threats and regime change.[44]

On August 6, 1990, after Iraq's invasion of Kuwait, the United Nations Security Council passed a resolution imposing a multilateral trade embargo against

Iraq, with exception only for humanitarian assistance. The sanctions on Iraq were extended and escalated until the U.S. invasion in 2003, preventing not only new investment in Iraq's oil industry, but even basic repairs and improvements.[45]

Sanctions Backfire

Ironically, these economic sanctions during the 1990s did little to stem the tide of terrorist financing or weaken the target regimes, which in fact profited from smuggling activities. Instead, the sanctions caused slower investment in the oil fields of Iraq, Iran, and Libya, which later resulted in shortages when global economic demand reached new heights 2003–8. Because of those sanctions, therefore, OPEC was unable to reach the planned production capacity targets that it had set for the mid-1990s.[46] Ironically, OPEC's ability to exercise market power after the price collapse of 1998 was in large part made possible precisely by this lack of excess capacity caused by sanctions.

There were other factors limiting investment in capacity as discussed in previous chapters, such as the rapidly expanding populations in many OPEC countries, which created intense pressures on state treasuries for expanded social services, leaving less money to be spent on oil sector expansion.[47] But there is no question that OPEC capacity has also been constrained by international and American economic sanctions policy. By 2000, OPEC's spare capacity was a negligible 2 percent of world oil demand and resided almost exclusively in Saudi Arabia, which contained roughly about 90 percent of world's spare capacity in 2008. Even today, oil markets remain extremely vulnerable to short-term disruptions because of this lack of excess capacity. Table 3.1 illustrates how total OPEC capacity had actually fallen between 1979 and 2005.

September 11 "Changed Everything"

The September 11, 2001, terrorist attacks on the United States gave renewed momentum to the importance of economic sanctions against what was perceived to be state-sponsored terrorism. The event also prompted increased calls for reduced U.S. dependence on Middle-East oil, citing a growing link between terrorism and petrodollar financing. This line of reasoning became the mantra of the neoconservative movement that would become an important fixture in the George W. Bush administration and was one reason frequently cited to support military intervention in Iraq.[48]

Summing up representative thinking on the potential dangers of heavy reliance on Middle East oil, former CIA director R. James Woolsey wrote:

The wealth produced by oil is what underlies, almost exclusively, the strength of three major groups in the Middle East – Islamists, both Shiite and Sunni, and Baathists – that have chosen to be at war with us. Our own dependence on that oil, and the effect this has had on our conduct over the past quarter-century, have helped encourage each of these groups to believe that we are vulnerable.[49]

Neoconservative thinker Ariel Cohen, key analyst at the conservative Heritage Foundation, explicitly argued that access to oil revenues was a critical aspect of the export of radical Islam:

The oil bonanza funded the worldwide export of radical Wahhabi Islam, the ideological breeding ground of Al-Qa'ida and the Taliban, over the last three decades. Government sponsored foundations, supervised by members of the Saudi royal family, fueled jihad from New York to Kabul, and from Miami to Manila, by funding brainwashing for violence in Wahhabi academies (madrassas), and terrorism training under the guise of charity. Hamas and Yasser Arafat's al Aqsa Martrys Brigades, which undermined the Oslo process and now are busily blowing the roadmap to bits with their weapon of choice brainwashed Palestinian suicide bombers are partially funded through Saudi telethons and hailed by preachers in Saudi government-supported mosques worldwide.[50]

Dreams of "The Oil Weapon" Resurface

For years, Saddam Hussein had argued that the United States, through corrupt puppet regimes in the Gulf, exercised its global hegemony and denied the Arab peoples their rightful earnings from their national oil resources. He characterized the Gulf War as part of this U.S. conspiracy to deprive the Iraqi people and other Arab nationals of the right to garner "fair" value for their national patrimony – oil resources.[51]

Simultaneously, Ossama Bin Laden had also urged the Arab Muslim masses to seek higher rents for oil. In his letter to the American people, he wrote:

You steal our wealth and oil at paltry prices because of your international influence and military threats. This is indeed the biggest theft ever witnessed by mankind in the history of the world.

As economic hardship and regional conflicts in the 1990s fed anti-Americanism, the latter became a major influence on domestic politics, affecting regional leaders' ability to cooperate with the United States and her energy companies. Surveys show that anti-American attitudes, although subsiding, are still pervasive. According to a 2004 survey by the Pew Research Center for the People and the Press:

In the predominantly Muslim countries surveyed, anger toward the United States remains pervasive, although the level of hatred has eased somewhat and support for the war on terrorism has inched up. Ossama bin Laden, however, is viewed favorably by large percentages in Pakistan (65%), Jordan (55%) and Morocco (45%). Even in Turkey, where bin Laden is highly unpopular, as many as 31% say that suicide attacks against Americans and other Westerners in Iraq are justifiable. Majorities in all four Muslim nations surveyed doubt the sincerity of the war on terrorism. Instead, most say it is an effort to control Mideast oil and to dominate the world.[52]

The Advisory Group on Public Diplomacy for the Arab and Muslim World, commissioned by U.S. Congress in 2003, reached similar conclusions, stating that:

Surveys show much of the resentment toward America stems from our policies. It is clear, for example, that the Arab-Israeli conflict remains a visible and significant point of contention between the United States and many Arab and Muslim countries and that peace in that region, as well as the transformation of Iraq, would reduce tensions.[53]

The Advisory group added that "official U.S. diplomacy is seen as frequently buttressing governments hostile to freedom and prosperity ... many Arabs and Muslims believe that such support [of repressive governments] indicates that the U.S. is determined to deny them freedom and political representation." This sentiment has affected otherwise friendly OPEC leaders' willingness to cooperate with the United States in the energy area. Driven by these political trends at home, OPEC was slow to expand capacity during 2003–8, seeking higher prices instead.

Escalation of U.S. Military Presence

The export of Middle-East geopolitical problems to the shores of the United States was closely tied to Al-Qaʻidaʼs outrage at U.S. military presence in Saudi Arabia. Paradoxically, the U.S. response to that threat, as it began withdrawing troops from Saudi Arabia,[54] was to intensify its overall military presence in the region, mainly through the invasion of Iraq. The United States currently runs the risk of becoming itself an entrenched regional combatant rather than a power broker.[55]

Ironically, one of the key benefits of the U.S. invasion of Iraq, as envisioned by then U.S. Deputy Secretary of Defense Paul Wolfowitz, was that a newly independent and democratic Iraq would develop its vast oil resources and thereby break the oligopolistic power of OPEC. On the contrary, Iraq's oil production capability actually fell – from 2.7 million barrels per day in 2002 to barely over 2 million. Far from weakening OPEC, the invasion of Iraq in fact strengthened it by enabling anti-U.S. countries such as Venezuela to gain an audience at the same time that long-term allies such as Saudi Arabia felt less compelled to help after their advice against the invasion of Iraq fell on deaf ears.

Within Saudi Arabia, the announcement of the U.S. withdrawal was followed almost immediately by an attack on Westerners in the Kingdom. The simultaneous suicide bombing attacks carried out by 15 Saudis on three compounds housing foreigners in Riyadh wounded 200 people and killed at least 34, including 8 Americans and 7 Saudis.[56] Seven of the Americans killed had worked for the subsidiary of a Virginia firm that was training the Saudi National Guard and civil-service officials, suggesting that the attack targeted the Saudi regime itself. The incident was one in a series of incidents in 2003 that added a "terror premium" to international oil prices.[57]

"The War on Terror"

September 11 and the subsequent "war on terror" brought new momentum to U.S. national concerns about the link between terrorism and the proliferation of weapons of mass destruction to the Middle East. Infamously, President Bush's call to arms against an "Axis of Evil" of Iraq, Iran, and North Korea in his January 2002 State of the Union address tied those countries to the threat of terrorism:

States like these, and their terrorist allies, constitute an axis of evil, arming to threaten the peace of the world. By seeking weapons of mass destruction, these regimes (Iraq, Iran, North Korea) pose a grave and growing danger. They could provide these arms to terrorists, giving them the means to match their hatred. They could attack our allies or attempt to blackmail the United States. . . .[58]

Within this framework, the U.S. administration's continued conflict with Iran over Tehran's nuclear aspirations has contributed to volatility in oil markets. Iran's pursuit of nuclear technology also hangs over regional stability, given the potential for a regional nuclear arms race, as officials at a March 2007 Arab summit meeting suggested, especially as a number of countries in the region are investigating civilian-purpose nuclear-power development. In the meantime, additional sanctions imposed on Iran for its failure to suspend uranium enrichment continue to perpetuate the dynamics that have restrained energy supply capacity growth for decades.[59]

Escalating rhetoric has led some Iranian leaders again to invoke the 1973 memories of an "oil weapon." Iran threatened to cut its oil exports to the West if a U.S.-led coalition imposed further sanctions. Iranian Supreme Leader Ayatollah Ali Khamenei in June 2006 warned the United States that Washington "should know that the slightest misbehavior on your part would endanger the entire region's energy security. . . . You are not capable of guaranteeing energy security in the region."[60] Saudi Arabia responded quickly to this rhetoric by increasing its investments in upstream oil production capability in order to be able to replace any lost Iranian exports.[61]

In early January 2008, the escalation almost reached the level of military hostility as U.S. warships had an altercation with five Iranian Revolutionary Guard speedboats that approached them in Gulf waters.[62] The possibility of an escalation in the U.S. conflict with Iran over its nuclear aspirations remains a wild card in oil price trends. Some analysts have argued that the widening U.S. presence in the Gulf has increased those risks. Conversely, in an endless causal loop, others in Washington have argued that U.S. military presence in the Gulf has become all the more critical precisely because the region is more conflict prone.

Regardless of the long-term resolution, it is clear in the short term that U.S. presence did contribute to higher energy prices through increased geopolitical risk premia and slower capacity building. In turn, renewed petrodollar flows to the region have ignited a new arms race that contributed to price escalation during 2003–8. Mounting U.S. debt, due in part to financing the Iraq war and in part to feedback through higher oil-import costs, also contributed to the declining Dollar, which in turn fed the spiral of rising Dollar-denominated oil prices and continued the downward pressure on the Dollar, to which we now return.

5

Dollars and Debt: The End of the Dollar Era?

The previous episode of globalization ended with World War I and a domino effect of protectionist measures leading into World War II. After World War II, the Bretton-Woods accord restarted global trade and growth by making the U.S. Dollar the first official universal currency with respect to which all other currencies fixed their exchange rates. Trade-surplus countries were thus incentivized to hold their excess reserves in Dollars and Dollar-denominated assets. The growth of debt, mainly denominated in Dollars, was thus at the heart of globalization.

The Dollar as Reserve Currency

Since the Dollar was still pegged to gold under the Bretton-Woods system, global economic growth, and its prerequisite growth in trade, were constrained by the global supply of gold between 1945 and 1970. Once the Dollar was divorced from gold in 1971, a credit-based system of global trade enabled accelerated growth in trade and economic activity, as Paul Volcker noted, with apparent puzzlement: "People were more willing to hold dollars that weren't backed by gold than they were willing to hold dollars that were backed by gold."[1] For decades, the mounting volume of world trade was made possible by mounting stockpiles of international reserves. Figure 5.1 shows the total accumulated official reserves in Special Drawing Rights (SDRs) of the International Monetary Fund (IMF). In fact, the bulk of those reserves were held in Dollar-denominated assets. During the 1970s, and again in the current decade, a significant part of this growth in international reserves has been accumulated in the coffers of oil-exporting countries. This, in turn, has eventually contributed to the resurgent flows of petrodollars that have been at the center of our analysis.

During the early years of the twenty-first century, globalization has continued to grow, but the Dollar's role has begun to shrink. In Figure 5.2, we can see that the role of the Dollar as an international currency, as measured by the percentage

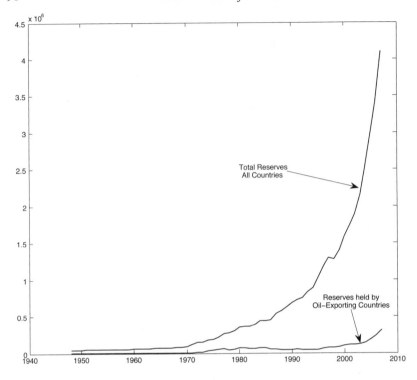

Figure 5.1. Total reserves in millions of SDRs. *Source*: IMF, IFS.

of official allocated reserves held in Dollars, had continued to grow with globalization through the millennium mark. As the United States continued to accumulate trade deficits and debts through the first decade of the twenty-first century (see Figure 1.3), doubts about the sustainability of the Dollar-centered international financial system continued to mount, prompting a number of countries to diversify their holdings away from Dollar-denominated assets.

If the current pattern continues, the post-Bretton-Woods Dollar-based international financial system could come to an end very soon. In the remainder of this chapter, we review the positive and negative systemic effects of the Dollar-centered system that has prevailed since World War II. In Chapter 6, we discuss the geopolitical and economic incentives that may hasten the end of the Dollar era. In Chapter 7, we discuss potential alternatives to the current international financial system that may arise and the likelihood of continued globalization under those alternatives. We begin this series of discussions with the official birth of the Dollar era at Bretton Woods, shortly after the end of World War II.

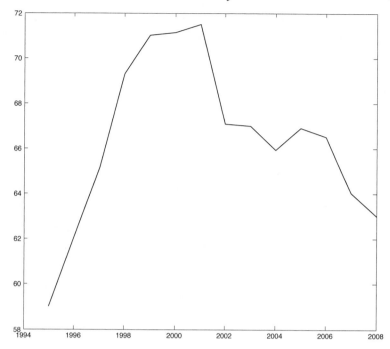

Figure 5.2. Percentage of allocated official reserves held in Dollars. *Source*: IMF, COFER.

Bretton Woods and Beyond: The Primacy of U.S. Debt

At the turn of the previous century, the British Pound played the same role as the Dollar plays today, with roughly two-thirds of the world's official reserves being held in that currency. As the American economy rose in prominence during the early decades of the twentieth century, especially after World War I, major central banks started to hold Dollars in increasing proportions.

The role of the British Pound continued to decline at an accelerating pace during the Great Depression, mainly because low interest rates that were intended to boost the faltering British economy increased pressure on the Pound, eventually forcing Britain to abandon convertibility of the Pound for gold in 1931. One of the great paradoxes is that the Pound suffered because of the gold standard, and the Dollar later replaced it in international dominance as the global currency after Bretton Woods precisely by appealing to the stability of its gold backing. However, the true potential of the Dollar was only realized after its convertibility for gold was abandoned during that fateful summer of 1971.

The Bretton Woods Accord made the U.S. Dollar the official global currency to which all other currencies were pegged. A fixed exchange-rate system was seen as the best means of restarting and accelerating world trade, as it reduced transaction costs and eliminated one of the main sources of risk in international transactions. In due course, the relative merits and drawbacks of fixed vs. flexible exchange rates became central subjects of academic and policy-maker debates, which any new recruit for the International Monetary Fund was expected to have mastered.[2]

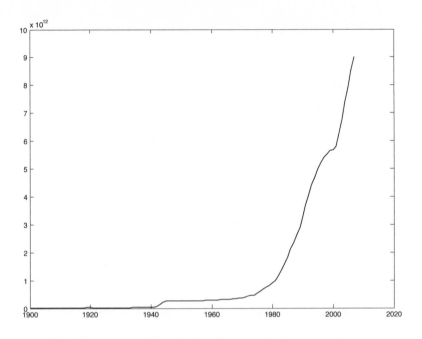

Figure 5.3. Total U.S. debt outstanding in Dollars. *Source*: U.S. Treasury.

A fundamental problem with the Bretton-Woods system irked many world leaders. Charles De Gaulle indicated on more than one occasion that he was flabbergasted that the Bretton-Woods system allowed the United States to force the rest of the world to hold its debt, regardless of fiscal discipline or lack thereof.[3] It is a common saying that if one owes the bank 1 million Dollars, then one has a problem, but if one owes the bank 1 billion Dollars, then the bank has a problem. Likewise, complaints of those sharing De Gaulle's views were dismissed by Nixon's Secretary of the Treasury, John Connally, who said famously to a group of European interlocutors that the Dollar is "our currency, but your problem."[4]

Unchecked Growth of U.S. Foreign Debt

For many decades, foreign governments as well as various public and private entities preferred to hold interest-bearing Dollar-denominated assets, rather than holding Dollars and forfeiting this interest as part of seignorage to the Federal Government of the United States. The total volume of outstanding debt grew exponentially fast during three episodes: (1) immediately following World War II and the Bretton-Woods accord, in part to finance the reconstruction of Europe through the Marshall plan; (2) shortly after the Dollar was decoupled from gold in 1971 feeding a spiral of global inflation; and (3) the most recent episode after 1998, featuring renewed petrodollar flows and global inflationary pressure. The latest episode of mounting debts during the twenty-first century has driven faith in the Dollar's viability as an international currency to previously unseen lows.

Global Economic Growth, Interest Rates, and Debt

The remarkable economic growth that the world has witnessed since World War II was in large part driven by globalization and the growth in global trade. Figure 5.4 shows the direct relationship between world GDP growth and world export growth. The importance of trade for growth has been more manifest in the past two decades, when greater increase in the volume of world trade was needed to produce a recognizable growth in world income. During that period, the Asian export-oriented model of economic growth has thus become global, as an increasing portion of global economic growth originated in the continent.

The causal link acts in both directions: economic growth enhances spending on imports, and the increase in exports contributes directly to economic growth. One way to sustain this cycle for an extended, albeit finite, period of time, is through debt financing of expenditure on imports.

Easy Money

During the early 1980s, the memory of 1970s stagflation was still fresh in central bankers' memories. Stagflation during that period made it clear that a lax monetary policy, with or without fiscal stimulus, need not translate into increased economic growth and reduced unemployment and may cause inflation. However, central bankers seemed to have forgotten that lesson only a decade later.

By the early 1990s, central bankers' primary inflation-fighting function began to give way to political-business-cycle and recession-fighting considerations. The resulting pattern of interest rates in major industrialized countries is shown in Figure 5.5. The case of Japan was extreme, of course, where even zero interest rates could not lift the country out of its deflationary spiral during the country's lost decade. Other industrialized countries that suffered milder recessions also used monetary policy to boost economic growth whenever necessary. The Taylor rule variation on inflation targeting, which began to gain popularity during the

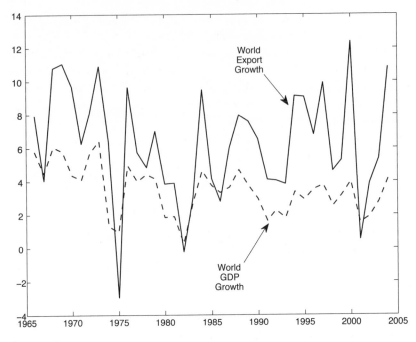

Figure 5.4. World GDP and export growth percentage. *Source*: World Bank, WDI.

1990s, thus modeled interest-rate policy explicitly as a function both of inflation and economic growth.[5]

The case of Japan notwithstanding, the experience that central bankers acquired during the late 1980s and early 1990s suggested that they could use monetary policy to shorten and reduce the severities of recessions without risking inflation. The mystique surrounding Federal Reserve Board Chairman Alan Greenspan, in particular, suggested that the risk of inflation was muted.

This gave the Fed Chairman and other central bankers further confidence in their efforts to use monetary policy to prevent financial market panics. In particular, the apparently successful handling of the financial crash on "black Monday," October 19, 1987, as well as the day markets opened after the terrorist attacks of September 2001, both through massive liquidity infusions, suggested that monetary policy can also be used to support financial markets without fear of triggering inflation.

During the early years of the twenty-first century, central bankers were continuously called upon to reduce interest rates as one financial-market bubble gave rise to another. Massive spending on information technology as the millennium approached, in part fueled by fear that old equipment would malfunction once

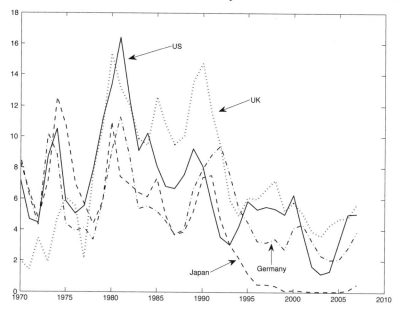

Figure 5.5. Money market rates. *Source*: IMF, IFS.

the calendar turned to January 1, 2000, fueled a bubble in technology stocks. As that bubble deflated, lower interest rates, meant to minimize the adverse effects of the bursting bubble, fueled another bubble in real estate. Massive volumes of cheap mortgages were repackaged into asset-backed securities which translated into a worldwide credit bubble that caused a financial crash in 2008, but has yet to be fully unraveled.

Uneasy Symbiosis: U.S. Consumers and Asian Savers

Global economic growth during the past decade was thus made possible through sustained consumption, which was in turn financed by cheap credit. That cheap credit was made possible through the patterns of investment of export surpluses, mainly of Asian countries, but eventually also of oil-exporting countries.

The savings rates in the industrial West have been systematically lower than those in the export-surplus East, as shown in Figure 5.6. During the early years of the twenty-first century, the bulk of those Asian savings were invested in Dollar-denominated assets, allowing U.S. consumers to continue borrowing at low interest rates to finance their consumption of imports from Asia countries. This trade pattern, in turn, allowed those Asian countries to continue their phenomenal export-led growth.

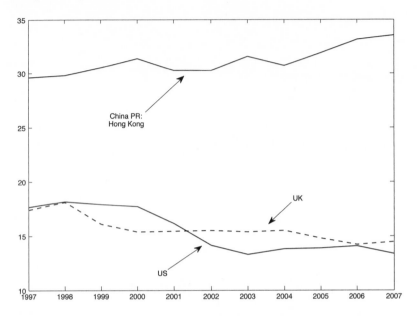

Figure 5.6. Gross national savings as percentage of Gross National Income. *Source*: IMF, IFS.

This symbiotic relationship between Asian exporters and U.S. consumers supported the Dollar for many years, despite mounting debts shown in Figure 5.3. Led by China, many of those export surplus countries did not allow their currencies to appreciate against the Dollar, concerned mainly about maintaing the competitiveness of their exports.

The resulting quasi-fixed exchange rate system resembled the Bretton-Woods Dollar-based system, which prompted a number of researchers to call the system Bretton-Woods II.[6] Some economists expected this system of global economic growth based on Asian exports and U.S. consumption funded with Asian savings to continue, while others expected it to collapse at any moment when those countries abandon the Dollar.[7] In fact, as Figure 5.2 suggests, diversification away from the Dollar has been a slow process, albeit noticeable, and the eventual end of the current financial system has been difficult to predict.

The Decoupling Hypothesis: Hard Landing vs. Transition

A number of prominent economists have been forecasting a soft landing for the global economic and financial system. This optimistic forecast was based on the assumption of continued growth in emerging economies, even as mature industrialized countries experience slower growth. In this regard, El-Erian predicted that "[t]he resulting long-term hand-off in economic growth [from developed to developing economies] will gradually reduce the world's sensitivity to variations in U.S. growth performance," based on "greater emphasis on domestic components of demand" in the developing world.[8] In contrast, Roubini and Setser predicted, prematurely but possibly accurately, that the burden of financing unsustainable U.S. debts may destabilize Asian domestic financial systems, thus preventing a soft-landing transition from export- to domestic-consumption-oriented growth.[9]

At the heart of this debate is the possibility of decoupling export-oriented economies, especially China, from the business cycle in mature industrialized countries, especially the United States. There is no doubt that the long-term potential for the Chinese domestic market is gargantuan. However, the short-term absorptive capacity of that domestic market may not be as substantial as some economists had assumed.

The limits on short-term absorptive capacity are evidenced by the direct relationship between the annual rate of growth of Gross National Income and Consumer Price Index (CPI) annual inflation rate for Mainland China, shown in Figure 5.7. As fuel and food prices increased during 2007–8, the National Statistical Bureau announced that Chinese annual inflation had reached 8.7 percent in February 2008, the highest level in more than a decade.[10]

It is generally accepted that high inflation is disruptive of economic growth, as evidenced by China's own experience in the late 1990s.[11] In this regard, Stanley Fischer (1993) estimated that every extra percentage point of inflation reduces the growth rate of an economy by one-tenth of a percentage point, on average.[12]

The threat of inflation may be compounded through its secondary effects on the financial system. The savings glut in China produced speculative bubbles in real estate, stock, and asset markets, some of which had begun to deflate before the crash of 2008, as shown for the Shanghai Composite Index (SSEC) in Figure 5.8. Speculative bubbles of the sort seen in the SSEC tend to attract irresponsible borrowing and lending practices, as banks lend to investors against appreciating assets of various types, including most notably real estate, only to witness multiple loans going bad simultaneously. Indeed, Japan learned this lesson the hard way as Asian prudence that was much celebrated during the 1970s gave way to the same Western-style speculative bubble culture to which Japan was supposedly immune.

Easy Money Revisited

In his classic explanation of financial *Manias, Panics, and Crashes*, Charles Kindleberger wrote two axioms:

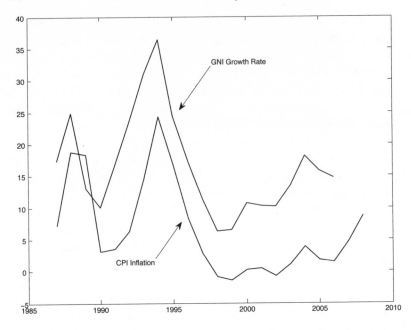

Figure 5.7. Mainland China Gross National Income and CPI percentage change. *Source*: IMF, IFS.

Axiom number one. Inflation depends on the growth of money.

Axiom number two. Asset price bubbles depend on the growth of credit.[13]

We have discussed earlier in the chapter how easy money, and the serial asset bubbles that it has facilitated, were in part caused by the accommodating monetary policy stance of the U.S. Federal Reserve. In this regard, by continuing to provide cheap credit to soften the effects of one speculative bubble's deflation, the central bankers of the world – with the Fed at the lead – have contributed to what Soros has called a super bubble, components of which span banking crises of the 1980s, emerging market crises of the 1990s, the technology bubble of 2000, and the most recent real estate and derivatives-driven credit bubbles.[14] Of course, when faced with the horrific prospect of a financial meltdown, it is difficult for any central banker to stick to inflation-targeting or other policy objectives, unless the latter are institutionally imposed.

Figure 5.8. Shanghai Composite and Dow Jones Industrial Average. *Source*: Yahoo Finance.

Contagion: Sequential Bubbles and Crashes

Soros identified three main forces behind the super bubble of the past two decades. The first was increasing credit expansion, in part to avoid recessions in the aftermath of financial bubble deflation or major economic or geopolitical events. The second factor was globalization of financial markets, which provided a greater marketplace for absorption of the generated credit. Finally, the third factor was increasing financial deregulation that allowed for new financial products that facilitated marketing the increasing supply of credit to the larger global marketplace. In his analysis, Soros dated the first factor back to the end of the Great Depression circa 1933, and the latter two factors to the 1980s.[15]

This is reminiscent to a large extent of Hyman Minsky's interpretation of Keynesian analysis of the Great Depression, which suggested that capitalist economic systems, with profit-oriented economic units in the real and financial sectors, are inherently unstable.[16] The story is a familiar one: A prolonged period of economic growth lulls investors into a false sense of security. The result is that appetites for risk begin to increase, as continued profitability and low rates of bankruptcy justify optimistic beliefs about the level of risk exposure. As a result, optimism gives way to euphoria (irrational exuberance, in the words of Robert

Shiller)[17] as investors bid up the prices of capital goods using borrowed funds that banks are happy to provide. The prolonged period of growth also suggests that prudential regulations should be relaxed to unleash the power of laissez-faire capitalism, thus setting the stage for financial disaster.

Minsky's Taxonomy: Hedge, Speculative, and Ponzi Finance

In this regard, Minsky provided a famous taxonomy of hedge, speculative, and Ponzi financing.[18] The three types of financing are distinguished by examining the cash flows of an economic unit. If cash receipts generally exceed contractually committed cash outflow, the unit is engaged in hedge finance. If financing contracts commit the unit to larger cash outflows (both principal and interest) than expected inflows, the unit is engaged in speculative financing, relying on the good will of financiers who will be happy to continue the provision of funds. Finally, if the level of speculation is such that new financing is required not only to repay the principal on earlier financing, but also to cover the interest payments thereof, then the unit is said to engage in Ponzi financing.

Transition from hedge to speculative or from speculative to Ponzi finance may occur for a number of reasons. Any catalytic event, no matter how short lived, may create the appearance of a trend in the prices of some assets. The bubble in technology-company stocks, for instance, began as investors anticipated the need for new software and hardware solutions as the millennium approached and older computers and programs were expected to malfunction. Once the positive trend in asset prices is established, speculators begin to buy those assets not only based on expectations of high intrinsic value, but merely to "get into" the market, confident that they will eventually be able to sell at even higher prices.

Credit markets play a crucial function in creating and sustaining such speculative bubbles, as suggested by Kindleberger's second axiom, quoted earlier. Obvious examples are provided by the real estate bubbles that have afflicted many economies over the past few decades. After a prolonged period of increasing real estate prices that border on speculative bubbles, bankers consider such assets to be very good collateral and therefore feel confident lending to individuals who are extremely likely to default were prices to fall. With banks competing to lend to individuals who are investing in those assets, the very act of lending becomes a self-fulfilling prophecy that the collateral value will continue to rise, thus ensuring the bank's interest against default.

As the bubble reaches obviously unsustainable levels, psychological market factors begin to raise doubts in the minds of investors, thus reducing the supply of funds. In turn, the reduced supply of funds raises interest rates and transforms the difference between cash inflows and cash outflows from positive to negative. Interest rates may also rise nominally due to central bank intervention, as well as to market forces, as earlier cheap funding drives asset price inflation. Psychological and economic factors thus eventually force market-euphoria-driven inflation to reverse course. However, since debts are denominated in nominal Dollars, the eventual deflation plays a critical role in creating a negative mismatch between cash inflows and cash outflows for economic units, causing investors to reduce their supply of funds and accelerating the inevitable economic downturn.[19]

The New Millennium's Minsky Moment

It bears repeating that Minsky, and according to him, Keynes, viewed this cycle as endogenous to capitalist economic systems. External shocks, such as the oil embargo of 1973 or the terrorist attacks of 2001, may provide catalysts for crisis development. However, the tendency for good economic performance to cause regulatory complacency and investor euphoria, which in turn fuels inflation through speculative and eventually Ponzi finance, is inherent in the system itself. Indeed, as Soros and Minsky have pointed out, the regulatory vehicles that were put in place in the United States to prevent another Great Depression from occurring were eventually seen as impediments to growth. In time, this view has given rise to a series of financial innovations to circumvent regulatory restrictions, as well as explicit deregulations in the United States intended to allow heavily regulated banks to compete with new nonbank financial institutions and market-oriented financial products.

Soros suggested that globalization forces in the 1980s allowed this Minsky scenario to repeat on the international stage, thus creating a global credit bubble. Suspension of disbelief, which leads to investor euphoria, requires faulty memory, or reasons to belief that "this time is different." The series of speculative bubbles that evolved around the turn of the century were in part fueled by beliefs that the Fed, especially under the stewardship of Alan Greenspan, would never allow a repeat of the Great Depression to occur.

This belief, dubbed "the Greenspan put," was reconfirmed by the Fed's ability to weather multiple financial storms, including the stock market crash of 1987 and the terrorist attacks of 2001, by infusing liquidity into the financial system without causing disruptive inflation.[20] Only much later were inflationary concerns voiced after years of continuous expansionary (low interest rate) monetary policies, meant to avoid deep recession after each of the serial bubbles deflated.

The balance of inflationary concern and fear of deep recession has thus consistently prompted the Fed to err on the side of expansionary policies, driving interest rates to all-time lows. One of the factors that was not taken into consideration was the new surge in petrodollars, which quickly rivaled the outflow of savings from Asia starting in 2003. In Chapter 7, we shall argue that this constant tie between long periods of economic growth, especially driven by inflationary monetary policies, almost always brings about an energy-price crisis as the rate of growth of fuel-production capacity lags behind the rate of growth of energy-demanding investment and consumption. This is a global resource curse, quite different from but connected to the resource curses of oil-and-gas-rich countries that requires careful analysis.

Latin America, Japan, Asian Tigers, and China

It is important to note that a similar move from hedge to speculative and eventually to Ponzi finance has taken place on the international scene. Most famous, perhaps, have been experiences in Latin America, first in the 1970s and early 1980s, when the maxim that "countries don't go out of business" fueled a credit boom financed by recycled petrodollars, and later in the mid-1990s. The oil-price-driven spiral in the 1970s and 1980s, in particular, is worth recalling: Expectations of continued high oil prices made loans to oil-rich Latin American countries a form of hedge finance. As expectations eventually gave way to inflationary speculative finance, the stage was set for reversal of the spiral in the 1980s, when the U.S. Fed raised interest rates to combat the resulting inflation.

The experiences of Asian countries in the 1980s and 1990s were different from the Latin American experience insofar as savings rates in Asian countries have been very high. Despite that main difference, Japan and later Asian-tiger countries were not immune to the Minsky syndrome described earlier. In all of those countries, hedge finance, both domestic and international, eventually turned speculative, as the prices of capital goods were driven upward through the familiar euphoria that multiyear growth paths always seem to inspire.

The most celebrated of the Asian euphorias in Japan eventually ended with a banking crisis that cost the country a full decade. Earlier wage and price inflation in Japan that caused the export of investment and growth to neighboring Asian countries ultimately caused the export of the same financial euphoria and eventual crisis in the mid-1990s. Surprisingly, the examples of financial-led crises in Japan and other Asian countries, not to mention Latin America and the rest of the world, did not prevent a new euphoria from developing: one that suggested continued Chinese and Indian economic growth and the concomitant demand for energy perpetually sustaining high energy prices. The latter fiction sustained the oil-price bubble through 2007 and the first half of 2008.

The Dollar and Bets on Chinese Growth and Oil

This brings us to reviewing the various economic stories that can sustain high oil prices, and the investment vehicles that speculators and Ponzi financiers are likely to utilize when such stories dominate investor expectations. In this regard, we note that the stories and players change from one euphoric episode to the next: The major players in domestic and global financial systems during the 1970s petrodollar-driven euphoria of Latin American finance were bankers. However, the direct role of banks in financial markets has been declining steadily overall.

Bankers continue to facilitate leverage for speculators, through lending as well as market-based finance, but the bigger market movers in recent years have been generally unregulated hedge fund managers. In this regard, understanding dynamics of the current oil-price bubble, and the corresponding financial dynamics of the U.S. Dollar, requires understanding how a hedge fund manager may sustain an oil bubble through beliefs about continued Chinese growth.

It is highly common that hedge fund managers monitor multiple markets in an attempt to hedge exposure to one set of assets with another. For instance, Long Term Capital Management (LTCM) famously hedged its exposure to emerging market debt with positions in U.S. Treasury markets. This particular strategy backfired when Russia defaulted on its debt in 1998, credit risk not having been taken into account sufficiently in the statistical models employed by LTCM.

The Oil Bubble and "Peak Oil" Theorists

Toward the end of 2007, oil prices began to skyrocket to the point where some analysts began to predict $200 per barrel as a long-term sustainable price level.[21] Many observers suggested that prices were merely bid up by speculators in futures markets, while others attributed the rise to a combination of sustained growth in demand (mostly from growing economies in Asia) and peaking supply.[22] The thesis that oil supply and demand would forever be out of balance – supply would peak and there would be increasing scarcity – gained even greater momentum than it had during the past oil boom cycles of the 1970s–1990s.

Peak oil theory, first introduced by Marion King Hubbert in 1956 (notably the same year as the Suez war caused a small-scale oil price crisis), postulated that oil production follows a bell-shaped curve of production with respect to time. Production rose rapidly as a field, basin, or region had its first major oil discovery, later hitting a peak rate of output after some period of exploration and exploitation, and finally declining sharply as field pressure drops and no more oil can be recovered. The theory gained significantly in credibility because Hubbert correctly predicted that U.S. oil production would peak in the early 1970s.

Around 1995, several analysts began applying Hubbert's method to world oil production, concluding that global oil production would peak relatively soon.[23] These analysts argued that the majority of the world's oil production is concentrated in mature fields from which the extraction of additional supplies will be increasingly costly as mechanical or chemical aids are used to induce artificial (as opposed to natural) lift. As each older field peaks and produces a dwindling amount of oil, world production, according to Peak Oil theory, will drop to a point where it will no longer be economical to use oil. In one particularly bleak assessment, geologists Colin J. Cambell and Jean H. Laherrere argued in a *Scientific American* article that "the next oil crunch will not be so temporary."[24]

When oil prices soared during the period 2003–8, such peak oil voices, previously shunned in the mainstream, gained credibility. Statistical evidence was mounting to support the thesis that financial players were fueling a speculative bubble in oil, which was increasingly treated as an asset class that diversifies away from the Dollar and other deflating assets. Ironically, the logic of peak oil, which argued that the rising prices were not caused by a speculative bubble, in fact helped to fuel a classical bubble mania in oil markets, by providing a story for why "this time is different."[25]

Of course, similar predictions that "this time is different" have been a mainstay of earlier oil crises, and in fact it is the story each time that is different. In the throes of World War II, the U.S. Department of the Interior proclaimed in 1939 that only thirteen years of oil reserves remained in the United States.[26] In 1972, James Akins, then director of the Office of Fuels and Energy at the U.S. Department of State, wrote an influential article in *Foreign Affairs* called "The Oil Crisis: This Time the Wolf Is Here," which similarly argued that oil demand was about to outstrip available oil supply permanently (adding the warning that it would create a dangerous and destabilizing transfer of wealth to oil-producing countries).[27]

Akins's 1970s oil crisis warning – that oil scarcity was a danger to the world order – resurfaced similarly in the postmillenium security literature under a new parlance of "resource wars." The concept, first popularized by Michael Klare, suggested that "diminishing supplies of vital materials" will raise the risk of conflict across the globe and "introduce new stresses into the international system."[28] As oil prices were rising toward their 2008 peak, Nader El-Hefnawy took the resource war argument a step farther, asserting that since the U.S. economy is the most oil dependent among world powers, "the United States could ultimately lose its position as a world power ... just as the UK's position declined along with the age of coal and steam that it (the UK) pioneered."[29]

Oil Futures as a Play on the Dollar and China

The oil bubble can be explained based on predictions of Dollar depreciation and expectations of Chinese growth. In this regard, oil has become literally "black gold," in the sense that investors can use it as a hedge against Dollar-denominated price inflation in other commodities. This hypothesis is supported by the fact that energy inflation was significantly more pronounced than inflation in other

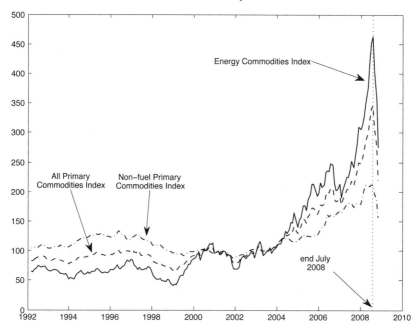

Figure 5.9. Commodities indices (overall, energy, and nonfuel). *Source*: IMF, IFS.

primary commodities during the commodity bubble 2003–8, as illustrated in Figure 5.9.

The temporal coincidence of rising fuel prices (Figure 5.9) and declining Chinese stocks (Figure 5.8) suggest that speculators could have placed simultaneous bets on continued Chinese growth, continued accumulation of U.S. debt and depreciation of the Dollar, and overvaluation of the Chinese stock market by shorting Chinese stocks and investing in oil futures. Once oil prices started to rise, trend-following speculators were likely to jump on the bandwagon, thus contributing further to the trend. When oil prices rose, they contributed further to U.S. deficits and downward pressure on the Dollar. As we have seen at the beginning of this chapter, the dominant role of the Dollar in the portfolio of currencies held as official reserves has suffered as a result. The question we face today is whether this rebalancing of official reserves will stabilize, or usher in the end of the Dollar era following the example of the Pound in the early part of the twentieth century.

Global Recession, the Crash of 2008, and Eventual Recovery

As the authors had suggested in May 2008, two months prior to the commodity indices' crash in July 2008, the cycle in oil prices did in fact continue.[30] Demand did not continue unabated as had been predicted. Fuel price subsidies that had insulated consumers in Asia, including China, were lifted, bringing a dose of reality back to oil traders, who had previously euphorically believed that nothing, not even high commodity prices and a U.S.-led recession, could curb growth in India and China. Like the Japan myth of the 1970s, China's economic miracle began to look less miraculous by the end of 2008, and Chinese oil demand growth began to recede.[31] China also lifted its subsidies on fuel prices, portending lower demand for oil in 2009.

Similar boom-related manic suggestions that American drivers were price in-sensitive to retail gasoline prices proved equally incorrect, as the price reached $4 per gallon and American drivers reduced their driving significantly. This is clearly illustrated in Figure 5.10, which shows that U.S. drivers' demand for gasoline has in fact fallen quite significantly following retail price spikes in 1973, 1979, 1990, and 2008. Contrary to popular belief, therefore, drivers' demand for gasoline, which may be inelastic at low to moderately high prices, in fact exhibits significant price elasticity near the threshold of $4 per gallon in 2008 prices. This thresh-old effect has significant policy implications, including support for gasoline-tax policies to prevent increased demand for fuel-inefficient vehicles following price moderation, which we discuss in Chapter 8.

By the end of summer of 2008, U.S. gasoline demand had fallen by 10 per-cent compared to a year earlier, as Americans traveled less and purchased more fuel-efficient cars. This trend is only expected to continue as the U.S. economic recession deepens in 2009.[32] Demand for oil within the OECD also fell by over 2 million barrels per day by the end of 2008 compared to a year earlier. Thus, over-all world oil demand has declined over the past year by at least 300,000 barrels per day.

Thus, the last in a series of bubbles – in technology stocks, then in real estate, and finally in commodities – came to an end. Starting in the 1990s and lasting into 2008, lax monetary policies had allowed economic growth to continue by fueling those bubbles, which in turn allowed U.S. consumers to spend their fic-titious wealth, thus preventing the economy from falling into a deep recession. Monetary policy has now reached its end, as the world appears to have fallen into a liquidity trap, with target interest rates of the U.S. Fed approaching zero.

Regardless of how long the ensuing global recession lasts, and the levels of suc-cess that stimulative fiscal and monetary policies around the world may attain, it is certain that the main cycle in economic growth rates and energy prices will

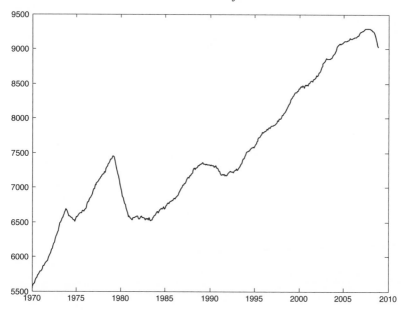

Figure 5.10. U.S. finished motor gasoline product supplied (thousand barrels per day, 12-month moving average). *Source*: U.S. Department of Energy, EIA.

continue. Because of financial and incentive misalignments, it is likely that investments in fuel-production capacities will fall short of the levels required to support the eventual renewal of global economic growth, especially in emerging markets. Oil prices would then skyrocket once again, preparing for the next episode of recession. The amplitude of those booms and crashes and their effects on economies and societies worldwide are likely to depend on whether or not the current Dollar-centered financial system that has amplified the past two cycles persists. We now turn to this issue, analyzing the potential for abandoning the Dollar and potential replacements thereof.

6

Motivations to Attack or Abandon the Dollar

Even before it came to exist, the Bretton-Woods system and the Dollar-centered financial system that it produced were not embraced universally. The main architects of the Bretton-Woods system, Keynes for the United Kingdom and White for the United States, had to strike a number of bargains between their competing interests. Financial historians recognize three main compromises.[1]

The Split Personality of Bretton Woods

The first compromise was on the tradeoff between monetary stability, which the United States sought to avoid the financial booms and crashes of the 1920s and 1930s, and flexibility of monetary policy, which the United Kingdom desired to avoid prolonged recessions. The Dollar was pegged at $35 per ounce, but convertibility of Dollars for gold was available only to central banks, not to private investors.

This quasi–gold standard restricted U.S. monetary policy and helped to establish the Dollar as a reliable currency for international trade. In order to reinvigorate international trade after the protectionist trade wars of the 1930s, the Bretton-Woods system stipulated that all other currencies were pegged to the Dollar. This frightened many Britons, who considered this system to be *de facto* return to "the tyranny of gold."[2] For that reason, a second compromise was embodied in the Bretton-Woods accord, whereby exchange rates relative to the Dollar could ostensibly be adjusted if necessary, under intentionally vague conditions.

The final compromise was reached to accommodate the United States' desire to have currency convertibility in order to promote international trade, and the United Kingdom's desire to maintain controls in order to avoid speculative attacks on currencies. In this regard, a speculative attack on a currency would normally be implemented by borrowing in the attacked currency and then selling for another. The compromise that evolved was to introduce current account convertibility while maintaining controls on capital accounts, thus preventing speculative attacks.

117

For most of the life of the Bretton-Woods gold-Dollar system, the United States realized current account surpluses and used them to invest long-term in the emerging economies of the time, including Japan and a number of European countries. For most of that period, therefore, the United States was the mirror image of its recent self: Whereas the United States has been recently the world's largest debtor and excess consumer, it was then the world's largest creditor and excess saver.

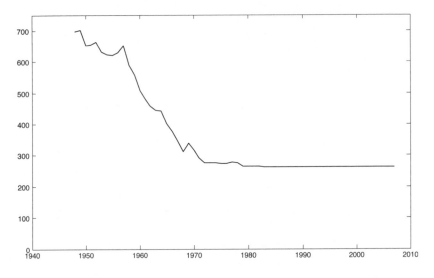

Figure 6.1. U.S. gold reserves in millions of fine troy ounces. *Source*: IMF, IFS.

Early Attacks on the Dollar

This is not to say that the Bretton-Woods period was exempt from worries about the Dollar. In fact, there have been periods when the United States current account ran into deficit, for instance in the years following the Suez crisis of 1956 – which coincided with and contributed to another oil crisis[3] – during which the United States angered its French and British allies by insisting that they and Israel needed to halt their tripartite attack on Egypt. The current account deficits of the United States together with the lack of good will on the part of European central bankers thus prompted a number of central banks to convert their Dollar holdings into gold, precipitating a significant decline in U.S. gold reserves. Fears of potential Dollar devaluation led to an increase in gold prices in London, which in turn prompted the Bank of England to lead a European effort to bring them back to $35 per ounce.[4] This was a precursor of things to come.

America's "Exorbitant Privilege" and Geopolitics

Charles de Gaulle, President of France during the last full decade of Bretton-Woods (1959–69), famously lambasted the Bretton-Woods system as an exorbitant privilege for the United States, which allowed her to print money with which she could import goods and services as well as engage in geopolitical exercises around the world. It was for this reason that France became the first of the large European countries to demand gold for its Dollar reserves, to the tune of $884 million and $601 million in 1965 and 1966, respectively, precipitating the eventual demise of the Bretton-Woods system in 1971.[5]

Eichengreen has argued that there was more to this trend than mere dislike for exorbitant U.S. geopolitical and economic privilege. He argued that there was in fact a fundamental problem with the fixed-exchange-rate system under Bretton Woods. Whereas central banks as a group may have seen an advantage in keeping the system intact to promote global trade and economic growth, each central bank had an individual incentive to defect and demand to convert its Dollars to gold.[6]

The incentive to defect increased as the level of U.S. gold reserves declined and an imminent devaluation was expected, eventually forcing the United States to close the gold window. As difficult as coordination to maintain the Bretton-Woods fixed-exchange regime may have been during the 1960s, Eichengreen argued, the current *de facto* quasi-fixed exchange rate regime, especially with fast-growing export-oriented Asian countries, would be much more difficult to maintain and therefore unlikely to survive for a similar period. We return to this issue later in the chapter.

Before turning to this issue, however, we need to consider one of the most significant blocs of countries that have continued to peg their currencies and their fortunes to the Dollar, Middle-East oil-exporting countries, and the geopolitical effects of this peg. As we have seen in Chapter 3, the Islamist radicals' grievance with the United States and their local regimes was in large part economic in nature. Bin Laden's letter and interview in 1995 and 1998, respectively, clearly expressed that grievance in economic terms, and the symbolism of targeting of the World Trade Center twin towers in New York City (repeatedly, with eventual catastrophic success) reaffirms this economic grievance.

Amplified Cycle and Militant Grievances

Although the militants' response has been absurdly criminal, it is important to understand the economic problems that result from the current crisis-prone financial system and the amplified economic cycle that it has caused in oil-exporting countries. As we discussed earlier, the initial decline in real oil prices leading up to 1973 was in large part caused by the inflationary deficit spending of the United States.

Paradoxically, that decline in real prices, and the coincidental factors described in Chapter 1, gave rise to a middle-class with great economic aspirations. Once those aspirations were dashed with the turn of the business cycle in the mid-1980s and again in the 1990s, a faction of that middle-class turned criminally militant.

The rhetoric of nationalist interest and the link to oil prices in fact did not originate with the Islamic militants of the Middle East or the leftist regimes of Latin America. It was Richard Nixon in 1974 who threatened France and other would-be opponents of the U.S. attempt to organize a cartel of oil importers: "Security and economic considerations are inevitably linked and energy cannot be separated from either."[7] It was natural for rising nationalist Islamism to adopt this worldview, together with the secular nationalist view of "the oil weapon" that emerged during the 1973 Arab-Israeli war and the contemporaneous oil embargo.

Middle Classes Sympathetic to Militant Grievances

As Figures 3.3 and 3.4 have suggested, the middle classes of the oil-exporting Arab countries have suffered substantially from the post-Bretton-Woods financial and economic roller-coaster. During times of expansion, massive petrodollar inflows led to substantial asset and commodity inflation, which impacts fixed-income middle-class workers disproportionately. Moreover, the investments of those workers tend to be concentrated in real estate and stock markets, which are susceptible to substantial bubbles, as evidenced by the Kuwaiti Manakh collapse in the early 1980s and the more recent bubbles of the mid-2000s.

Perhaps the most devastating realization for the middle classes of oil-exporting countries and their neighboring labor-exporting countries of the Middle East is the pattern shown in Figures 2.1 and 2.3. With every cycle of petrodollar flows, those middle classes lose some of their savings in stock and real estate market bubbles, and then realize that their real incomes will never recover to their earlier values, as terms of trade continue to move against primary-commodity exporters. As the 1995 bin Laden letter to King Fahd suggested, economic discontent has also resulted from poor investment of the oil proceeds during boom times and the inability of oil exporters to diversify their economies sufficiently to avoid this resource curse.

As we shall see in the following section, the same sentiments previously expressed by De Gaulle have thus resurfaced not only in the rhetoric of Islamic militants, but also in the rhetoric of leaders of other oil-exporting countries. To recap, De Gaulle had emphasized the unfairness of the international financial system that gives the United States the unique privilege of printing cash to pay for goods, services, and geopolitical influence. The petrodollar system that evolved during the 1970s has made oil exporters particularly vulnerable to the economic and financial crises that inflationary U.S. policies have produced.

Petrodollar Recycling and the Dollar-Pricing of Oil

In the early 1970s, as the value of the dollar was devalued against gold by 7.89 percent, a newly empowered OPEC pressed the major international oil companies to adjust the Dollar-price of oil to match its depreciation. The suggestion was to link the price of oil to a basket of nine currencies (Belgian, Swiss, and French francs, German Mark, Italian Lira, Japanese Yen, Dutch Gulden, Swedish Krone, and Pound Sterling).[8] This formula (known as Geneva I) was adopted in 1972 and included provisions for further adjustments but was never successfully implemented.

By the next round of Dollar devaluation in February 1973, the OPEC countries reopened negotiations for an adjustment of Geneva I. At the time, the October 1973 oil embargo swept all previous pricing accords away, and the drastic changes in the absolute price made debate about the matter of the numeraire immaterial. Thus, ironically, the crisis reinforced the Dollar as the main unit of account and means of payment for international crude-oil transactions. The Dollar's centrality was reinforced by the need for petrodollar recycling, because it was the only currency with enough liquidity for the task.[9]

The Beginning of Petrodollars

OPEC surplus countries became vested in the Dollar's health because any action that could weaken the Dollar, such as an abrupt end to Dollar-pricing of oil, would simultaneously cause losses in accumulated Dollar holdings. Exploiting this conundrum was U.S. Secretary of Treasury William E. Simon and National Security Advisor Henry Kissinger, who each strongly believed that America would be greatly disadvantaged, both economically and geopolitically, unless it could attract the petrodollar revenues to Dollar-denominated assets and recycle them through the United States.

In Simon's case, the worry was how to reduce America's soaring balance-of-payments deficit, created by rising oil import prices. Kissinger had different worries. Arab oil exporters were considering in public the possibility of moving their funds from one country to another based on judgments about foreign policies toward the Arab world.[10] Kissinger wrote in his memoirs: "For a few years, the oil producers even threatened the stability of the world financial system by accumulating enormous surpluses, which they could move from the financial institutions of the industrialized democracies to those of more accommodating states."[11]

The Petrodollar Recycling Scheme

The United States strategy included tethering moderate oil nations to the U.S. economy. Thus, Kissinger wrote: "Our primary goal was to create incentives for the producing nations to become responsible participants in the international economy. To do so, we sought to elaborate clear distinctions between the moderates and more radical members of OPEC."[12]

To weaken OPEC solidarity, the United States created bilateral economic commissions at the cabinet level with Iran and Saudi Arabia. The commission's goals were, according to Kissinger, to "encourage the use of surplus dollars for development projects, to reduce producers' free funds for waging economic warfare or blackmail against the industrialized democracies, and to return some of the extorted funds to our economy."[13]

Indeed, Kissinger's plan was particularly successful in the case of Saudi Arabia, which "seized the opportunity" to build new economic and military ties to the United States.[14] Under the rubric of Kissinger and Simon's Joint Commission on Economic Cooperation and Joint Security Cooperation Commission, Saudi Arabia developed a major economic infrastructure development and military modernization plan that employed a large number of large U.S. multinational corporations such as Bechtel, Parsons, and Fluor Corporation.

The U.S. financial sector also embraced Saudi investors. By 1976, Saudi Arabia had invested $60 billion in the United States. By 1979, the Saudis were the largest holders of Dollars and U.S. Government securities.[15] U.S. military sales to Saudi Arabia jumped from $305 million in 1972 to over $5 billion in 1975.

Saddam Hussein, Ahmadinejad, and Dreams of Petroeuros

The success of the Kissinger-Simon petrodollar recycling strategy, combined with appreciation of the Dollar against other currencies in the early 1980s, stifled serious questioning of Dollar-pricing in oil markets for almost two decades. Earlier, in the mid-1970s, OPEC had discussed the adoption of Special Drawing Rights (SDRs) as a unit of account but in the end settled instead for a simple price increase of 10 percent.[16] The issue of Dollar denomination resurfaced seriously only when Iraq's Saddam Hussein revived it.

Announcing that Iraq no longer wanted to deal in "the currency of the enemy," Iraq announced in 2000 that it would no longer accept Dollars for oil payments.[17] Hussein favored receiving Euros for Iraq's oil despite the substantial cost of this switch. Currency conversion fees alone would have amounted to millions of Dollars. Losses on accumulated interest at the United Nations (UN)-monitored escrow account in New York would have adversely affected the United Nations budget as well, under the UN-managed oil-for-food program.

According to news reports of the time, Iraq in fact continued to keep its existing deposits in Dollars, muting any impact of the shift and suggesting that the move was merely symbolic.[18] In this regard, the Euro was in fact at a historic low at that time. However, the move seemed to signal dissatisfaction with the United States and the United Kingdom, who were favoring tighter sanctions against Iraq, in contrast to Euro-zone France and Italy, who favored relaxing the sanctions.

OPEC's Recent Contemplation of Petroeuros

Saddam's foray into Euro pricing of oil sold under the UN oil-for-food program might have remained a mere historical curiosity. However, the Dollar's decline in 2007–8 reignited calls from within OPEC to consider a switch to Euro pricing. Iran and Venezuela urged OPEC to abandon Dollar pricing at the November 2007 meeting in Riyadh, Saudi Arabia. The argument rested mainly on the rapid depreciation of the Dollar at the time and the resulting inflation of imported-good prices in OPEC countries.

The proposal was rejected by Saudi Arabia, which argued that such a move could potentially backfire by causing even larger depreciation in the Dollar and "complicating the problems we are facing from the Dollar's fall."[19] This is one of the fundamental paradoxes of a currency peg, which we discuss in the following section. The Saudi commitment to pricing oil in Dollars may have been partly driven by the earlier petrodollar-recycling political agreement of the 1970s.

Iranian President Mahmoud Ahmadinejad, expressing displeasure with the outcome of the OPEC meeting, complained that a falling Dollar meant that oil producers like Iran were inadvertently being forced to subsidize the U.S. economy: "They [the United States] get our oil and give us a worthless piece of paper," he told journalists, echoing similar remarks by Charles De Gaulle in the 1960s; "we all know that the U.S. Dollar has no economic value." Venezuelan President Hugo Chavez concurred: "The empire of the Dollar has to end," he said, making clear the geopolitical component of the argument.

Iran Moves Unilaterally

Iran has been pressing OPEC to price oil in a basket of currencies, rather than the Dollar, and confirmed to the media that OPEC countries had set up a committee to study the impact of the Dollar on oil prices at the November 2007 head of states summit.[20] Of course, Iran itself had already shifted away from pricing its oil in Dollars in response to the U.S.-led sanctions, which have become progressively more painful financially in recent years.

In this regard, U.S. efforts have continued to punish Iran for its purported support of international terrorism, including refusal to discuss Tehran's ostensibly peaceful nuclear aspirations. As part of this effort to tighten sanctions, the United States Securities and Exchange Commission (SEC) published a report on oil, banking, and export credit agencies that conduct business with "countries deemed to sponsor terrorism." The U.S. pressure on the banking community, combined with a possible future UN resolution that would call on countries to avoid entering into new agreements that would contribute to the "proliferation of sensitive nuclear activities," has prompted many international banks and export credit agencies to suspend or cut back their dealings with Iran.[21]

As a result, Iran has had to look for supplies elsewhere and also to finance fuel imports more creatively. Iran reportedly has begun negotiating open credit lines with sellers, with the transactions settled in Euros rather than Dollars to avoid U.S. scrutiny.[22] In April 2008, Iran finally announced that it had stopped conducting oil transactions in U.S. Dollars.[23] In fact, China's state-owned Zhuhai Zhenrong Corp., one of Iran's largest crude buyers, has been paying for oil in Euros since late 2007. In addition, Indian banks have been reportedly using letters of credit in different currencies to circumvent trade restrictions.[24]

Saudi Arabia Holds the Peg

The Dollar's depreciation during 2007–8 caused significant inflationary pressures in other OPEC countries, whose oil revenues were denominated in Dollars, but whose imports were mostly denominated in other currencies. With mounting twin fiscal and trade U.S. deficits and corresponding debt burden, the Dollar's decline was widely expected to continue for the foreseeable future. Saudi commitments to continue selling oil in Dollars notwithstanding, the pressure on OPEC to switch to Euro pricing was continually increasing into mid-2008. This led to a confrontation between Saudi Arabia and other OPEC countries.

In February 2008, OPEC's Secretary General Abdullah El-Badri said in an interview that OPEC might switch to Euro pricing within a decade to combat the Dollar's decline. "Maybe we can price the oil in the Euro," El-Badri said. "It can be done but it will take time."[25] Several weeks after that, Muhammad al-Jasir, Vice Governor of the Saudi Arabian Monetary Agency (SAMA), said that calls to price oil in Euros were politically motivated and added that Saudi Arabia would continue to price its oil exports in Dollars and maintain the Dollar-peg for the Saudi Riyal.[26]

Petrodollar Recycling Redux?

The Saudis' insistence on pricing oil in Dollars and maintaining their currency peg may have been in part to honor the decades-old agreement of financial support for the U.S. currency in exchange for military security and other privileges. However, SAMA's decision was also very much part of a larger investment strategy that aligned Saudi financial incentives with a strong Dollar. In this regard, pricing oil in another currency would not by itself reduce demand for the Dollar substantially to cause further depreciation of the Dollar and decline in the value of the country's Dollar-denominated investments. However, were oil to be priced in another currency, the incentive to continue to hold and invest oil proceeds in assets denominated in that other currency would be increased because of transaction costs of currency conversion as well as the aforementioned incentive to reduce dependence on a depreciating currency.

We shall return to the general issue of diversification of trade-surplus countries' asset holdings toward the end of this chapter. In the short term, signs of 1970s-style petrodollar recycling were evident. Most notable, perhaps, was the Abu Dhabi Investment Authority's purchase of shares of Citicorp in 2008 and announcements of new military sales to Saudi Arabia. However, only "20 cents of each $1 in increased purchases from oil exporters came back directly to the United States in the form of higher purchases of U.S. goods" as compared to 41 cents of each $1 purchase from oil exporters back in the form of Euro purchases and 60 cents of each $1 sent abroad returned to purchase Chinese goods.[27] Consequently, the U.S. Federal Reserve Bank estimated that net investment by oil exporters in the United States represented only one-fourth of the more than $1.3 trillion that oil exporters have invested worldwide between 2003 and 2006.[28]

The Paradox of Pegged Currencies

The fixed-exchange-rate regime of the Bretton-Woods Accord came to an end in the 1970s. However, a number of countries have continued to fix their exchange rates, mainly relative to the Dollar, for a variety of reasons. One of the primary reasons, which had prompted the Bretton-Woods format in the first place, was to eliminate currency risk from the calculations of foreign-trade participants, as well as portfolio and direct foreign investors.

Export-Oriented Growth in Asia: The Japanese Experience

For Asian countries that pursued an export-oriented growth path, intervening in foreign exchange markets to maintain an undervalued currency relative to the Dollar was particularly useful. The United States had not only the largest unified market to which those countries could export their goods, but also the unique financial ability to print Dollars, which continued to be universally accepted through multiple episodes of mounting U.S. indebtedness. This export-oriented growth formula proved most successful first for Japan during the 1970s and '80s, and then for other Asian countries in later decades.

The export-oriented growth formula leads to international interdependence that at various times has led to cooperation or confrontation. As shown in Figure 6.3, Japan realized spectacular growth rates in the early 1970s in large part through competitiveness of its exports to the United States, as her currency remained generally above 200 Yen per Dollar (Figure 6.2). In the mid-1970s, the

Figure 6.2. Japanese Yen per U.S. Dollar. *Source*: IMF, IFS.

Yen appreciated relative to the Dollar, and Japan gradually lost competitiveness in U.S. markets and experienced lower growth rates.

However, as the Fed Chairman Paul Volcker raised interest rates to combat inflation in the early 1980s, the Dollar appreciated again relative to the Yen and other currencies, and U.S. current account deficit reached an alarming 3.5 percent of GDP. On September 22, 1985, at the Plaza Hotel in New York City, the United States and her major surplus-trading partners in Europe and Japan agreed to intervene in currency markets to orchestrate an orderly depreciation of the Dollar relative to their currencies (the Plaza Accord). The group met again in February 1987 to halt the depreciation of the Dollar (the Louvre accord).

As shown in Figure 6.2, the Japanese Yen has never depreciated back to its pre-Louvre-Accord levels, in large part due to continued intervention by the Bank of Japan. Because Japan's economic growth in the 1970s and early 1980s was primarily export driven, the country feared falling into a severe recession following the appreciation of its currency under the Plaza Accord. Consequently, it did not sufficiently sterilize the expansion of its money supply as it purchased Dollars with Yen, hoping that the expansionary monetary policy might allow domestic growth in consumption to sustain overall economic growth. Instead, the expansionary monetary policy resulted in credit-driven speculative bubbles that caused severe

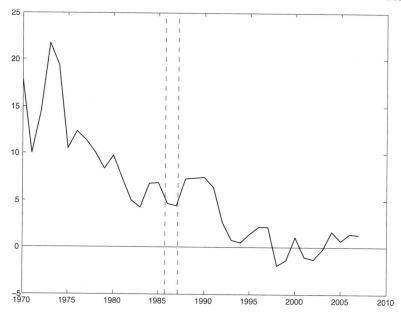

Figure 6.3. Japanese nominal GDP growth percentage. *Source*: IMF, IFS.

problems for the Japanese banking system and resulted in a catastrophic "lost decade" during the 1990s.

The Chinese Approach

In contrast to the Japanese experience shown in Figures 6.2 and 6.3, the Chinese currency has generally depreciated relative to the Dollar throughout the 1980s and early 1990s, allowing Chinese exports gradually to replace their Japanese counterparts in U.S. markets. Although the Yuan has been allowed to appreciate slightly to the Dollar starting in the late 1990s, the rate has been extremely slow, intentionally, to maintain China's export competitiveness and remarkable export-based growth. As a result, China had accumulated more than US$2 trillion in reserves by the end of 2008.

We have discussed the symbiotic relationship between the U.S. consumption-based growth and China's export-based growth throughout the book. However, as the level of overall U.S. indebtedness has increased, and especially as the United States fell into recession starting at the end of 2007, the pressure on China to revalue its currency and turn to domestic-oriented growth has mounted. Perhaps in part because of the lessons that China has learned from Japan, it has continued its policy of protecting the undervalued Yuan and preventing it from appreciating.

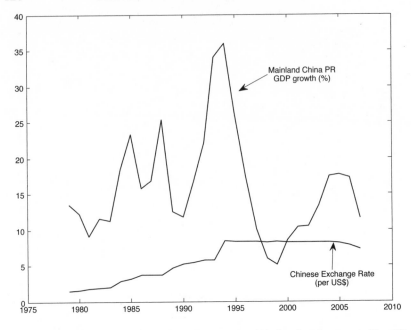

Figure 6.4. Mainland China, PR: Nominal GDP growth (%) and exchange rate (Yuan/$).
Source: IMF, IFS.

Bretton Woods II

It remains unclear whether the global recession that started in 2008 will force China and her trading partners to reach a new agreement on the international financial order. It is important in this regard to understand that Chinese-style export-oriented growth (or lack thereof) have important social and political as well as economic and financial roots.

In a series of influential papers, Dooley, Folkerts-Landau, and Garber have argued that the pursuit of export-oriented growth, and the concomitant international financial system to support it, has been a matter of necessity for some Asian countries. The same logic, applied here to China, can be extended to a number of other countries in "the periphery," as the authors have revived the neo-Marxist language of the mid-twentieth century:

China has about 200 million unemployed or underemployed workers to bring into the modern labor force. For political stability, there is a need for 10–12 million net new jobs per year in the urban centers. A growth rate of around 8+% has served to employ about 10 million new workers each year. About 3 million have been in the export sector.[29]

The core-vs.-periphery language of mid-century neo-Marxism was justified by the following observations: By maintaining an undervalued currency, China and countries that follow her example have kept their labor relatively impoverished, thus allowing for ever greater capital accumulation and economic growth. Because the domestic financial market of those developing countries cannot efficiently allocate capital without fueling destructive bubbles, as the Japanese experience has shown, those countries were better off using their domestic savings to finance consumption in the United States. This is done in part by purchasing U.S. Treasury bonds, thus depressing interest rates and allowing for credit-induced consumption in "the core country." The resulting current account surplus was balanced with a capital account deficit representing direct foreign and other growth-inducing investment.[30]

In the series of papers where they described what they called the revival of the Bretton-Woods system of Dollar-centered fixed exchange rates, Dooley et al. argued that the system can survive well past 2010.[31] In contrast, Eichengreen argued that there is a fundamental coordination problem between countries in the periphery (emerging markets of the early twenty-first century, especially in Asia), which makes the Plaza and Louvre-style coordination struck by the earlier European and Japanese periphery highly unlikely.[32] Therefore, he expected the system to expire earlier than Dooley et al. had suggested.

Petrodollars Tip the Balance

The debate between believers and disbelievers in the longer-term sustainability of Bretton Woods II missed an important element. As global economic growth, consumption-based in the core and production-for-export-based in the periphery continued under the revived Bretton-Woods system, demand for hydrocarbon fuel grew much faster than output could. In turn, this sluggishness in output, which was caused by insufficient investment in production capacity during the low-fuel-price period of the 1990s, led to reduction in spare productive capacity and a spike in crude oil prices that rivaled its predecessor in 1979.

We have shown in the previous section that direct petrodollar recycling to the United States was not as significant in the later episode as it was in the earlier. However, that is increasingly immaterial in a highly globalized world, as then presidential candidate Obama suggested when he discussed in his debate with McCain "borrowing $700 million from the Chinese to pay the Saudis."

Money is fungible, and it makes little difference for the financial system whether the oil-exporting countries invest their trade surpluses directly in U.S. Treasury bonds and other Dollar-denominated assets, or indirectly through investments and trade with emerging countries who invest in those assets. The net result in either of those two cases is sufficient demand for U.S. Dollars to prevent the currency from depreciating substantially.

What matters significantly for the international financial system, and the three-decades-long period of global trade and economic growth that it has supported, is the extent to which the latest surge in petrodollar flows has caused acceleration of U.S. debt accumulation and potentially hastened the end of the Dollar-centered financial system. Eichengreen had argued that shifting away from the Dollar should be easier before 2010 than it would have been circa 1985.[33] However, the financial crash of 2008 showed that the Euro is far from ready to assume the role of global currency, as we discuss in Chapter 7. In fact, the Dollar and the Yen appreciated relative to the Euro as a consequence of investors' flight to familiar safety following the crash. The Dollar's safety, however, is predicated on sufficient belief that others believe in its safety, ad infinitum. We now turn to this problem.

Pegged Currencies and "The Balance of Financial Terror"

Lawrence Summers, Secretary of the Treasury during the Clinton era, described the financial and geopolitical component of the uneasy symbiosis discussed in Chapter 5 as a "balance of financial terror."[34] This system can thus be seen with various degrees of concern, depending on the time horizon of our analysis and various assumptions about dynamics beyond that time horizon. For long-term analysis, this core-periphery relationship seems benevolent. For medium-term analysis, it appears unsustainable but beneficial for as long as it lasts. For short-term analysis, as Summers has suggested, it is a source of mutual financial terror.

Foreign Direct Investment and "Convergence"

During the golden days of Bretton-Woods II, Barro and Sal-i-Martin and a host of other writers proclaimed that the prevailing international economic system would lead to international "convergence."[35] The idea was rather straightforward: Mature societies with larger per capita GDPs can sustain only a slower rate of growth, while emerging-market economies can grow at substantially faster rates. The latter can be attained through foreign direct investment by mature-economy corporations, which is commonly associated with technology transfer, improved managerial skills, and other factors that can allow those emerging markets not only to employ their hordes of unemployed and underemployed labor, but also to employ them more efficiently.[36]

The convergence hypothesis suggested long-term declines in international as well as within-country per capita incomes based on a simple linear relationship between economic growth and initial income. At extremely low initial incomes, it amounted to little more than arithmetic truism: starting near zero, any growth looks significant. Many economists who used more sophisticated models of income dynamics found the evidence in favor of convergence less than compelling, concluding instead that there may be increased stratification into rich and poor "clubs,"[37] both within and between countries.

There was clearly an ideological component to this ongoing debate, as advocates of convergence hypotheses were implicitly defending globalization against its detractors. This was evidenced by the title that Stanley Fischer chose for his article in response to the "clubs" literature: "Globalization and Its Challenges."[38] Fischer performed his analysis by using population-weighted real per capita GDP data, thus giving enormous weight to China and India, which happened to be growing extremely fast over the post-Bretton-Woods period, thus lending credibility once more to the convergence hypothesis.

In fact, there has not been a uniform trend of convergence or divergence over time or across regions. Within the Organization for Economic Cooperation and Development (OECD), there has been indeed a consistent trend toward convergence or declining inequality. However, African countries have shown a consistent trend of divergence or increasing inequality, and Latin American countries have shifted from declining to increasing inequality after the 1980s, as East and South Asian countries have switched in the opposite direction.

Indeed, the United Nations Development Programme's (UNDP) Human Development Report in 2005, entitled *International Cooperation at a Crossroads – Aid, Trade, and Security in an Unequal World*, focused primarily on continued or increasing inequality between and within countries as the primary barriers preventing the attainment of the Millennium Development Goals.[39] As the study shows, the main focal point of the "convergence" debate, per capita income, is a very poor measure of welfare as measured by the UNDP's Human Development Index (HDI).[40] Therefore, although economists can continue to slice and reanalyze the growth and income inequality data of the past few decades to prove the benevolence or malevolence of globalization and the international financial system that has made it possible, the long-term "convergence" benefits of this international financial system have been doubtful to many in the developing world.

The international social contract of global capitalism promised eventual convergence for workers in emerging economies, who endured lower than possible living conditions in order for their savings to finance consumption in advanced economies, which consumption allows their own economies to continue to grow through exports. The promise of this social contract is that workers in emerging markets are essentially trading their own consumption for better living standards for later generations.

This requires patience which it may not be possible to muster during global business cycle downturns. Moreover, the status quo may be politically untenable even if the global economic system delivered on promises of growth and future consumption but "convergence" proves to be a myth.

With the most recent financial and economic crisis unfolding during 2008–9, many in the United States have come to doubt the long-term benefits, not only the sustainability, of the model of global economic growth built upon U.S. consumption and emerging-market investment. As most arguments on the long-term benefits of the status quo have begun losing credibility everywhere, we are left with the medium-term Bretton-Woods II argument, and the short-term fear of complete global financial collapse.

Medium-Term Sustainability of Bretton Woods II

As we have seen earlier in this chapter, the proponents of the renewed Bretton-Woods system, with the Dollar and the American consumer at its heart, never saw it as a long-term prospect. Some economists – most notably Barry Eichengreen – doubted that the current system could be sustainable even in the medium term. At the other extreme, some prominent economists have argued for the long-term sustainability of U.S. dual fiscal and trade deficits, which are required for the system to operate. Indeed, Richard Cooper has even argued that any coordinated effort to reduce the U.S. trade deficit may cause a financial distress and an economic slowdown more severe than what would develop as a result of "disorderly market adjustment to the trade deficit."[41]

Perhaps adherents to this latter view, which was ironically published just prior to the financial meltdown in summer 2008, would continue to view the historical counterfactual of a 2007–8 Plaza-Accord style coordinated effort to depreciate the Dollar relative to the Chinese Yuan as potentially more dangerous. However, both adherents of this view and more skeptical adherents of renewed Bretton Woods as a transitory phenomenon must adjust their beliefs about that system's time horizon significantly.

Sustaining the system during the first eight years of the new century required constant generation of U.S.-based Dollar-denominated assets for purchase by the countries with whom the United States had a trade deficit. The resulting credit binge to generate those assets resulted in one of the most spectacular debt crises in history. The need for replacing the current international financial system has thus become obvious. Consequently, the prospect of sudden collapse or the short-term "balance of financial terror" remains as fearsome as ever.

Balance of Financial Terror

The most troublesome aspect of the current global financial system is the massive volume of U.S. Federal debt, which is climbing ever closer to the size of the U.S. GDP. A big portion of this debt is held by major Asian economies, including most notably Japan, China, and South Korea, as well as a number of oil-exporting countries. The "balance of financial terror" is the bilateral short-term threat between the United States and her creditors, as well as among the various creditors of the United States, which Eichengreen astutely noted do not necessarily share the same objectives or act in unison as a bloc.[42]

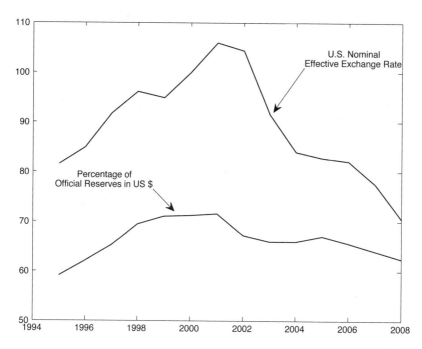

Figure 6.5. U.S. nominal effective exchange rate and percentage of official reserves in U.S. Dollars. *Sources*: IMF, COFER, and IFS.

The United States has *de facto* been gradually depreciating the value of her creditors' accumulated savings, and those creditors have been gradually diversifying their reserves away from the Dollar, as shown in Figure 6.5. The nominal effective exchange rate, weighted by trade with various countries, has declined significantly since 2001, the brief bump after the financial crash of 2008 notwithstanding. However, this depreciation and the decline in the Dollar's percentage of official reserves have been generally muted.

Were the United States to depreciate her currency significantly, perhaps to enhance competitiveness in international markets and begin reversing the current trend of significant trade deficits, she would not only reduce the growth potential for her trading partners, but also massively reduce the purchasing power and value of their savings. The effect of such a massive devaluation, or a sustained program to depreciate the Dollar significantly against the currencies of her trading partners, would not be substantially different from an outright default.

Although the United States has never defaulted on her Federal debt, one may consider closing the gold window in 1971 as the equivalent of a default in the Bretton-Woods gold-based system – one that had been long anticipated by Charles De Gaulle and other detractors of that regime. The possibility of an outright default is extremely remote. However, a major depreciation, especially relative to the Chinese Yuan, would have a similar effect.

Japan and the major European trading partners of the United States cooperated in the 1980s to depreciate the Dollar relative to the Japanese Yen in this exact manner. As we have discussed, China has been consistently unwilling to pay the price that Japan agreed to pay two decades earlier. However, that does not preclude the possibility of a unilateral move by the United States, either of her own accord or as a reaction to other central banks' actions.

The latter is a fundamental coordination problem between the various creditors of the United States. If those countries believe – with some good reason – that the current system is unsustainable, then each would like to avoid being the one left with steeply depreciating Dollars as the endgame approaches. Although those countries have generally maintained the current system and continued to hold Dollars and to invest in Dollar-denominated assets, a catalytic event – perhaps one that is precipitated by a smaller creditor that wishes to attack the Dollar for geopolitical as well as financial reasons – may force them all to race for the exit as a result of self-fulfilling prophecies of the Dollar's collapse.

The Threat of Renewed Protectionism and Mercantilism

As many analysts began comparing the financial collapse of summer 2008 to the Great Depression, policy makers were scrambling to comfort the world, and perhaps themselves, that nations have chosen a path of continued trade and cooperation. The greatest threat, those leaders warned and reminded themselves, would be a wave of protectionism similar to that which prevailed during the period between World Wars I and II. Those protectionist policies, as well as the fear to implement aggressive fiscal stimulus plans that may become inflationary in the medium-to-long term, were in fact the reasons that a severe but potentially manageable financial crisis turned into the Great Depression.

Perceived Fairness of Trade Policies

The UNDP's Human Development Report 2005 explained that freedom of trade and its benefits may be in the eye of the beholder. In a section entitled "The limits of convergence," the report's authors wrote:

One of the prevailing myths of globalization is that increased trade has been a catalyst for a new era of convergence. Expanded trade, so the argument runs, is narrowing the income gap between rich and poor countries, with the developing world gaining from access to new technologies and new markets. Like most myths, this one combines some elements of truth with a hefty dose of exaggeration. Some countries are catching up, albeit from a low base. But successful integration is the exception rather than the rule—and trade is a driver of global inequality as well as prosperity. For the majority of countries the globalization story is one of divergence and marginalization.[43]

It is well known that terms of trade consistently move against exporters of low value-added goods, brief periods of spiking oil and raw material prices notwithstanding. With the notable exceptions of China and a handful of other countries, increased exports have been consistently low-value-added and thus have not delivered on the "convergence" promise of globalization, even for many Latin American countries.

Following the spectacular failure of import-substitution policies of the 1960s and the equally spectacular success of Asian export-led growth models, many countries and policy advisors have adopted the view that increased exports are an end in themselves:

In other areas most policy-makers accept in principle that economic growth and consumption are not ends in themselves but means to advance human development. In trade the logic of development is inverted. Success is typically measured in terms of export growth, changes in trade to GDP ratios and the speed at which import barriers are falling.[44]

Few in this day and age would doubt the importance of economic openness – as measured, say, by the ratio of total trade (exports plus imports) to GDP – for growth and development. However, openness is increasingly viewed as a necessary but not at all sufficient condition. Otherwise, Latin America, which has led the world in trade liberalization, would have been an unequivocal success story over the past two decades, which it clearly has not.[45]

The same questions regarding the usefulness of trade openness apply equally to foreign direct investment flows. It is true that foreign direct investment is generally superior to portfolio and debt investments because of its relative permanence and invulnerability to hot-money speculation, in addition to technology and managerial-skill transfer and increased access to advanced-country export markets. However, there are instances in many developing countries where foreign direct investment is merely a form of tariff hopping.

For example, in Egypt, where hefty tariffs were levied upon automobile imports, assembly plants were set up by foreign car manufacturers with minimal domestic value added as most parts were imported at lower tariff rates. The net result was lower tariff income for the Treasury with minimal prospects for developing a domestic automobile industry as other countries such as India and Malaysia have done successfully over the same time period.

The virtues of trade openness and the measurement of economic success by rates of growth of exports are similarly questionable for exporters of raw materials, especially crude oil and natural gas. In order to avoid return to poverty in the long term as terms of trade continue to move against their current exports, those countries need to exercise concerted efforts toward industrialization and diversification of their economies.

We have argued in earlier chapters that hasty industrialization plans result in unproductive white-elephant projects and fail to enhance overall long-term economic growth. This warning notwithstanding, it is true that long-term growth requires industrialization and eventual export of higher value-added goods. The primary comparative advantage of those countries in undertaking diversification efforts would be their access to cheap fuel and raw materials, which advantage is eroded by the very export of those goods in the short term.

Resource Economics of Oil-Exporting Countries

In other words, the resource-economics calculation for a developing country is somewhat complex. For example, the decision whether to extract oil and sell it now does not only depend on the current price, the rate of return on investing the proceeds, and the expected future price. Those factors alone have been sufficient to convince some policy makers in Kuwait, for example, to argue that they should keep oil in the ground because its current price is too low, the rates of return on investment are too low, and the expected future price is very high.[46]

We now need to add the development-economics complication of low value-added exports and high value-added imports: Even when the oil exporter gets a high financial rate of return on its investments in the advanced industrialized economies, this financial return does not easily translate into long-term economic growth and development. In fact, the recycling of petrodollars for investment in the industrialized nations further reduces the cost of funds to the producers in those nations and erodes potential long-term competitiveness of potential or nascent industries.

It is easy to see how this line of thinking can lead to infant-industry protectionism, which has been practiced with success in the industrial West itself, as evidenced by the success story of Airbus, which would not have achieved competitiveness with American Boeing were it not for early subsidies by European countries. As global economic growth declines significantly following the latest financial crisis, the incentive to pursue protectionist policies, beyond the predictable reduction in oil production and sales by OPEC countries, will become increasingly difficult to resist.

Indeed, this is likely why many policy makers have continued to remind us of the painful lessons of the Great Depression. However, advocates of protectionist policies are expected to gain a louder voice in the face of increasing economic hardship. Those advocates include groups as different as labor unions and other disaffected groups in developing nations on the one hand, and autocratic regimes aiming to continue social and geopolitical programs despite declining revenues, on the other. The level of protectionism is therefore likely to increase, and thus further to erode the Dollar's role as a global currency, setting the stage ultimately for transition to a different international financial system, smoothly or otherwise.

Energy Mercantilism

The cycle in energy prices is likely to continue as we have argued throughout the book. Moreover, it is clear that unless investment in production capacity by national oil companies increases substantially during the contractionary phases of the global business cycle, the frequency and amplitude in that cycle are both likely to increase substantially. Unprecedented spikes in energy prices as the global economy recovers from the current recession are widely predicted. However, the credit freeze associated with the recession has prevented investors from capitalizing on the lower cost of increasing production capacity, as steel and other prices have fallen significantly.

This means that when the global economy recovers, immediate access to energy resources can make the difference between continued growth and crippling stagflation. Rhetoric in the latest United States election cycle about weaning the country off "imported oil" is particularly informative: It's not just addiction to oil that is problematic for national security, but addiction to oil that is imported from countries with different geopolitical agendas. It is in this framework that the appointment of retired Marine General James Jones as National Security Advisor for incoming President Barack Obama was described by a *Wall Street Journal* blogger as "putting energy first," based on earlier statement by General Jones that "energy is a national security issue, and it is an international security issue of the highest order."[47]

It is within this context that China's national oil company's investment in Sudanese oil infrastructure has been increasingly viewed through a geopolitical lens. The political debate is informed by humanitarian considerations, including for example the widely cited Human Rights First report on a perceived "oil for guns" trade pattern between China and the perpetrators of genocide in Darfur.[48] The official Chinese position – that their national oil company should seek investment opportunities anywhere in the world – is viewed with increasing skepticism especially when China seeks deals with Sudan and Iran, both of which have been ostracized by the Western coalition of nations led by the United States.

China's move has thus been generally criticized on geopolitical and humanitarian grounds. However, the debate has also been increasingly about economics, characterizing China's motivation and strategy as a form of energy mercantilism.[49] China's response has been that the United States poses a greater threat to global energy markets, because of her consumption patterns and geopolitical strategies.[50] Likewise, Russia's attempts to control a larger share of natural gas market infrastructure in Europe and larger interests in Western economies are viewed with alarm in the West as geopolitical and mercantilist and viewed by the Russians as an effort to obtain some measure of security for their economy.

Energy mercantilism is hardly a new phenomenon, as the title of Daniel Yergin's Pulitzer Prize–winning history of oil suggests – *The Prize: The Epic Quest for Oil, Money & Power*. Likewise, Kevin Phillips has argued in *American Theocracy: The Peril and Politics of Radical Religion, Oil, and Borrowed Money in the 21st Century* that every great empire was built upon control of the most efficient source of energy. Thus, he argued, the Dutch empire was built on wind power and was superseded by the British empire built on coal and steam power. The latter in turn was superseded during the American century by an economy built on oil, which was abundant within U.S. borders. Continued and increasing dependence on oil, which is mostly imported in the twenty-first century, Phillips argued, has become a major source of potential weakness and a driver for neo-mercantilism.[51]

In the post-Bretton-Woods era, many shared Volcker's surprise that the world was willing to hold more Dollars without any backing than Dollars backed by gold. In large part, the Dollar's success in expanding its role as global currency was tied to the Kissinger-Simon program for petrodollar recycling, which included investing the proceeds of oil exports in Dollar-denominated assets and pricing oil in Dollars. To some degree, therefore, the term "petrodollar" has also served as a reminder that Dollars were essentially backed by oil, as Saudi Arabia and smaller oil-exporting countries in the GCC have continued to support the Dollar both as a store of value and as a medium of exchange.

The Dollar's support is thus eroded by the increasing mercantilist trends to make bilateral oil trades, including with countries that have limited market access such as Sudan and Iran, as well as others that engage in such deals for geopolitical or economic reasons – which trades need not be denominated in Dollars. The relationship has also strained between oil-importing Western countries and the main oil-exporting countries in the Middle East, which themselves have been increasingly viewing oil trade through a mercantilist lens. During periods of low oil prices, the oil-importing countries decry OPEC strategies as protectionist and contrary to free market policies. Conversely, when oil prices are higher, those importing countries pressure major OPEC producers to actively reduce prices through increased production.

The role of the Dollar has been particularly problematic in the most recent phase of the cycle, as oil-exporting countries in the Middle East experienced significant inflationary pressure because of the Dollar's decline against the Euro and the denomination of most of those countries' imports in the latter. Thus, the debt-based expansionary policies of the United States, which have angered European leaders at least since De Gaulle, are increasingly becoming a source of discontent in Middle-Eastern countries. This discontent reached its peak in 2003, when the perceived geopolitical gains of supporting the Dollar at their own economic cost were proven nonexistent as the United States invaded Iraq against Saudi and other regional protests.

Thus, the new wave of energy mercantilism has reduced the incentives of both Asian and Middle-East surplus trading partners to support the Dollar as a store of value or as a medium of exchange. The "balance of financial terror" continues to be a major concern for all three blocks in the short term. However, it is clear that the long-term diversification away from the Dollar has already begun, as evidenced in Figure 6.5. Therefore, the road toward a new international financial system remains as unclear as its destination is unknown. The criteria for selecting a new destination must include the ability to sustain at least a significant portion of the recent successful globalization-driven growth, and the road thereto must include avoidance of quick collapse of the existing system.

Globalization with Multiple Currencies: Bretton-Woods III?

In some sense, the world has had a multiple currency system for most of recorded history. The Biblical image of a bimetallic world was immortalized in the image of exchanging Roman coins for silver Shekalim at the Temple in Jerusalem. In addition to precious metals, base metals such as copper have been commonly used for lower denominations, and a variety of storable commodities, such as salt in North Africa and dried dates in Arabia, have been used as commodity monies.

Gold and silver coins were often alloyed with cheaper metals and yet traded for the weight equivalent of the pure precious metal, thus creating fiscal revenue for the sovereign in the form of seignorage. Debasement of the coins, by reducing the percentage of precious metals therein, was a standard inflationary policy to finance fiscal spending. Perhaps the most infamous ancient spiral of currency debasement was started by Emperor Nero's debasement of the Denarius.[52]

From Bimetallic Standards to Multiple Currencies

The history of money in Western Europe and the United States is checkered by oscillation back and forth between silver-based currency, gold-based currency, and bimetallic standards. Great Britain's adoption of the gold standard for the Pound

Sterling at 7.32 grams of gold for a Pound, for instance, was attributed to Sir Isaac Newton, who was master of the mint in 1717, setting the price of silver too high relative to gold – thus forcing silver coins out of circulation.[53] Similarly, the United States adopted a "hard money" tie to both gold and silver in the mid-nineteenth century, oscillating during the post-Civil War period between gold and silver, before settling on a gold standard toward the turn of the century.[54]

The advantage of a standard that fixes the metallic content of coins or equivalence of paper or electronic money is the imposition of financial discipline. The government and the banking and quasi-banking systems in such a system are restricted in the amount of money that they can create, thus putting a limit on inflationary policies. The disadvantage is that the volume of available and easily extractable precious metals becomes a constraint on economic growth, precisely for the same reason that it constrains expansionary monetary and fiscal policies.[55]

The world returned to a quasi gold standard under Bretton Woods, rhetorical statements to the contrary by Keynes notwithstanding. As we have seen previously, the United States was able to pursue inflationary policies (De Gaulle's "exorbitant privilege") and yet was protected under that system from speculative attacks by private investors, who were not allowed access to the gold window. However, when central banks' demand for gold mounted, first by France and then by England and other major creditors, the gold window was closed indefinitely in 1971. From that moment onwards, and despite the continued centrality of the Dollar, the world was essentially operating again in a multiple-currency environment, with a variety of floating, flexible, and pegged exchange rates.

Multiple-Currency Anchoring vs. International Lender of Last Resort

Abandoning the last remnants of the *de facto* gold standard under Bretton Woods was a primary contributor to the ensuing inflationary spiral, which created a fundamental problem for recycling petrodollars – a problem that we have argued will continue to recur periodically. Without the anchoring effects of gold balances in surplus and deficit countries, and interest-rate policies to prevent massive gold flows, the amplitude and frequency of the cycle can reach very damaging levels.

During the first major petrodollar-recycling crisis, the International Monetary Fund tried to play a central role of the world's banker and global lender of last resort. Johannes Witteveen, then Managing Director of the IMF, made his case to the oil-exporting countries flush with petrodollars, especially Saudi Arabia, as follows:

It is in your interest [to loan the IMF money, as banks in various countries would lend to their central banks] because you want to maintain the healthy international economy. It is in your interest because you have to have somewhere to put the money, and the IMF is a secure place.[56]

The IMF met some mixed success in this effort, with conditional agreement by the Saudis and condescension by Kuwait. Ultimately, however, the attempt to make IMF Special Drawing Rights the *de facto* monetary anchor would have robbed the United States of her exorbitant privilege as the world's banker, at a time when most countries, including those flush with petrodollars, were willing to let her continue playing that role. Therefore, although "it is not unreasonable to expect that the IMF should have provided a cooperative solution to recycling if any meaningful cooperation is to be expected in the future . . . , at every step of the way, IMF policies were blocked by the United States. Witteveen felt that he was in direct competition with the U.S. Treasury."[57]

Consequently, the Dollar has continued to reign supreme as the ultimate anchor of the international financial system. When U.S. policies were extremely inflationary, as in the late 1970s, even the recipients of petrodollars, as represented by the major forces in OPEC, contemplated anchoring to a basket of currencies instead of the U.S. Dollar. As we have seen, Kuwait has continued to price its oil in Dollars but now anchors its Dinar to a basket of currencies after appreciation relative to the Dollar. The discussion of abandoning the Dollar pricing of oil, revived in the 2008 meetings of OPEC, are very reminiscent of earlier discussions circa 1980, as several voices were advocating "the case of a basket of currencies as numeraire" to tackle "the Dollar crisis" and "exchange rate risks" brought about by inflationary U.S. monetary policies during that period.[58]

Multi-Currency Anchoring Would Not Prevent the Cycle

The gradual diversification of official reserves away from the Dollar, shown in Figure 6.5, may be seen as a natural trend toward the use of multiple currencies for store of value of various trade-surplus countries' savings. This transition has been gradual – holding fewer new trade-surplus revenues in Dollar-denominated assets – in order to minimize the "racing toward the exits" effect of outright dumping of currently held Dollar-denominated assets.

Because of the developments that we have already discussed, the Dollar's role is likely to continue declining not only as a store of value, but also as a medium of exchange, as more countries trade merchandise including oil in other currencies. The centrality of the U.S. consumer and public debt would have to decline accordingly. If global growth were to continue at the same path, those private and public consumers would have to be replaced by others in emerging economies, as El-Erian has suggested in adopting the decoupling hypothesis.[59]

If this gradual shifting from export-to-advanced-countries-oriented growth to domestic and export-to-other-emerging-markets-oriented growth does take place, then the current economic recession could be short-lived and global growth could resume at its previous high levels. Alternatively, if new sources of demand are not easily found to replace the American borrowers, then the world could be set for slower global growth in the medium to long term.

Regardless of the scenario that materializes for the current phase of the cycle, the hope is that we can shift to an alternative financial system that would be less likely to amplify the cycle through credit-driven bubbles. We also hope that we can make the transition to that system gradually – that is, avoiding total collapse of the current system in the transition.

In Chapter 7, we argue that the fundamental forces that drive the cycle, financial, energy-economic, and geopolitical, will continue regardless of the financial system in place and the one to which we hope to make a transition. In the process, we also analyze the factors that can amplify the cycle and/or increase its frequency. We use this analysis in Chapter 8 to make suggestions on all three fronts for destinations and roads thereto that may help to ameliorate this inevitable cycle.

7

Resource Curses, Global Volatility, and Crises

Hyman Minsky wrote during the late twentieth century, explaining why political rhetoric has masked the financial forces that have caused significant amplification of economic cycles since the collapse of the Bretton-Woods system. The primary target of his attack was the (still) dominant neoclassical school of economic thought, which has continued to deny many of the economic dimensions of the financial crisis that started during 2008 as "myths."[1] In criticizing this neoclassical school's adoption of "real business cycle" models that abstract from cycles driven by financial markets, Minsky wrote:

A theory that denies what is happening can happen, sees unfavorable events as the work of evil outside forces (such as the oil crisis) rather than as the result of characteristics of the economic mechanism, may satisfy politicians' need for a villain or scapegoat, but such a theory offers no useful guide to a solution of the problem....

The economic instability so evident since the late 1960s is the result of the fragile financial system that emerged from cumulative changes in financial relations and institutions of the years following World War II.[2]

In writing this book, we have at times focused on Minsky's favorite link between economic activity and financial market structure and regulation. However, we have also suggested, perhaps in the same spirit, that understanding the overall cycle, and the potential for severe crises if the cycle was not regulated properly, would require understanding the links to resource economics, especially energy markets, and geopolitical developments in the part of the world where most of those resources are located.

Borrowing from Minsky, we can also suggest that political rhetoric that explains Middle-East geopolitical developments in terms of "evil groups," and blames energy-market problems on an evil-like cartel, "offers no useful guide to a solution of the problem." Therefore, we aim in this chapter to understand the fundamental three forces underlying the cycle and its potential severe-crisis swings, in the hope that this can help us to find solutions to this recurring problem.

Continued Regional and Global Resource Curses

The fact that the oil-and-gas-rich Middle East continues to be plagued by the resource curse was made obvious in the latest episode of petrodollar inflows during 2003–8. All the symptoms of the region's resource curse during the 1970s, analyzed for instance by Amuzegar (see long quote in Chapter 1), were evident during this latest episode.[3] Construction booms are the mainstay of rent seeking for contractors, cement and steel merchants, and various municipal and national administrators. In this regard, the construction boom in the Gulf region was so conspicuous that many reports suggested that half of all the world's construction-site cranes were deployed in the region.

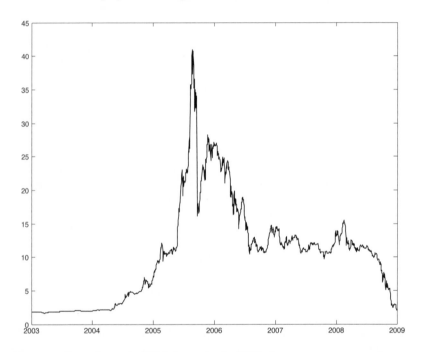

Figure 7.1. Emaar Properties PSJC share price (in AED). *Source*: www.emaar.com investor relations share price lookup.

Stock Market, Financial, and Construction Bubbles

White-elephant projects are rarely characterized thus by their advocates. The latest construction boom was in part justified by 1970s-style suggestions of diversification of the Gulf economies, building infrastructure, and so on. However, residential and office-building construction grossly exceeded any reasonable expectations of population and economic growth, thus building up a real estate bubble that burst early in some countries (e.g., Kuwait, as shown in Figure 3.3) and later in others. The Dubai bubble burst later, with luxury real-estate prices reported to drop nearly 19 percent month on month by November 2008, and prices of moderate housing fell approximately 5 percent during the month of October 2008.[4]

The stock price of Emaar Properties PSJC, one of the region's greatest real-estate-developer success stories, was slashed by nearly 85 percent over the course of 2008, as shown in Figure 7.1. This collapse in 2008 was only the latest manifestation of the petrodollar-driven real-estate bubble in the Middle East. The earlier collapse circa 2006 coincided with the collapse of all regional stock markets, as previously shown in Figures 3.4 and 4.1.

In other words, the regional bubble that began in 2003 has collapsed in two phases: the first when investors circa 2006 recognized that share prices were unsustainable, and the second when the oil bubble that sustained the inflow of petrodollars eventually collapsed. The first collapse initially fueled commodity-price bubbles in precious metals and eventually a speculative bubble in the oil price itself, as funds flew from regional investors to hedge fund managers in Europe and the United States, who in turn invested the funds in speculative oil futures bets. The resulting rise in oil prices contributed further to inflows of petrodollars that allowed the bubble to feed upon itself, until it finally burst in summer 2008. The buildup of the commodity bubble following the first partial collapse of the regional bubble circa 2006 and the eventual simultaneous collapse of both bubbles is illustrated in Figure 5.9.

In this regard, it is important to note that regional stock markets provide investors very few diversification benefits. Those markets' listings are dominated by petro-sector companies, construction-sector firms including the likes of Emaar and also cement and steel companies, and financial firms. The last obtain profitability by extending credit to the first two sets of firms, therefore creating near-perfect correlation between the different listings on those markets, and translating bubbles in oil prices into real estate and financial bubbles, all of which eventually collapse simultaneously.

Education Cities as White Elephants

Just as financial bubbles are motivated by illusions that "this time is different," Middle-East construction and financial bubbles are premised on false hopes of having learned lessons of the past. In this regard, the absence of appropriate investment in education to build regional human capital has been a mainstay of economists' and international financial and development institutions' criticism for decades. The incorporation of this advice into the regional investment environment during the last bubble has been nothing less than shocking.

In a typical display of the folly of trying to run before one can walk, regional countries have been competing feverishly for establishing satellite campuses of globally renowned universities, such as Georgetown and Cornell in Qatar and New York University in Abu Dhabi, as well as standalone graduate-research oriented universities such as the King Abdullah University for Science and Technology (KAUST) near Jeddah, Saudi Arabia.

Regional monarchs have been more than generous in their financial support of those higher education efforts: The Qatari Emir Hamad bin Khalifa Al-Thani dedicated the revenue from an entire natural gas production line to fund research, and the Saudi King Abdullah bin Abdul Aziz Al Saud established a $20 billion endowment for KAUST. Nonetheless, many of those campuses have been prime examples of the construction boom in the region, with "occupancy" rates rivaling the lows of skyscraper office buildings.

The failures of those pretentious forays into state-of-the-art higher education betray the lack of appropriate elementary and secondary education, not to mention proper undergraduate training to staff graduate-research centers with local talent. Those efforts therefore are typical of white-elephant projects that attempt to skip some of the earlier steps of development, thus resulting only in construction and financial booms.

A Singapore-style educational-investment effort would start at the level of elementary education, begin identifying promising students at the preparatory or middle-school levels, and eventually begin to produce first-rate university graduates in 20–25 years. Attempts to establish first-rate undergraduate and graduate education before or simultaneously with investments in those earlier phases is akin to starting a building at the fifteenth floor with faith that the first fourteen floors will materialize in due course.

Financial Centers, "Islamic Finance," and Other White Elephants

A number of Western universities have been more than happy to accept the money to establish those satellite campuses, as the immediately accrued revenues and enhancements to their endowments are guaranteed regardless of the success of those universities. In this regard, those universities have behaved in a manner that is very similar to HSBC, Citi, and other multinational banks that have been more than happy to populate some of the offices in "financial centers" established in Dubai, Doha, and Manama, ostensibly to rival regional financial centers in New York, London, and Singapore.

One of the ostensible distinguishing features of those financial centers, with which Kuala Lumpur was eager to compete with great success, has been the growth in so-called "Islamic Finance." The latter is a product of the marriage of the ideological writings of Abu Al-Aʿla Al-Mawdudi and the other fathers of contemporary political Islam, which gave rise to a large literature on "Islamic economics" on the one hand, and the techniques of financial engineering created for regulatory arbitrage and perfected by the United States and the United Kingdom lawyers starting in the 1980s on the other.[5]

Crude methods of legal arbitrage, based on buy-sell-back and lease-sell-back, were introduced to the Middle East by indigenous banks during the first petrodollar boom in the 1970s. Western institutions were quick to exploit this field as soon as petrodollars began flowing back to the region after 1998. They began to offer everything from retail-level banking and investment products, such as auto loans and mutual funds, to corporate and government bonds that are structured via sale and lease contracts.[6]

The international bankers' interest in the region is no different from the world-class universities' interest: both are tied to the glut of cash caused by the spike in oil prices and the limited absorptive capacities of the regional economies.[7] Dreams of developing financial or educational centers that can survive beyond petrodollar-rent seeking notwithstanding, the resource curse of the Middle East therefore seems to be as much a factor during the latest petrodollar boom as it was three decades earlier. One of the factors that have changed during those three decades, however, is the increased integration of financial markets through technological and financial advancement. This has made the global resource curse, which is closely related to (but distinct from) the regional one, all the more dangerous as we move forward.

The Global Resource Curse

In the remainder of this chapter, we shall argue in three sections that all three components of the cycle that we have analyzed in previous chapters are set to continue: The world will continue its dependence on hydrocarbon fuels for the foreseeable future, geopolitical forces that fuel international conflicts and radical groups' terrorism are likely to continue and intensify, and the increased contagion in financial markets will exacerbate rather than ameliorate the propensity for speculative bubbles and crashes. We conclude the chapter with an analysis of how those three factors interact to perpetuate the cycle, and potentially to increase its amplitude and/or frequency. Before proceeding to this analysis, however, we need to reconsider how the regional and country-specific resource curse of the Middle East (and to a lesser extent other oil-exporting countries in Latin America, Africa, and Asia) has given rise to a "global resource curse."

The classical resource curse, for instance as studied in a series of papers by Jeffrey Sachs and Andrew Warner, is comparative: Countries that are rich in natural resources, especially oil and gas, tend to grow more slowly relative to the rest of the world, even when other geographical and economic variables are taken into account.[8] The global resource curse that we wish to discuss is closely tied to this regional resource curse. Rather than manifesting itself in the form of lower average global economic growth, although it might, the main feature of the global resource curse that we wish to highlight is its contribution to the cycle in oil prices that amplifies the global business cycle.

Petrodollars and the Investment Cycle

The global resource curse, especially as it relates to oil and gas extraction and refining, stems from the construction cycle of production and refining capacity and the divergence of short-term and long-term incentives. Taking the regional resource curse as a given, as we have argued, we should expect significant petrodollar flows from oil-exporting countries during the boom years. A global economy that is well managed would sterilize the inflationary effect of petrodollar outflows, investing them in long-term securities that are tied inversely to oil prices. The income from those securities would accrue when the world economy falls into recession and oil prices decline. Those accrued revenues would be dedicated to building more extraction and refining capacity to reduce the magnitude of the next spike in oil prices when a period of sustained economic growth resumes.

We discuss the benefits of such a system, and possible mechanisms for making it operational, in Chapter 8. For now, we recognize that the world suffers from a global resource curse because such a mechanism does not exist. Consequently, the world has been investing in the creation of oil extraction and refining capacity during the boom years, when it is most expensive to do so. Moreover, because of the lag between the commencement of such capacity-enhancement investments and the ultimate production of fuel, the existing system creates an asynchronicity that we discuss further later: New production and refining capacity comes online at a time when fuel prices are already low because of the recession caused in part by the high fuel prices at the time of investment.

In other words, the existing system is wasteful of global resources, because it encourages investment in building excess capacity when the petrochemicals industry has to compete with other thriving sectors of the economy. Moreover, the system amplifies the cycle, because of both adding to investment spending during boom times and reducing investment during recessions. Thus, the petrochemical investment cycle moves pro-cyclically with the global business cycle, contributing to steeper declines in oil prices as available supply increases when demand is declining and vice versa.

Our analysis in this regard is hardly novel or surprising. At the 2008 Oil and Money conference in London, the Secretary General of OPEC, the Secretary General of the International Energy Agency (IEA) (representing major oil-importing industrial nations), and almost every other speaker at the conference all seemed to agree that the cycle of oil prices will continue, at least through the next economic recovery, which is expected to take place within the next few years. They all agreed as well on the need for continued investment in production and refining capacity during the current recession to avoid an even steeper spike in oil prices, which could be potentially quite destructive. They all expressed the need to pursue cooperative rather than adversarial policies to ameliorate the cycle in oil prices. However, the representatives of oil-exporting countries and those of oil-importing countries had very different views of how such cooperation would take place.[9]

Whither Cooperation?

The problems of petrodollar recycling, investment in production and refining capacity, and market supply-and-demand management (by OPEC and tax policies of importing countries, respectively) are fundamentally similar to a repeated prisoners' dilemma. In a single prisoners' dilemma, each player can choose to cooperate or defect. Unfortunately, each player has the incentive to defect, seeking instant gratification at the other's expense, regardless of what the other player does. Consequently, the unique equilibrium in that environment is for both parties to defect, even though they would both be better off had they both been able to precommit to mutual cooperation.

Acting at each point in time as if the game was played only once, OPEC is myopically tempted to keep prices high when it can, perhaps justifying its action as compensation for the years of low prices and revenues. When the opportunity arises, importing countries are similarly tempted to act myopically to keep prices low to the extent possible. Importing countries may also go beyond economic calculation to encourage long-term destruction of demand for fossil fuels, for both geopolitical and environmental reasons.

Viewing the problem coherently as a repeated game, both exporting and importing countries can choose to sacrifice instant gratification for mutual long-term benefit. Precommitment mechanisms to ensure mutual cooperation, with possible penalties for deviation therefrom, can therefore make both groups better off.

Unfortunately, when one side adheres to its commitments, the other side, which answers politically to a very different constituency, may be tempted to betray long-term agreements by pursuing its own short-term benefits of "using the oil weapon," or "ending addiction to *imported* oil," the emphasis on *imported* highlighting the geopolitical dimension of this energy strategy. In this regard, although repeated prisoners' dilemmas allow for long-term cooperation through a variety of long-term strategies, it is the nature of political elections in the West and rent seeking in the oil-exporting countries to favor short-term benefits over long-term strategies, especially if the latter appear to benefit the perceived adversary.

This suggests that theoretical results that prove the feasibility of long-term cooperation may be of little value for securing actual long-term cooperation between oil exporters and importers.[10] This limitation of the theoretical results stems from their requirement that players must be sufficiently patient, so that contemplation of future benefits from cooperation and punishments for defection can allow them to resist myopic instant gratification.

Another complication is the fact that technological constraints restrict the ability of consuming nations to punish oil exporters in the short term, and political considerations limit the abilities of various countries to inflict mutually painful penalties on others. For example, as we have seen in the previous chapter, international bodies such as the International Monetary Fund have failed to play the central role of smoothing the cycle by serving as lender of last resort, precisely because long-term-oriented policies may contravene the short-term strategies of some major players, including both oil importers such as the United States and oil exporters such as Kuwait.[11]

We discuss the consequences of this current regime toward the end of this chapter, and potential coordination mechanisms to enhance global efficiency, and thus to reduce the impact of this global resource curse, in Chapter 8. We now turn to establishing that the various components of this global resource curse: (i) continued dependence on hydrocarbon fuels, the bulk of which will continue to be located in the Middle East, (ii) continued geopolitical animosity, and (iii) continued financial amplification of business and oil-price cycles are all likely to remain with us for the foreseeable future.

Continued Global Dependence on Oil

Under the *status quo*, the dampening of demand through global recession ultimately sows the seeds for the oil crisis scenario to begin anew, as falling oil prices hinder company and oil-producing country revenues, and hence production-capacity investment in oil-producing areas. Low oil prices also tend to derail progress of conservation and the promotion of energy-efficient practices and technology in major oil-consuming nations. So, just as demand, stimulated by cheap energy costs, starts to recover along with economic growth, new oil supplies are shrinking due to the delayed aftereffects of lower investment while prices were low. As oil prices rise and oil-supply concerns resurface, producers respond simultaneously by rushing into the limited market for drilling rigs, skilled personnel, and capital, thus creating bottlenecks and cost inflation. In this manner, the boom-and-bust oil cycle perpetuates itself.

The Most Recent Cycle in Oil Prices

This cycle of high oil prices to economic contraction to low prices is a long-standing one that has repeated more than once since the 1970s oil crises. Those episodes include the shrinkage of OECD oil demand for almost a decade in the aftermath of the 1979 oil crisis, as well as the more recent effects of the 1997 Asian financial crisis. The effect of the financial crisis known colloquially as "Asian flu" is shown in Table 7.1.

Table 7.1. *Oil Demand by Region 1996–8 (mm b/d and % change)*

Region	1996	1997	% Change	1998	% Change
World	72.03	73.9	2.6	74.24	0.5
US	18.25	18.62	2.0	18.7	0.4
EU-15	13.03	13.10	0.5	13.39	2.2
Asia	17.74	18.53	4.5in	18.18	-1.9
China	3.55	11.5	11.5	3.95	-0.3

Source: Baker Institute for Public Policy Energy Program.

The sudden economic meltdown in much of Asia precipitated an even more unexpected drop in Asian oil consumption during 1997–8. Asian oil demand fell by 1.9 percent in 1998, after a 4.5 percent rise between 1996 and 1997. The slowdown in Asia contributed to a major change in the global oil supply-demand balance, limiting the growth in worldwide oil demand to 74.24 million b/d in 1998, which was only 0.5 percent higher than its level in 1997. This minuscule increase in global oil demand pales in comparison to annual growth rates averaging 2 to 3 percent over the course of the mid-1990s.[12] The sudden decline in global demand contributed to downward pressure on oil prices, which crashed to $10 per barrel.

Soon after the Asian flu effects subsided, the global economy began to recover, contributing to resumed demand growth and fueling a sustained recovery in oil prices. As we have discussed in previous chapters, by 2003, prices were on a major ascendancy, driven by OPEC cohesion in the face of a booming global economy that caused corresponding increase in global oil use and ever-rising forecasts of future demand for oil.

The current economic contraction and corresponding oil-price drop of late 2008 fits this same pattern. Thus, as long as the world's eventual recovery will be dependent on oil, it would be a mistake to consider the falling prices of 2008–9 as a sign of permanently low oil prices. The main objective of this section is to establish that economic dependence on oil is most likely to continue at the same or very similar levels as in previous waves of the cycle. Thus, we can safely anticipate that the next upswing in economic growth will lead to significant shortages and a renewed episode of soaring oil prices, which will eventually lead to another recession, and so on.

Emerging Economies, Car Ownership, and Oil Demand

Economic development in the current era has been and continues to be highly correlated with increased urbanization, electrification, and growth in the use of private automobiles. In this regard, studies have shown that as per capita income in a developing nation rises to reach the range of $5,000 to $12,000, the number of vehicles per person tends to increase dramatically. For example, if a country started with per capita income below $5,000 and 25 vehicles per 1,000 people, as per capita income rises above $5,000, vehicle stocks may very well increase to 500 vehicles per 1,000 people, a factor-of-20 multiplication.[13]

This correlation is very important because many emerging economies, including most notably China and India, are expected to experience per capita income growth to this critical "launching point" for private car ownership. Thus, there is a tremendous potential for an uptick in oil demand to resurface quickly as the global economy expands anew.

Per capita primary energy use in the developing world remains markedly lower than the industrialized West, and therefore the countries with the highest rates of economic growth are also those most likely to increase their oil demand significantly. For example, India's total primary energy consumption per person averaged roughly 0.38 tonnes of oil per person in 2006, and China's corresponding statistic is 1.29. This is in stark comparison to the United States where total primary energy consumption per person averaged 7.79 tonnes of oil per person, and Germany where the statistic is 3.98 tonnes per person.[14]

Shifting Source of Oil Demand Growth

Because of the higher forecasted rates of per capita GDP growth in Asian emerging economies, and the aforementioned significantly lower levels of per capita income and energy consumption in those countries, forecasters such as Cambridge Energy Research Associates have featured scenarios under which "the center of global economic and political gravity shifts to Asia." Under one such scenario, the average growth rate in future global oil demand would be 4 percent a year to reach 124 million b/d by 2030, with Asia accounting for 51 percent of rising oil use and representing 42 percent of world energy consumption and 54 percent of world GDP.[15]

The IEA has also projected similar trends in its 2008 forecast, with a reference scenario under which China and India account for just over half of the increase in world primary energy demand between 2006 and 2030. In line with the "launching point" hypothesis, the IEA projected that non-OECD countries will account for 87 percent of the increase in demand over the coming 25 years.[16]

According to the IEA 2008 reference case, approximately three-quarters of this projected increase in world oil demand by the year 2030 would be attributed to the transport sector. In this regard, it must be noted that the transportation sector is the biggest contributor to oil demand growth in non-OECD countries. Therefore, under the IEA's 2008 scenario, transport sector oil use will account for 57 percent of global primary oil consumption by 2030, compared to 52 percent currently and 38 percent in 1980.[17]

In particular, the IEA has projected Chinese oil demand to rise from 7.5 million b/d in 2007 to 16.6 million b/d in 2030, and Indian oil demand to rise from 2.9 million b/d to 7.1 million b/d over the same period. The IEA 2008 forecast for total world demand was more conservative than previous forecasts because it took into account the possibility of higher prices leading to economic slowdown and demand reduction, which have in fact materialized. Within this framework, the IEA reference case forecasted total world demand rising to 106.4 million b/d by 2030, compared to 85.2 million b/d in 2007, at an average rate of 1 percent per annum.

Future U.S. Oil Demand: The Ultimate Wild Card

Although Asian economic growth is generally expected to be the main driver for oil-demand growth, the U.S. role in sustaining that demand growth remains substantial. In this regard, there are currently more than 242 million road vehicles in the United States, for an average of one vehicle for every person. On average, each vehicle is driven over 12,000 miles annually, and virtually all vehicles are powered by petroleum-based fuels, either gasoline or diesel. As a result, despite the fact that the United States accounts for only 5 percent of the world's population, it consumes over 33 percent of all the oil used for road transportation in the world.

The United States imported 13.2 million b/d of oil in 2007 or about 65 percent of its total consumption of roughly 20.2 million b/d. That is significantly up from 35 percent in 1973. Prior to the 2007–8 oil price crisis, the share of imported oil for the United States was projected to rise close to 70 percent by 2020, with the United States becoming increasingly dependent on supply from GCC countries.[18]

New projections made by the U.S. Department of Energy and the IEA in 2008 predicted that U.S. oil demand will flatten by 2030, based on new car-efficiency standards and an aggressive biofuels program for the United States. The IEA projects that U.S. imports will drop to 11.9 million b/d by 2030, as higher prices and legislative policies dampen demand growth. This prediction may prove to be excessively optimistic, especially given the failure of U.S. ethanol use to reach its targeted levels in 2008. Nevertheless, the relevance of future U.S. legislation for determining oil demand cannot be overstated.

Increasing U.S. reliance on imported oil has been a significant factor in strengthening OPEC's oligopoly in international oil markets. U.S. net oil imports rose from 6.79 million b/d in 1991 to 10.2 million b/d in 2000 during a period when global oil trade (that is, oil that was exported across borders from one country to another) rose from 32.34 million b/d to 42.67 million b/d. In other words, the U.S. share of the increase in global oil trade over the period was a substantial 33 percent. For OPEC countries, the U.S. import market was even more significant – representing over 50 percent of OPEC's export growth between 1991 and 2000.

Between 1995 and 2006, U.S. gasoline demand grew on average at about 1.7 percent per year, reflecting factors such as growing per capita income, low gasoline prices and a commensurate increase in driving less fuel-efficient SUVs and other larger cars, and increasing urban sprawl. However, U.S. gasoline demand began falling in 2007 in response to high prices, economic slowdown, and improving fuel efficiency of automobiles.

U.S. Legislation and Its Potential Effects

In 2007, the U.S. Congress passed new Corporate Average Fuel Efficiency standards (CAFÉ). According to a study by the James A. Baker III Institute for Public Policy, the new 35-mile-per-gallon fuel efficiency standard will cause reduction in U.S. oil demand of 2.3 million b/d by 2020.[19] A stricter CAFÉ standard of 50 mpg would reduce demand by 6 to 7 million b/d. Conversely, if lower gasoline prices and more lax legislation spur a return to 2 percent per annum growth in U.S. oil demand, the U.S. contribution would exceed 15 percent of the total world consumption growth.

Because of her large share of the market for internationally traded oil, incremental U.S. acquisition of oil has a significant effect on the market price. This is problematic because U.S. consumers base their demand on the average, rather than marginal, cost of the last barrel of oil acquired to satisfy their demand.[20] In the meantime, the fact that the United States faces a rising supply curve for oil gives her some monopsony power.

Therefore, to the extent that the United States and other major importers can coordinate their policies, they can have some control over the price of oil. The path of oil demand growth for the United States will, therefore, be a critical factor for the future of the oil-Dollar cycle. The degree to which the U.S. Congress can pursue aggressive policies to curb demand growth, for instance imposing gasoline taxes when oil prices fall to penalize consumers who drive inefficient vehicles, will have a significant effect on oil-price dynamics. We return to this issue of demand-side domestic as well as multinational policies designed to ameliorate the cycle in Chapter 8. We now shift our focus to the supply side of oil-market dynamics.

Oil Supply Dynamics I – The International Oil Companies

A major source of concern that a new disruptive spike in oil prices may occur in the near future is that at the same time that fuel demand could take-off in the developing world, growth of conventional oil supply within major oil-consuming regions is expected to slow down. In this regard, it is notable that between 1980 and 2000, more than 40 percent of the increase in world energy supply was produced within industrialized regions such as the United States (mainly Alaska and the Gulf of Mexico), Europe (U.K. and Norwegian North Sea), and Australia.

In contrast, new within-OECD oil supplies are expected to decline significantly over the next 25 years, merely accounting for less than 10 percent of new conventional oil supplies. In this regard, domestic oil production has already peaked in the United States, falling to 5.12 million b/d in 2005, compared to 6.48 million b/d ten years earlier. Similarly, North Sea production, the leading local supplier to Europe, has declined from 6.39 million b/d in 2000 to under 2.11 million b/d at the end of 2005.

Greater contributions to oil supply from within the OECD could come in the form of higher-cost, unconventional resources such as tar sands, oil shale, coal to liquids, and gas to liquids.[21] However, exploitation of these unconventional resources may involve the release of higher amounts of greenhouse gases than in the production of conventional oil and gas, creating political opposition to their widespread use on environmental grounds.

Despite the ascendancy of national oil companies (NOCs), the international majors (IOCs) still possess a large market share of 20 percent of non-OPEC production. Although these IOCs have access to massive capital that could have been invested in expanding productive capacity, they have failed to invest sufficiently in exploration when oil prices were rising at the turn of the century. In part, this was because they had not been able to sustain access to prolific oil regions, as many countries have grown increasingly protective of their oil resources and have been turning away foreign investment.[22]

Since 1998, the exploration spending of the five largest IOCs, which are Exxon-Mobil, Chevron, Conoco-Phillips, Shell, and BP has been relatively constant despite soaring profits and rising cash flows. Adjusting for the rise in costs of materials, personnel, and equipment such as drilling rigs, the five largest IOCs have in effect cut spending levels in real terms over the past ten years. This is in contrast to the 1970s and 1980s when strong IOC exploration spending spurred large increases in non-OPEC production. These legacy assets of the majors are naturally

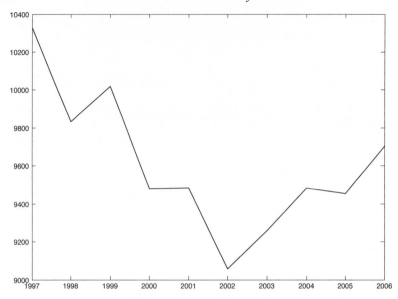

Figure 7.2. Production of the Big 5 Oil Companies (mm b/d, excludes production from Candian tar sands). *Source*: Baker Institute for Public Policy Energy Program, SEC.

declining, thus raising serious concerns about what new resources will be available to replace them.

As a result of this lack of exploration spending, oil production for the five largest oil companies fell from 10.3 million barrels a day in 1997 to 9.4 million b/d in 2005 before rebounding weakly to 9.7 million d/b in 2006, as shown in Figure 7.2. In the meantime, even as their production has failed to grow with demand, the five international majors have come to control over 80 percent of the oil reserves of the top 25 publicly traded oil companies in the United States, up from 69 percent in 1993.[23] This pattern suggests that the IOC have generally favored short-term profitability over long-term shareholder-value creation.

Oil-Supply Dynamics II – The Growing Power of OPEC and NOCs

Conventional oil and natural gas geology is such that approximately 62 percent of the remaining proven resources lie in only five countries. In the case of oil, the five largest resource holders are all Middle-Eastern countries, and Russia is sixth. In projecting future supply potential, more than half of that volume is projected to come from just three countries: Iraq, Iran, and Saudi Arabia.[24] Forecasts that these three countries will be able to meet the growing energy needs of an economically prosperous Asia might prove unrealistic given the region's political and social conditions.

In this regard, optimistic projections that OPEC can meet increased Asian demand by increasing capacity an additional 10 to 20 million b/d over the next two decades run counter to historical experience. OPEC's capacity has actually fallen, not increased, over the past 25 years, from 38.76 million b/d in 1979 to roughly 33 million b/d currently.[25] In addition, with low oil prices expected well into 2009, investment spending within OPEC is likely to fall as demands for social spending take priority facing relatively limited government revenues. Indeed, Venezuela's state-run oil industry's production capacity has declined in recent years by over 1 million b/d, and Nigeria has been unable to expand production, mainly because of social and political problems.

More generally, the growing control of global oil resources by NOCs, which are used to serve social agendas (such as domestic fuel subsidies) rather than dedicating their resources to oil field maintenance and expansion, means that these companies tend to operate at technical efficiency levels well below those of the international majors.[26] Noncore, noncommercial activities not only have imposed costs upon the NOCs, but also have in some cases hindered them in raising internal or external capital for oil field investment.

National Oil Companies, Price Distortions, and Excess Oil Demand

Socially motivated price distortions contribute not only to slower growth in supply, but also to faster growth in demand. Fueled by large consumer subsidies, the Middle-East Gulf region has become the second largest region of growth in oil demand after Asia, with consumption rising by more than 5 percent a year since 2003. The Gulf region's demand for oil now represents over 7 percent of total world oil demand, and consumption growth is being driven by economic expansion, high population growth, and extremely large subsidies of electricity and gasoline prices.[27]

Distortionary effects of energy-price subsidies include the incentive for growth in energy-intensive sectors and reduced energy efficiency. In high-population societies, this exacerbates the budgetary problems faced by the NOCs' governments, leaving fewer funds to reinvest in expanding oil production. This dynamic has transformed OPEC member Indonesia from a net oil-exporting country to an oil importer. Indonesian fuel subsidies by the late 1990s had reached almost one-quarter of the government's entire federal budget, causing a massive economic dislocation and ending the long-time rule of President Suharto.[28] The same dynamic is at work in Mexico and Iran, which are likewise expected to become net oil importers in the next decade.

Biofuel – Hopeful Myths and Discouraging Facts

The first major U.S. attempt to develop alternative energy sources to "replace" imported oil has been a dismal failure, mainly because it was hijacked by special interests and political lobbying. The U.S. Midwest plays a pivotal role in early primaries for U.S. presidential elections and that region's farm lobby, especially the corn lobby, has a particularly strong influence in Washington, D.C. With strong pressure from Midwest congressmen and the farm lobby, the U.S. Congress passed extensive "energy" legislation in 2005 and 2007 that focused heavily on corn-based ethanol, less because it would be an effective substitute for oil and more because it would represent a financial subsidy to Midwestern states.

In effect, this ethanol gambit has been singularly ineffective. In late 2008, the United States was producing around 640,000 b/d of ethanol, mainly from corn. However, current U.S. ethanol production is but a small fraction of the 9.5 million b/d of gasoline fuel consumed during the peak summer driving season. For technical and regulatory reasons, 6 billion gallons a year of ethanol are needed in the United States to replace carcinogenic chemical MTBE as a fuel additive to comply with clean air regulations for reformulated fuels. In other words, current ethanol production to date has not replaced any refined-oil-based gasoline per se, but has merely replaced additives that are being removed from the fuel system.

Ethanol production is targeted to reach 1 million b/d by 2012 under the new 2007 Energy Independence and Security Act. However, logistical and technical barriers have already led Congress to relax targets for 2008 and 2009, and it re-mains unclear whether the United States will ever be able to meet the final targets of the 2007 energy bill. Worldwide, biofuels represented only 1.5 percent of total road transport fuel in 2006, and the IEA projects that biofuels at best will only meet 5 percent of total road fuel demand by 2030.[29]

Pessimistic Forecasts of Renewable Energy Contribution

The cost and time to move renewables into the global energy system to provide non-oil energy for heating and powering non-gasoline-burning automobiles will be formidable, even with strong government intervention. In the United States, thirty-seven states have passed renewable energy portfolio standards requiring that renewable energy constitute a minimal percentage of fuel used to generate elec-tricity in the state. Many states are still struggling to meet the ambitious early targets. On the aggregate, wind power still represents less than 2 percent of all electricity generated in the United States to date.

Based on current OECD policies, the IEA is projecting that total cumulative investment in renewable energy will have to reach $5.5 trillion 2007 Dollars to move renewable energy from 7 percent of total world primary energy supply to 10 percent, or from 18 percent of total electricity generation output in 2006 to 23 percent in 2030.[30] In energy consultant Cambridge Energy Research Associates' (CERA) "Breakpoint" scenario analysis, which favors aggressive policies to promote alternative fuels and technologies, growth in hydroelectric and renewable energy capacity accounts for 28 percent of additional generation capacity built from 2006 to 2030. But even under this alternative-technology-friendly scenario, CERA predicts oil demand to grow from 88 million b/d in 2010 to 108 million b/d in 2030 (as compared to 92 million b/d in 2010 to 124 million b/d in its Asian Phoenix scenario).[31]

This is not to say that investment in alternative energy sources and the pursuit of higher energy efficiency in consumption are futile efforts. On the contrary, as we have discussed, improvements in automobile corporate average efficiency standards to 35 miles per gallon in the United States alone could eliminate 2.3 million barrels a day from oil demand. In its study "Reducing U.S. Greenhouse Gas Emissions: How Much at What Costs?" consultants McKinsey & Co. have argued that there are sizable low-cost gains that can be achieved through energy efficiency.[32] The Center for American Progress has also emphasized that a fiscal stimulus package of $100 billion, combined with a federal loan guarantee program, could boost private-sector investment in energy-efficiency technology, create 800,000 lost construction jobs in the United States, and "produce an annual reduction in global oil demand of 1.2 percent."[33]

In fact, all of those efforts to reduce dependence on oil, both on energy supply and demand dimensions, will be revisited in our discussion of strategies to ameliorate the cycle in Chapter 8. Nonetheless, the inescapable conclusion of the evidence on energy supply and demand trends presented in this section is that the world will continue to depend on oil for at least 30 percent of its energy needs in the coming decades. Increasingly, that oil will be sold by countries in the Middle East, which is one of the most volatile regions geopolitically.

Global Conflicts, Radicalisms, and Terrorism

There are very few intervals in modern history during which we are not reminded of the volatile nature of geopolitics in energy-rich regions. As we write this section, military hostilities have flared up again in the Middle East, as the ceasefire in Gaza between the Hamas government and Israel expired without reasonable hope of renewal, contributing to a moderate spike in oil prices at the end of 2008. The dramatic collapse in oil prices during the second half of 2008, which was not slowed down significantly by OPEC promises to cut production significantly, did react moderately to geopolitical strife in the Middle East. This potential for a geopolitical premium in oil prices is likely to remain for the foreseeable future.

This direct relationship between geopolitical problems and energy prices is particularly alarming because the decline in oil and gas prices has direct economic and political effects, especially for the leaders of Russia, Venezuela, and Iran.[34] Perhaps to relieve some of those pressures, Russia's Gazprom has acted once again, incidentally during the same week when hostilities had resumed in the Middle East, to halt supplies of natural gas to and through Ukraine, creating great anxieties within the European Union.[35]

Geopolitical Strife and Energy Prices

The potential for social, political, or even military problems in the region, fueled by rising religious fervor, sectarian conflicts, and media sensationalism, becomes ever greater as oil prices decline. Geopolitical problems in the Middle East need not begin as international disputes. Rather, many domestic problems may be the initial culprits. In this regard, even before oil prices began to slide, migrant workers from South Asia were increasingly staging demonstrations to protest dire working conditions and the negative impact of inflation on local wages during the first half of 2008.[36] Such problems are expected to escalate as millions of migrant workers from Pakistan and India lose their jobs and need to be repatriated home, escalating unrest in the Gulf and potentially in Pakistan and India as well.[37]

Moreover, many countries within the region are vulnerable to domestic unrest or political crises, ranging from leadership succession problems to radical revolutionary challenges to existing regimes, which could lead to another 1979-style disruption to oil production in an oil-producing country or disruption of transportation routes for tankers. Moreover, oil exports could be easily curtailed by work stoppage or strikes by oil workers, possibly motivated by political trends involving power sharing or human rights issues. Last, but not least, and extremely tight security arrangements notwithstanding, instability inside oil-producing countries in the Gulf could spur terrorist attacks on regional oil facilities or Western contractors working on oil facility expansion projects, reintroducing the so-called terror premium in international oil markets.

Return of the "Oil Weapon" Possibility

The threat of an oil or energy weapon has emerged into international discourse in recent years, though no such prolonged cutoff of oil has actually ensued. Two oil producers, Venezuela and Iran, have specifically made public statements threatening to cut off oil supplies as a matter of state policies that they perceived to be legitimate defensive and retaliatory responses to political or commercial conflicts.[38]

European countries have expressed concerns that Russia's resumption of its aggressive strategy in 2006 against Ukraine may again produce significant spikes in local natural gas prices. Russia's winter 2006 effort to forcibly renegotiate prices, ostensibly to reflect the fair market value of natural gas in Europe, greatly affected consumers in both Ukraine and Western Europe. While the motivation for the cutoffs both in 2006 and 2009 may have been commercial, the moves were widely interpreted as attempts by Moscow to undermine the anti-Russia, pro-NATO (North Atlantic Treaty Organization) stance of the newly elected government of Ukrainian President Viktor Yushchenko. Thus, the periodic disruptions, short enough not to prompt sufficient diversification away from Russian gas, but long enough to cause panic and introduce a geopolitical premium in energy prices, can serve Russia's economic and political goals simultaneously.

Iran, Israel, and the Arab World

Perhaps nowhere is the potential for a geopolitical and/or terror premium in oil and gas prices as evident as in the many conflicts to which Iran is a party directly or indirectly through agents in Syria, Lebanon, and elsewhere. Iran's strategic location, as well as its important role in the supply of oil and potential as a major gas supplier, gives it leverage to assert itself in global energy markets. Moreover, Iran's role as an indigenous historical superpower in the Gulf region has great bearing on the stability of the Middle East as a whole, and by extension oil security. In this regard, Iran's active support for such subnational groups as Hizbullah is a major factor in regional politics and raises the risks of an escalated Iranian-Israeli confrontation.

Already, the Iranian pro-Palestinian posture has put many Arab rulers in very difficult bind, as the argument that the Shi'ite Iranian threat exceeds the Israeli threat during the Israeli war with Hizbullah during summer 2006 failed to gain traction among the Arab masses. Exactly the opposite occurred, as the Arab masses viewed Hizbullah much more favorably than their own regimes – in no small part because the militia had been more successful against the formidable Israeli war machine than all of their Arab-country armed forces combined.[39] Tensions between Israel and Iran were a key element of a summertime oil price spike in 2006 and harken back to earlier Israeli warnings that Tel Aviv could hit vulnerable oil export facilities such as Kharg Island and other offshore regions instead of preemptively attacking the Bushehr nuclear plant. [40]

Tensions between Iran and the West over Tehran's nuclear aspirations are also viewed as a threat to oil markets. An important factor in this regard is the possibility of expanded economic sanctions against Iran, which could result in a ban on Tehran's oil exports to the international market. In addition, Iran's geographical leverage on the Strait of Hormuz also raises the risks that its ongoing conflict with the United States over its alleged nuclear weapons aspirations could lead to a temporary closure of the Strait. The Strait is the main passageway for 16 to 17 million barrels of oil a day, roughly two-thirds of total world oil trade by tanker and 20 percent of total world daily oil demand.[41]

Renewed Middle-East Arms Race

As noted earlier, petrodollar flows to the Gulf region are often accompanied by arms races. Three factors make the current round of arms race in the Middle East different from earlier ones:

  (i) U.S. military involvement in the region has become much more direct, with hundreds of thousands of American troops on the ground in Iraq and Qatar, making the United States a direct military participant instead of an international diplomatic broker and distant arms supplier.

  (ii) The United States and Russia are selling nuclear technologies to regional participants in addition to conventional arms, airplanes, and missiles. This activity sows the seeds for a nuclear arms race in the already unstable Middle East.

  (iii) Existing regional conflicts are being complicated by the violent participation of nongovernmental radicalized subgroups such as Al-Qa'ida and Hizbullah whose interests differ from regional governments and are less susceptible to diplomatic pressures or initiatives.

Thus, the petrodollar-driven military-buildup wave of 2003–8 has greatly increased the chances of a nuclear confrontation in the Middle East. This, in turn, has raised the chances of increased regional tension and distrust and contributed early in the cycle to the geopolitical-strife premium in oil prices.

Iran's nuclear aspirations – claimed to be for peaceful electricity generation but widely believed to be for military ends – have been central to recent confrontations in the region. The Gulf Cooperation Council (GCC) contributed to this fear of a nuclear arms race in late 2006, with an announcement that it too would embark on a nuclear energy program. By February 2007, the GCC and the International Atomic Energy Agency (IAEA) agreed to work together on a nuclear power plan for the Gulf Arab states. The IAEA was to provide technical expertise and the GCC was to hire a consulting firm to speed its nuclear discussions.[42] So far, unlike Iran, GCC countries have proposed that uranium enrichment would be undertaken in a neutral country, reducing some of the potential crossover with a nuclear arms development program.[43]

Rhetoric between Saudi Arabia and Iran was building up in early 2007, and a statement was made during an Arab summit in March 2007 suggesting that Iran's ambitions could begin "a grave and destructive nuclear arms race in the region." The rhetorical war between Iran and Saudi Arabia extended also to the issue of Palestine, with each side trying to undermine the other's credibility. Iranian and

Hizbullah propaganda against Saudi Arabia and other Sunni regimes were also decried by the latter to be a form of Shi'ite proselytism.[44]

The conventional-weapons component of the Gulf-region arms race was made semiofficial in July 2007, when the Bush administration announced plans to offer a $20 billion arms package for Saudi Arabia and its Gulf Arab neighbors. U.S. Undersecretary of State Nicholas Burns described the arms package as aimed to "enable these countries to strengthen their defenses and therefore to provide a deterrence against Iranian expansion and Iranian aggression in the future."[45]

By spring 2008, the United States, seeking Saudi support for the U.S. Dollar and a lower oil price, went further and issued nuclear aid proposals. President Bush visited the region and announced new cooperation agreements under which the United States would assist Saudi Arabia in developing nuclear power for medical and industrial civilian uses as well as generating electricity. The agreement will expand cooperation to better safeguard the kingdom's vast oil reserves and its pipeline distribution system, as well as its borders. As part of the deal, the White House stated that Saudi Arabia is to join a global initiative to combat nuclear terrorism, to enhance the protection of nuclear systems, and to improve her ability to detect and confiscate illegally held nuclear material.[46]

This reemergence of an arms race in the Persian Gulf in recent years should come as no surprise, as similar military buildups have been typical by-products of the earlier oil-petrodollar-conflict cycles. However, the current brewing conflicts could be more virulent and harmful than in the past, as the strategic escalation to weapons of mass destruction and the heightened involvement of subnational groups raise the stakes.

Continued Geopolitical Strife: Inevitable and Intentional

Therefore, we can see that in the most energy-rich parts of the world, the Middle East and Central Asia, regional powers have been mired in multiple geopolitical conflicts that are likely to continue well into the future. In this regard, it is paradoxical that problems, including military altercations and even economic sanctions, can add a hefty premium to energy prices, thus enriching the coffers of regional countries, including both observers and instigators. In other words, a little bit of trouble, even a little bit of terrorism, is good for regional business.

Why would leaders in the region kill the goose that lays that golden egg? In fact, as energy prices decline precipitously, it becomes ever more expensive for the regional states to dedicate resources to peacekeeping and law enforcement, just as cuts in social programs and lack of job opportunities help to incite militant activities within their borders. In other words, not only is it advantageous for some of those problems to surface, in order to reintroduce the geopolitical premium in oil prices, but it is also more expensive to prevent this scenario from unfolding.

Therefore, for the foreseeable future, we can expect geopolitical problems to contribute to the rebound in oil and gas prices, with a lag coinciding more or less with the lag that is needed for low energy prices to drive a global economic recovery, as we shall discuss later in this chapter. Before proceeding to the final section that integrates all three drivers of the cycle, we establish that the recurrence of financial mania and crises, as Minsky and Keynes had argued, is also likely to be a permanent fixture of the increasingly deregulated capitalistic global economic and financial system.

Serial Amnesia, Greed, and Financial Crises

In Chapter 5, we summarized some of the main features of Hyman Minsky's analysis of financial booms and busts, in which he suggested based on the analysis of John Maynard Keynes's writings that financial instability is a fundamental feature of free-market capitalism. In this regard, we have discussed the forces of greed and hubris that allow markets to progress from hedge finance to speculative finance and then ultimately to Ponzi finance. In this manner, the most recent financial bubble gave rise to the largest Ponzi scheme of all time – a $50 billion scheme spanning multiple continents and envisaged by Bernard Madoff, the ex-Chairman of NASDAQ and highly acclaimed fund manager.[47]

Paul Krugman went further by suggesting that the Madoff scandal, rather than being an exception, was in fact part and parcel of what Soros has called a super bubble, to which Krugman referred as "The Madoff Economy."[48] This phenomenon, which started in the 1980s and lasted until the most recent credit bubble collapsed, is a natural consequence of the financialization of the economy. In this regard, the financial sector has reached a peak of 8 percent of U.S. GDP, which when compared to its earlier size of roughly 5 percent would suggest the existence of "about $400 billion a year in waste, fraud and abuse."[49] In this regard, it is noteworthy that Kevin Phillips had considered excessive financialization of an economy – along with depletion of its domestic access to the current dominant fuel – as central forces of decline of empires.[50]

Serial Amnesia, Greed, and Hubris

Henry Blodget, one of the culprits in the technology-stock bubble around the turn of the century reflected on the most recent credit bubble by arguing that we are collectively bound not to learn the lessons of financial booms and busts because of a combination of serial amnesia and "this time is different" assumptions. He quoted the well-known investor Jeremy Grantham as saying that "we will learn a great deal in a very short time, quite a bit in the medium term, and absolutely nothing in the long term." Blodget concluded his analysis of the current and previous bubbles and crises by agreeing with Minsky and Keynes:

[B]ubbles are to free-market capitalism as hurricanes are to weather: regular, natural, and unavoidable. They have happened since the dawn of economic history, and they'll keep happening for as long as humans walk the earth, no matter how we try to stop them. We can't legislate away the business cycle, just as we can't eliminate the self-interest that makes the whole capitalist system work.[51]

Experimental Evidence

The Experimental-Economics literature has investigated the emergence of bubbles over the past two decades. Lack of common knowledge of rationality, in other words believing in the "greater fool" hypothesis in order to buy an asset above its fundamental economic value only in the hope of selling it to someone else, was demonstrated to be a primary driver of the phenomenon of speculative bubbles. In this regard, experienced subjects who have previously seen a bubble forming in the same market are less likely to sustain a similar bubble in later iterations of the market environment.[52]

However, later analyses have confirmed that the cause for bubbles is not merely lack of common knowledge of rationality, but in fact an intrinsic level of irrationality of humans.[53] A major element of this irrationality should be attributed to human greed, which allows us to sustain the belief that prospects that seem too good to be true may in fact be anything other than just that. In other words, bubbles may arise for the same reason that otherwise perfectly rational individuals who have managed to accumulate some savings would give those savings away to a nice banker from Nigeria who emails asking for their bank account information in order to transfer millions therein.

Financial Crises, Recessions, and Limits of Keynesianism

Contrary to some ideological streams of economic thought, the occurrence of financial bubbles and the ensuing financial crises when those bubbles implode or burst have very "real" economic consequences. Households that lose home and portfolio values reduce their consumption spending and therefore reduce cash flow to businesses. Reduced sales cash flow and accumulating inventories, together with reduced access to credit markets, force firms to reduce their investment spending, which in turn has adverse effects for other business that provide capital goods and intermediary products.

As Japan experienced during its "lost decade" of the 1990s, this can push the economy into a deflationary spiral as households, businesses, and banks hoard cash and reduce all aspects of their spending. Attempts to re-inflate the economy, as the U.S. Fed and other central banks around the world are attempting in the aftermath of the financial crash of 2008, can easily backfire and produce 1970s-style stagflation.

Intelligent vs. Panic-Mode Keynesiansim

In this regard, it has been well known at least since John Stuart Mill that increasing demand for final products and services through fiscal stimuli and accommodative monetary policies that fail to sterilize the rise in money supply may result merely in rising prices of the final products but fail to translate into increased demand for factors of production. This was one of the central critiques of Keynesian economics leveled by Frederich von Hayek, who made the argument that fiscal stimuli may therefore result in stagflation – higher prices but continued high rates of unemployment.[54]

In an interesting article commemorating the Keynes centennial, Hayek suggested that Keynes was in fact aware of this problem, but that he had cynically aimed to sell the world on fiscal stimulus as a solution for the Great Depression through oversimplified modeling. Hayek warned that economists and policy makers may carelessly assume that fiscal stimulus can thus solve the problem in any severe recession, to which Keynes replied that he could always write another book to correct that "Keynesian" misinterpretation. Unfortunately, Hayek noted, Keynes passed away shortly thereafter, leaving us with many adopters of this Keynesian misconception.[55]

Indeed, Nixon's concession in 1971 that "we're all Keynesian now" paved the way for the aforementioned decade of stagflation. Consequently, the January 2008 repetition of the same concession by none other than the *Wall Street Journal*, favoring fiscal stimulus in addition to accommodative monetary policy, is particularly worrisome.[56] The fear of falling into a deflationary spiral is so severe that economists who are fully aware of the inflationary dangers of the fiscal stimulus packages surely to be implemented around the world over the next few years are still supportive of those strategies.

Regulatory and Policy Cycles

As Minsky and Keynes would have it, the point of being Keynesian is not to wait until a crisis erupts and then to implement fiscal stimuli in panic mode, but rather to put in place sufficient regulatory constraints and counter-cyclical automatic stabilizers to avoid the occurrence of severe crises in the first place. Prevention, in economics as in medicine, is always better, and less costly, than treatment. Of course, as we have discussed previously, the temptation to remove strict regulations and automatic stabilizers that slow down growth during an upswing of the business cycle acts in the same way for policy makers as engagement in an obvious financial bubble does for investors. Therefore, we can expect the cycle of financial booms and busts, as well as the associated cycle of regulatory restrictions and deregulations, to continue for the foreseeable future.

Peaks and Troughs: The Need to Ameliorate the Cycle

The dynamics of our cycle, as discussed over the course of this and the preceding chapters, are rather straightforward. Assume that we start the analysis with low energy prices and strong economic growth. Eventually, that growth causes three patterns to emerge:

(i) Demand for fuel rises, both to sustain production and to accommodate increasing consumption, eventually leading to higher energy prices,

(ii) Stock prices, real estate prices, and eventually commodity prices begin to rise, eventually leading to financial bubbles, as speculators "follow the trend,"

(iii) Urbanization increases in developing countries, as the size of the middle class and its level of education, and commensurate economic aspirations, continue to rise.

Economic Growth Leads to Sharp Rise in Energy Prices

All three developments contribute to a sharp rise in energy prices, which may begin gradually, but eventually spikes. First, with limited capacity for producing more fuel, and lags in building more capacity, the increased demand bids up prices. Second, the wealth effect of rising financial values of financial and real assets increases consumption, which also contributes to further growth. This is partially translated into an increase in retail consumption of energy as fuel for transportation and travel, heating and cooling larger residences, etc. The latter effect is amplified in emerging economies, where urbanization generally starts at lower levels and therefore grows at much higher rates, with commensurate growth in energy demand.

Geopolitical factors often contribute further to the energy-price bubble, as happened in the aftermath of the U.S. invasion of Iraq in 2003, which was mistakenly assumed to reduce prices through increased oil production significantly and quickly in post-sanctions Iraq. Moreover, although pressure from militant groups and disgruntled workers is generally held in check during such periods – in part because the treasuries of oil-exporting countries, such as Saudi Arabia and Kuwait, have the funds available to mollify potential malcontents and to increase efforts on law enforcement – remnant malcontent groups from the previous bust of the cycle may continue to contribute to a "terror premium" in energy prices.

As energy prices continue to rise, the financial sector begins gradually to shift from hedge finance to speculative finance. Initially, the rise in various asset prices and corresponding wealth effects on consumers continue the pattern of economic growth and asset-price inflation, thus providing grounds for the hypothesis that "this time is different," and that the business cycle had been tamed. As this hubris spreads widely, the financial sector shifts from speculative to Ponzi finance, and the bubble builds to clearly unsustainable levels. The high prices eventually lead to economic recession, thus reversing expectations and fueling a crash in energy prices and other financial markets, as discussed next. Thus, the boom phase of the cycle has the roots of the bust phase within its own dynamics.

Very High Oil Prices Cause Recessions

Historically, there is a very strong negative correlation between oil prices at one point in time and soon-later macroeconomic output in oil-importing countries. In this regard, Hamilton pointed out shortly after the 1970s oil-price bubble that every recession but one since the end of World War II has been preceded by an increase in the price of oil.[57] Many later studies have similarly presented empirical evidence that energy price shocks reduce the rate of economic growth and either cause, or are catalysts for, recessions. In this regard, it is generally agreed that oil price variability is an important determinant of economic growth.[58]

The 1970s were, of course, a strong case in point, as economic recession was deep once interest rates rose in the 1980s. OPEC's restriction of global oil supply in 1973, followed by the subsequent second supply shock after the Iranian revolution in 1979, affected economic stability by contributing to higher inflation and lower economic growth throughout the developed world for at least a decade. Strong labor unions during the 1970s demanded that wages rise with inflation, contributing further to this inflationary spiral.[59]

In the early 1980s, the costs of the oil shocks were estimated at $1.2 trillion in lost economic growth for the seven largest industrial countries in the world.[60] In the aftermath of the oil shocks, the growth rate for the industrial world came to a halt, after witnessing a strong period of 5 percent per annum expansion during the 1960s. Monetary and fiscal policy may further contribute to deepening the recession following high oil prices. For example, the Federal Reserve Bank's restrictive monetary policy that began to curb inflation in 1980 was blamed as a key channel causing the economic slowdown that ensued.[61]

Recessions Reduce Oil Prices and Eventually Lead to Recovery

Consequently, it is clear that if growth in energy production does not keep pace with economic growth, the latter will eventually cause excess demand for energy resources, which results in higher energy prices and a quick end to economic growth. Therefore, Daniel Yergin had a partially valid point when he wrote during the 1970s that the energy question is "a question about the future of Western society," noting that in in the past, "stagnation and unemployment and depression tested democratic systems in the years between World War I and World War II" and asserting that if there wasn't sufficient oil to drive economic growth, the "possibilities are unpleasant to contemplate" for the contemporary era.[62]

Yergin's warnings circa 1980 proved excessively pessimistic because the economic slowdown was accompanied by an equally sharp drop in oil demand, which moderated prices considerably just a year or two later. In the period between 1980 and 1983, world oil demand fell by about 20 percent, even more sharply than the mid-1970s' decline of 6 percent.[63]

The Asian financial crisis circa 1997 had a similar effect on oil demand, as we have discussed previously. In this regard, the sudden economic meltdown in much of Asia precipitated an even more unexpected drop in Asian oil consumption 1997–8. Asian oil demand fell by 1.9 percent in 1998, after a 4.5 percent rise in Asian oil demand between 1996 and 1997.[64]

The same scenario seemed to repeat in 2008: U.S. oil demand declined 4.3 percent in the first quarter of 2008 relative to the previous year, while EU-15 demand declined 1.1 percent relative to spring 2007. Oil demand in Pacific industrialized nations (Japan, South Korea, Taiwan, Australia ,and New Zealand) also declined by more than 4 percent. Although Chinese demand remained healthy during the first half of 2008, this was mainly due to stockpiling reserves in anticipation of the Olympics. Those stockpiles are no longer necessary, as evidenced by 2 percent decline in Chinese demand for unregulated fuels, and global oil demand is likely to experience little or even negative growth during 2009.[65]

Reversal of the Financial Accelerator and Geopolitical Forces

During the global recession caused by previously high oil prices, financial speculators reverse course and follow the price trend of financial assets, real estate, and commodity including energy prices by short selling. Thus, the financial accelerator that helped the bubble to build to its peak serves to overshoot on the bubble deflation. Lower prices of fuel, raw material, and real estate, together with accommodating monetary policies that incentivize banks to provide credit at low interest rates, help to initiate economic recovery and renewed growth.

Because of stockpiles of fuel that were built up during the recession as well as increased capacity from investments during the previous boom coming online, growth initially puts little upward pressure on energy prices. This provides perverse incentives to invest in energy-intensive sectors and otherwise not to pursue more energy-efficient consumption and investment, and yet economic growth continues. Lower revenues force governments in oil-exporting countries to reduce their spending on social programs and security, thus contributing to increased anger among the newly minted middle classes, as well as reduced spending on security. Those factors of lagged increases in energy consumption and militant behavior eventually contribute to rising energy prices, and the cycle continues.

8

Ameliorating the Cycle

During the four decades covered in this book, we have witnessed two full phases of the cycle. We began writing this book (and rewriting various chapters, as the pace of change accelerated) in late 2006, when we noticed that the surge in petrodollars was left out of the Bretton Woods II sustainability debate. As it turns out, the crash of 2008–9 did not usher in the end of that system, in large part because U.S. creditors have recognized the "balance of financial terrors" problem and therefore have continued to invest substantially in Dollar-denominated assets, albeit more nervously and more vocally about that nervousness.[1] In other words, cooperation and coordination of investment policies have allowed the international financial system to remain intact through its latest crisis.

Moreover, although signs of increasing protectionism have been evident, including among G20 countries that have repeatedly warned against it, the early signs suggest that 1930s-style collapse of international trade and finance is unlikely: A recent World Bank Trade Note warned that despite signing a pact in November 2008 to avoid protectionism, seventeen out of the G20 countries had in fact implemented some protectionist policies, forty-seven in all, by March 2009.[2]

The World Bank note suggested steps that should be taken by the World Trade Organization (WTO) and G20 to avoid further escalation of protectionist policies worldwide. So far, despite significant reduction in global trade because of the severe global recession, and despite the isolated incidents discussed in this World Bank note, cooperation and coordination, including protection of a relatively strong Dollar, have prevented, the death of globalization empowered by trade and foreign direct investment.[3]

In the short to medium term, as countries struggle with the pain of global recession, the world's ability to escape another Great Depression through continued cooperation and coordination remains to be seen. In this regard, multilateral monitoring through G20, WTO, IMF, and other bodies, inevitably with greater representation and power given to Asian and oil-exporting creditor countries, may serve as precommitment devices to prevent the world from repeating the mistakes of the early twentieth century. However, greater long-term challenges lie ahead.

Inherent instability of free-market capitalism has once again taken center stage in global conversation. The Keynesian solution advocated by Hyman Minsky and others has been "big government," which both regulates financial markets to prevent severe swings of the cycle and implements automatic stabilizers through fiscal and monetary policies toward the same end.[4] This earlier literature has received a boost from recent advances in behavioral economics and finance, which increasingly advocate interventionist "libertarian paternalism" in order to protect individuals and societies from myopic idiosyncrasies, albeit within a regulated capitalist framework.[5]

The role of Keynesian "animal spirits" in governing financial market players and regulators has thus continued to receive further attention at the macroeconomic level, suggesting further regulatory paternalism at the national and global levels.[6] European members of the G20, especially Germany and France as well as the United Kingdom, have thus emphasized the importance of global financial regulation and empowerment of the International Monetary Fund as a lender of last resort for smaller countries that are suffering in the aftermath of the global crisis.

Free-Market Capitalism and Growth

Alarmed by the increasingly loud chorus of economic and political calls for heightened regulatory and direct government intervention to prevent similar mania, panics, and crashes from recurring, Gary Becker and Kevin Murphy, two Chicago-school free-market advocates from two generations, urged the world to stay the course.[7] Although many have ridiculed their views as ideologically driven denial of reality, Becker and Murphy had in fact stressed a very important point about financial regulation:

The claim that the crisis was due to insufficient regulation is also unconvincing. For example, commercial banks have been more regulated than most other financial institutions, yet they performed no better, and in many ways worse. Regulators got caught up in the same bubble mentality as investors and failed to use the regulatory authority available to them.

This argument should not be taken to the extreme of suggesting that there is no need to reverse recent deregulation trends and improve regulation of novel highly leveraged financial institution such as hedge funds. Indeed, recent pronouncements by government officials in the United Kingdom, the United States, Germany, and other centers of international finance have suggested that greater regulation of such financial institutions is inevitable.

However, the Becker-Murphy argument does highlight a fundamental tradeoff that individual countries and the global economy face. On the one hand, the existence of regulation does not guarantee that there will be no mania, bubbles, panics, and crashes, because regulators and regulated entities can be fooled equally by stories regarding why "this time is different." Indeed, as we have argued in earlier chapters, regulation and deregulation cycles suggest similarly that legislators and regulators are subject to the same "animal spirits" that afflict market participants. On the other hand, Becker and Murphy are correct in warning that excessive regulation and restriction of the animal spirits of market participants rob market capitalism of one of its greatest growth-inducing assets: financial innovation and appetite for risk justified by the promise of higher return.

Becker and Murphy reminded the world of the remarkable growth rates sustained over the past three decades, which remain remarkable on average even if we adopt pessimistic projections of the adverse effects of the latest crash. They argued further, along the familiar lines of "the rising tide raises all ships," that this sustained global growth was instrumental in reducing world poverty, most notably in China. In summary, they have argued that increased intervention and regulation "would risk damaging a system that has served us well for 30 years."

This alarmist message seems inappropriate, precisely because the authors were correct in declaring market capitalism "the only game in town." The danger of reverting to socialist models that had in the past century damaged economic growth in China, the Soviet bloc, India, and other countries, seems minimal. The issue being debated is how to fine tune this system of market capitalism. Indeed, the past 30 years have witnessed unprecedented growth, despite frequent market crashes and economic recessions. Trying to attenuate the cycle may lead to slower average growth rates in the short to medium term. However, because of the volatile nature of the three interlinked processes studied in this book, we have argued that the risks associated with severe downswings in the cycle have become too great to warrant gambling on growth.

Cycle Attenuation and Balanced Growth

Lower degrees of regulation and government intervention in financial and economic markets may indeed yield faster rates of growth, but only at the expense of distributional inequity. In this regard, the leading development economist Angus Deaton has argued that poverty should be measured in relative rather than absolute terms.[8] The issues that Deaton raised were not restricted to technical problems of measurement in terms of pricing nontradable goods and the like. Rather, he highlighted human-psychological aspects of welfare in terms of differentials in lifestyle, especially in an increasingly integrated world where the poor can observe consumption patterns of the rich more than ever before. This view is closely related to our analysis of religiously motivated terrorism-related geopolitical risks, which depend less on absolute poverty levels of potential terrorists and more on frustrated expectations and perceptions of inequity and exploitation.

Perceptions of inequity and exploitation have ignited populist anger in the United States against Wall Street professionals who received millions of Dollars in compensation despite contributing substantially to the financial market crash that has endangered the livelihoods of millions of families. With years and decades of similar outrage at the international stage, and with the aid of religious rhetoric and lack of economic opportunities for upward social mobility, individuals, groups, and rogue nations may resort to violence. With preponderance of weapons of mass destruction and increased global integration, the global cost of inequities (real or perceived) has become too high to justify the free-marketers' willingness to tolerate global instability and inequity as prices of faster average rates of growth.

Extreme risks are particularly high when states fail to provide opportunities for their citizens or to spend sufficiently on law enforcement. As we have argued, Middle-East oil-exporting countries and their neighboring labor-exporting countries are particularly vulnerable to this risk because of limited economic absorptive capacity, which leads to distortionary bubbles and poverty-inducing crashes as petrodollars flow and stop. The investment cycle in energy-production capacity has also been shown to work in a pro-cyclical manner, thus contributing further to geopolitical risks and commensurate energy-market volatility.[9] Geopolitical risks, especially near massive oil and gas traffic such as the Straits of Hormuz, are also approaching cataclysmic proportions in the current era of globalization.

Finally, we have seen that global financial systems that are deemed stable and sustainable in the short to medium term, such as the Bretton Woods II "balance of financial terrors" between Asian surplus-trading countries and the United States, may be undermined severely by petrodollar flows. Attempts to recycle petrodollars have failed in the past two phases of the cycle – contributing materially to the Latin American debt crisis of the 1980s, and the U.S.-centered global credit crisis of the new millennium. We have been fortunate so far that the "balance of financial terror" has sustained the current Dollar-centered global financial system. However, with increasing acknowledgment of the unsustainability of this financial system worldwide, and without an immediately viable alternative system in sight, the risk of global financial meltdown remains catastrophically high.[10]

Therefore, on all three fronts of energy markets, financial markets, and Middle-East geopolitics, the downside risk of wild cyclical oscillations has become intolerably high. Attenuation of the cycle may come at the cost of slower (if more balanced) average rates of economic growth worldwide. However, that cost appears well worth paying to avoid the risk of total systemic failure in financial, economic, or political spheres. Of course, with the potential reduction of those extreme risks, long-term investment in real economic growth may become more inviting once again, thus enabling us to assess the tradeoff not merely between short-term growth and stability, but also between short-term unbalanced growth and sustainably balanced long-term growth that is more immune to catastrophic disruptions, and thus contributes more substantially to global welfare.

Technical Solutions and International Cooperation

Unfortunately, everyone's incentives are not aligned in this quest for balanced growth. More importantly, there is a fundamental misalignment between the short-term goals of political and economic leaders and the long-term goals of their societies. Current calls by regulators to reward financial players for long-term rather than short-term financial performance seem particularly ironic in light of the political-regulatory leadership's own incentive to manufacture a quick economic recovery through fiscal stimuli that some European partners, especially hyperinflation-wary Germany find irresponsible.

In this regard, myopia may hinder the quest for cycle attenuation on multiple dimensions. The first, and perhaps the most important, is fixation on "technical" regulatory and institutional solutions. This "quick fix" syndrome has plagued the pages of various publications such as the *Wall Street Journal* and the *Financial Times*, various corners of the blogosphere, and even testimonies of senior officials before various legislatures.[11]

In this regard, we must remain cognizant of the cat-and-mouse nature of the regulatory cycle, where regulators tend to overreach after major crises, putting in place excessive regulatory restrictions that hinder efficient functioning of markets. At first, financial innovation enables market participants to enhance systemic efficiency through various legal and regulatory arbitrage activities. Eventually, marginal efficiency gains from such arbitrage activities decline and become negative when adjusted for increased systemic risk. In due course, a new crisis results from this increased risk, and the regulatory cycle – again as studied by Minsky and others – repeats.

Myopic Expectations of Controlling Myopia

Myopia thus contributes to the overall cycle in two ways. The first is deferment of regulatory adjustment in favor of avoiding severe recession, which has contributed to perpetually accommodating monetary policy following one bubble crash after the next. The second is inherent in the regulatory overreaction followed by complacency when accommodating regulatory, monetary, and fiscal responses fail to jump-start growth. The first phase of regulatory overreaction, currently in full display as we write this chapter in early 2009, aims primarily at creating a new level of trust in the stability of an inherently unstable system.

The quick-fix technical-solution approach relies on a historical illusion: All we need are a few technical adjustments to the system, such as forcing hedge funds to register with the Securities and Exchange Commission, regulating forward contracts and forcing their execution through regulated clearing houses, and the like. Perhaps most ironic is the expectation, suggested by Secretary Geithner in his testimony before the U.S. Congress in late March, that it is possible to regulate the system by forcing financial-sector compensation to be tied to long-term rather than short-term performance. The irony in this framework can be analyzed on two levels – pertaining to its sustainability and its effects.

First, Secretary Geithner's own motivations are themselves short-term oriented, as he aimed to calm financial markets sufficiently to restart credit extension and economic growth. Of course, if those efforts are successful, then the proposed regulatory framework, short-term-oriented as it was, will be quickly forgotten. In this regard, it is instructive to recall earlier repeated promises of regulating hedge funds and the non-bank financial sector. As it turns out, those promises of stricter regulation were forgotten shortly after the crises that prompted such promises – the failure of Long Term Capital Management in 1998, and of Enron in 2000, to name only the most obvious.

Second, even if the recession proves to be sufficiently deep and prolonged to give rise to far-reaching regulatory constraints, which will be inevitably excessive in the short-term if history proves to be a good guide, there is no way that short-term oriented financiers will be restricted by the long-term objectives of regulators. The problem is especially problematic because regulators, like all other humans, are subject to the same "animal spirit" short-memory limitations that affect bankers and other financial actors. In other words, even if the system that we put in place is not simply a fixed set of rules that are easy for financial practitioners to circumvent, but a regulatory framework that allows various regulators to adapt to financial innovation, the fundamental problem of time inconsistency and vulnerability to manias, panics, and crashes will persist.

In the remainder of this chapter, we begin by discussing the general classes of obvious technical solutions for cycle attenuation in the three spheres discussed in this book: energy markets, financial markets, and Middle-East geopolitics. After discussing those general "technical fixes," we shall turn to the fundamental problem of time inconsistency that renders those temporary fixes impotent in the medium to long term. Leveraging the competing interests of various nations and regions appears to be conducive to longer-term cycle attenuation, but implementations through international bodies such as G20, WTO, IMF, and the like are themselves merely supertechnical solutions that eventually fall prey to the same problems of time inconsistency. Consequently, we turn now to general classes of technical solutions with this disclaimer, and general suspicion of all technical solutions, regardless of their apparent cleverness and immunity to long-term arbitrage and eventual subversion to amplify rather than attenuate the cycle. We focus mainly on the energy cycle because it has been shown to be the nexus between the other two cycles, financial and geopolitical, and because we have shown in Chapter 7 that it is almost certain to repeat at least one more time.

Attenuating the Energy-Markets Cycle

The recurring cycle of oil prices and financial crises has been associated with competitive and sometimes hostile relationships between oil producer and consuming countries. This negative dynamic had its unfortunate genesis during Europe's colonial rule of the Middle East and Africa, when virtually all economic rents from natural resources found in the colonies were transferred to Europe in order to hasten her economic development. After World War II, this pattern of plunder was resisted by local nationalists, and thus began the struggle for control of the rents from rich resources in the deserts of Arabia and deltas of Africa.

Sins of the Colonial Past

The period from the 1950s through the 1973 oil crisis witnessed the gradual migration of control of national resource rents away from European companies and their governments to the newly independent nations of the Third World. The process, not always peaceful, left a bitter taste that lingers today as a latent force in North-South relationships. This toxic past was reawakened, to some extent, by the unilateralist policies and pronouncements of the U.S. administration of President George W. Bush toward festering conflicts in the Middle East and Africa and the "with us or against us" rhetoric of the "war on terror."

Although colonization and its legacy have generally faded to history books, a competitive attitude remains regarding who will reap the rents of underground black gold. Oil producers have maintained that they must receive a "fair price" for their oil in order to enable them to catch up to more advanced economies of the industrialized West. The West decries its dependency on imported oil, which is seen as a perennial danger for the economic security of its citizens. Leaders on both sides foster dissatisfaction and distrust of the other side of this fatally symbiotic relationship. The latter relationship remains dominated by the producing countries' quest for higher oil revenues and the importing countries' counter quest for faster growth through lower oil prices – a short-term zero-sum game.

Mistrust and Dysfunctional Energy Policies

This conflict is exemplified by OPEC's warnings in recent years that a shift to alternative energy sources inside major oil-consuming economies will discourage investment in future oil supplies, potentially forcing oil prices "through the roof" in the short to medium term. Speaking before a G8 meeting in June 2007, OPEC Secretary General Abdullah El-Badri said that OPEC was considering cutting its investment in new oil production: "If we (OPEC) are unable to see security of demand ...we may revisit investment in the long term." He warned that the U.S. and European biofuels strategy would backfire because "You don't get the incremental oil and you don't get the ethanol," alluding to the view that biofuels strategies may prove unsuccessful.[12]

When the United States repeatedly called on OPEC to increase its oil supply to assist U.S. consumers and potentially prevent a severe recession, OPEC responded by holding its oil output levels unchanged and criticizing the U.S. President instead for "mismanaging" the U.S. economy.[13] Both OPEC and U.S. strategists were at fault to frame the problem in short-term zero-sum-game terms and then demand cooperation from their declared opponents. By continuing to ignore the cyclical nature of economic growth, oil prices, and financial-asset markets, both have lost.

Economic Ramifications of Global Recession

In the fourth quarter of 2008, U.S. GDP fell 6.2 percent, costing the country 3.6 million jobs that were lost between December 2007 and January 2009, and the trend has continued through the first quarter of 2009. In the meantime, major oil-producing countries have not faired much better.

For example, despite large foreign currency reserves in 2008, Venezuela is expected to experience balance-of-payment difficulties by late 2009. Mexico's Central Bank has already devalued the Mexican Peso in fall 2008 and has borrowed $30 billion from the U.S. Federal Reserve Bank to boost liquidity and finance a major economic stimulus package. Even Dubai, ostensibly the beacon of financial acumen in the Arab Gulf, has suffered severely starting in late 2008, with real estate prices collapsing over 30 percent, requiring the UAE to tap resources of oil-rich Abu Dhabi for a $10 billion bailout to the once-booming emirate.

With oil prices at least $30 per barrel below Russia's most pessimistic budget scenarios for 2009, Russian hard currency reserves were depleted in desperate efforts to support the Ruble and to finance bailouts for various strategic corporations. Furthermore, for a variety of financial and political-risk factors, in part because of the recent Georgia war, Russia has also suffered from massive capital outflows. This capital flight was fueled both by the exodus of foreign and domestic investors, in part to save other parts of their portfolios.

Unanticipated Shocks

Several studies have shown that the *unanticipated* speed and magnitude of oil price fluctuations in the 1970s were the main contributors to adverse effects on global economic stability and growth. In other words, gradual and predictable appreciation of oil prices would have been less damaging because businesses and consumers would have been able to adjust their fuel consumption gradually without adversely affecting productivity and growth.[14] More recent analyses indicate that price volatility itself, regardless of the ultimate value of the commodity, can be debilitating by causing delays in investment.[15]

Gradual and predictable price movements would also eliminate the problem of unabsorbable petrodollar flows that flood oil-producing countries when prices rise radically. When the next phase of the petrodollar-flow cycle arrives, one hopes that elites in the Gulf will be more cognizant of their governments' inability to spend or invest the money "wisely" and might be more amenable to smarter policies that create sustained growth and the opportunity for gradual diversification of economic activity. The pattern during the last two phases of the cycle has been disastrous for those countries: Dramatic oil-price spikes have destroyed demand, forcing inventories to grow and prices to collapse suddenly, leaving governments desperate to adjust to suddenly lower revenues.

Mutual Benefits of Cycle Attenuation

From an oil producer's standpoint, smoothing the cycle in global oil demand is therefore critical for systematic fiscal spending and investment plans that are conducive to long-term economic growth and development. Those plans have, once again, been disrupted by the latest global recession: U.S. oil demand fell last year to its lowest level since the late 1990s, and the drop represented the largest annual decline in U.S. oil demand since 1980.[16] Meanwhile, with pre-Olympics fuel stockpiling well behind it, China's oil demand also began to decline precipitously in late 2008.[17]

Overall, OECD oil demand has declined by more than 5 percent and developing world demand growth has declined to less than 1 percent. This sinking demand has proved difficult for OPEC to manage, with both on-land and floating inventories of oil contributing further to lower oil prices.[18] In early 2009, the expectation of continued economic contraction worldwide has thus continued to put downward pressure on oil prices, despite announcement of OPEC production cuts exceeding 3 million barrels a day.

For net oil importers, the need to smooth the oil-price cycle is equally important to prevent financial crises and economic growth disruptions. In this regard,
studies have shown that countries with lower energy-consumption-to-GDP ratios
experienced less costly inflation-induced GDP loss, especially if oil-price inflation
is short-lived. Thus, for oil-consuming countries, reducing the energy intensity
of their economies is one way to attenuate their economic growth cycle and to
protect it from oil-price fluctuations.[19]

Diversification of fuel sources would also help oil importers to insulate their
economies against adverse oil-price shocks and short-term fluctuations. The success of energy efficiency and oil-intensity-reduction policies is exemplified by the
Japanese experience: Japan did not experience a severe recession after the 1979–
80 price shock, whereas the United States, the United Kingdom, and Germany,
all of which consumed more energy per unit of GDP, did experience painful losses
in economic output.[20]

Energy-Source Diversification

Thus, it has been shown that ameliorating the oil cycle can be good for both consumers and producers. With this reality in mind, the development of alternative
energy sources should not be seen as an effort to "harm" producers in a zero-
sum-strategy of "independence from imported oil." Instead, the effort should be
framed as a means of ameliorating the global resource-curse cycle that has been
harming the economic prospects of all economies. In this regard, gradual weaning
of the world from dependence on fossil fuels can be viewed as a planning tool for
oil exporters as well as importers.

Diversification of energy sources will play an important role in ameliorating
the oil-price cycle through supply-and-demand effects. On the oil-supply side,
the threat of new fuels reducing long-term oil demand creates an incentive for oil
producers to invest in adequate oil production capacity in order to prevent faster
price-induced migration to alternative fuels.[21] More stable oil prices, in turn, will
make it easier to plan capacity expansion more effectively, without falling victim
to severe liquidity and credit shortages that prevent such investments from taking
place during severe price downswings.

On the demand side, an increasingly diversified portfolio of energy fuels would
stabilize energy costs, thus contributing to greater economic stability. In this regard, investment in nuclear power during the 1970s, especially in Japan, was an
excellent example of how alternative energy served to protect economic growth in
the face of rising oil prices. The value of investing in nuclear energy is enhanced
by the fact that uranium prices are only very weakly correlated with oil prices,
thus providing substantial diversification effects for energy costs and economic
growth.[22]

Ongoing Efforts and Transportation-Sector Challenges

This diversification strategy is a major component of the U.S. Obama administration's fiscal stimulus package, which includes $10 billion in federal loan guarantees for renewable energy systems and electric transmission projects, and $6 billion for research and development on carbon sequestration technology. The planned stimulus package also includes a three-year extension to the investment tax credit for renewable energy production (totaling around $13 billion) from various qualifying U.S. facilities producing wind power, biomass generation, and geothermal and hydropower. Funds were also allocated for energy efficiency improvements at federal and state levels.[23]

However, a major challenge looms large: There is no major substitute for gasoline that can be quickly and broadly disseminated during a major disruption or oil price shock. In the longer term, an aggressive policy to promote the use of plug-in hybrid cars may provide long-term diversification effects in the United States This is particularly the case because the United States is experiencing a broadening base of fuels for power generation, with oil representing less than 2 percent of generation fuel. Natural gas, nuclear power, coal, and renewable sources such as hydroelectric have dominated the electricity generation sector in recent years.[24]

This challenge is particularly difficult because global oil consumption growth is mainly expected to be in the transportation sector, which may constitute more than 70 percent of demand growth. As we have discussed in Chapter 7, CAFÉ standards and possible international extensions thereof can be instrumental in improving gasoline efficiency of automobiles and thus reducing world dependence on oil. Higher consumer taxes on gasoline, similar to those imposed in Europe and Japan, may also discourage wasteful fuel consumption and simultaneously introduce automatic stabilizers for oil prices and their economic effects. As we have also discussed in Chapter 7, inefficient oil consumption and global risk can be reduced by eliminating distortionary fuel subsidies in oil-producing countries and replacing them with other, less distortionary income redistribution mechanisms.

Energy Market Regulation and Multilateral Intervention

Energy and commodity markets have become increasingly intertwined with financial markets through the accelerated growth of futures trading that started in the late 1970s, shortly after the dissolution of the quasi-gold-standard Bretton-Woods system. Thus, we have discussed in Chapter 5 how hedge-fund managers may have bet simultaneously on continued Chinese economic growth and precipitous decline of the Dollar through investment in oil futures. Indeed, it has been the central theme of this book that energy markets and financial markets should be considered jointly, especially in the post-Bretton-Woods world when "oil price" movements often say more about the numeraire currency (the Dollar) than the priced commodity itself.

In this regard, intervention by central banks in financial markets has been a mainstay of the post Bretton Woods world. We have reviewed, for example, the coordination among U.S., European, and Japanese central bankers gradually to devalue the Dollar relative to the Yen in 1985 and then to halt the trend in 1987, through the Plaza and Louvre Accords. Similarly, many central banks have intervened individually and in cooperation with others in foreign exchange markets to stabilize their exchange rates within target bands, for example in preparation for the European Monetary Union. Of course, central banks also engage in open market operations (trading their own governments' bonds) to adjust interest rates closer to their monetary policy targets.

International Cooperation in Oil Markets

By comparison, individual-country and internationally coordinated interventions in oil markets have been more sporadic. The main tools for intervention in oil markets have been government-controlled emergency strategic stockpiling systems and oil-producer spare-capacity control. However, those tools have been used mainly during times of great market imbalances because of wars or natural disasters, and international coordination therein has been severely lacking.

The International Energy Agency (IEA) was created in 1977 as one of the main tools intended for OECD countries to coordinate their responses to short-term energy-market fluctuations and formulate long-term energy and environmental policies. IEA experience proved successful during the 1990 Iraqi invasion of Kuwait, and the resulting loss of more than 4 million b/d in oil supply. Coordination between major oil importers and key oil producers with spare productive capacity helped to prevent 1979-style speculation-driven price spikes.[25]

In coordination with the IEA and Saudi Arabia, the United States used "test sales" from the Strategic Petroleum Reserve (SPR) to stabilize oil markets, with great success. Several years after this successful experience in 1990, the Clinton administration also used a unilateral "test sale" strategy to prevent oil prices from rising above $40 a barrel. The United States had thus signaled to oil markets repeatedly during the 1990s that it would use sales from the SPR to discourage speculative activity that might amplify price fluctuations, with repeated success in punishing speculative buying of oil futures sufficiently to prevent price spikes.

Coordination and Regulation Failures 2003–8

Despite this historical success, the U.S. administration of President George W. Bush refused to use the SPR as part of a coordinated economic strategy that aims to discourage long-position speculation. Policy coordination with major oil producers, especially Saudi Arabia, was likewise compromised by the Bush administration's rejection of Saudi warnings against the invasion of Iraq in 2003. The Bush administration's policy to restrict the use of SPR stocks to situations of war or natural disaster coincided with new rules on the New York Mercantile Exchange (NYMEX) system that removed prudential controls on position limits for speculators.[26] Thus, market speculators no longer feared unilateral U.S. test sales from SPR or policy coordination with Saudi Arabia and IEA to regulate prices, fueling the commodity-price bubble that eventually contributed to the financial crash and ensuing global economic recession.[27]

Initial NYMEX rules set in the 1980s had set strict position limits for speculative traders (those who are not trading to hedge existing price-risk exposure). Only hedgers were exempt from position limits on the grounds that their physical market positions exposed them to massive losses if they engaged in short-term speculative behavior. However, the Commodities Futures Modernization Act (CFMA) of 2000 – intended to serve newly emerging "clearing house" electronic trading facilities managed by companies like Enron who provided "risk management services," ostensibly – made it easier for financial players to obviate position limits and other regulations intended to prevent excessive speculation.[28]

Regulations by the Commodity Futures Trading Commission (CFTC) were undermined in part through foreign exchanges that allowed contracts for physical delivery within the United States to be traded outside the CFTC's jurisdiction – a phenomenon known as the *London loophole*. NYMEX and CFTC amplified the problem by extending exemptions from speculative position limits to swaps dealers who used the futures exchanges to hedge purely financial price risk exposures from financial contracts with institutional investors such as hedge funds or pension funds. This phenomenon, known as the *Swaps loophole*, has allowed institutional investors to take larger positions than they would have been allowed had they traded futures contracts directly on the exchange. The two regulatory *loopholes* thus allowed unlimited speculative investment in oil as a financial asset, contributing materially to the price bubble formation and crash.

Rebuilding Regulation and Coordination Frameworks

One of the arguments commonly used against stricter regulation of futures exchanges has been based on the fear that such strict regulation would drive most parties to use bilateral over-the-counter (OTC) transactions, which Secretary Geithner has thus suggested should also be regulated and executed through approved clearing houses. This argument is valid in principle, but only at the extreme, because exchanges such as NYMEX provide many advantages, especially in the forms of liquidity-based price discovery and insurance against counterparty risk.

In fact, investment bankers are very unlikely to underwrite large OTC transactions if they cannot hedge their risk exposure on formal exchanges.

An obvious technical correction to the excesses introduced by the CFMA would be to reinstate the CFTC definition of hedgers in terms of exposure to price risk in positions involving physical delivery. Speculative limits should apply to all other players with pure financial-risk exposure such as indexed funds. This strict definition of hedgers in commodities-futures markets keeps the latter tied to physical and economic fundamentals, which are restricted by storage and transportation capacity, and the like. Otherwise, futures exchanges become akin to fantasy-market gamesmanship and gambling, albeit gambling with occasionally catastrophic real-economic consequences.

In order to eliminate phenomena similar to the *London loophole*, a higher degree of coordination among regulators across the Atlantic and beyond will be required. This coordination can be framed in national-security terms, because loopholes that allow contracts with delivery in one nation to be manipulated by speculators in other markets can be severely disruptive of the delivery-country's real economy as well her financial markets.

Of course, this coordination of domestic and international market regulations is not easy. Competition among mature financial centers (such as London and New York) may be easier to control in mutual consultation to harmonize regulatory standards. However, the possibility of luring investors to emerging financial centers has often been predicated on providing less cumbersome regulation (as well as tax advantages). Thus, our recurring theme of the need for a grand North-South bargain must be invoked to establish a global regulatory framework that would allow energy markets to function more efficiently through derivatives trading to hedge parties' risk exposure while limiting potentially disruptive speculation to the minimum.

Petrodollar Recycling and International Lender of Last Resort

As we have argued in Chapter 7, no reasonable amount of investment in alternative energy would be likely to reduce global dependence on fossil fuels sufficiently over the next two or three decades to lead to the "independence" used rhetorically to motivate such investments. We have argued in the previous section that investment in alternative energy must be indeed a valuable part of any strategy to ameliorate the cycle, but it will not eliminate one of the main contributors to cycle amplification in the last two phases of the cycle: petrodollars.

We have shown that Middle East oil-exporting countries' economies continue to exhibit low absorptive capacities, suggesting unequivocally that the next phase of the cycle will again exhibit a surge in petrodollars, which will fuel some type of credit bubble and amplify the upswing and then crash of the cycle. Consequently, any successful program for cycle attenuation must include a significant petrodollar recycling scheme.

Limits to Pre-commitment Role of IMF

It is tempting to assume that empowerment of the International Monetary Fund as a global financial regulator and lender of last resort, as proposed recently by the Chinese Central Bank and several others, may be a solution to global financial imbalances generally – including petrodollars as well as trade surpluses in China and elsewhere. However, this one-size-fits-all approach to global financial imbalances is highly unlikely to work.

Already, Germany has pointed out that similar approaches to the shorter-term fiscal stimulus plan are mistaken because they do not distinguish between Chinese trade surpluses and excess reserves on the one hand, which can be ameliorated by increasing domestic consumption of the generally poor nation with massive reserves of approximately $2 trillion, and the very different economic and external financial positions of Germany on the other hand, which Chancellor Merkel characterized as having "negative reserves."[29] Likewise, petrodollars must be treated differently from other export surpluses in China and elsewhere.

Attempts by the IMF as international lender of last resort to recycle petrodollars during the first phase of the cycle in the late 1970s and early 1980s were frustrated by U.S. policy makers eager to recycle those same petrodollars through the U.S. financial system and arms-manufacturing industry and to restrict the control given to creditor countries such as Saudi Arabia at the IMF Board.[30] Likewise, current Prime Minister Gordon Brown's eagerness to make London the global capital of "Islamic Finance," even years ago when he was Chancellor of the Exchequer, can be seen in part through the mercantilist lens of petrodollar recycling.[31]

With the emergence of Sovereign Wealth Funds in Middle-East oil-exporting countries, including most recently the Saudi initiative that took place at the same time as the 2008 financial crisis, competition with the IMF to recycle petrodollars for objectives other than systemic stability continues to grow.[32] Unfortunately, the lesson learned from past cycles has been the need for greater independence.

As we write in early 2009, the lending capacity of the IMF has been enhanced significantly, adding hundreds of billions of Dollars to its proverbial war chest. Despite this enhancement, and any others that may follow, the limits of the IMF as a precommitment mechanism in the international financial system remain. Like WTO and other international bodies, the balance of powers in the IMF make it an effective precommitment tool only for smaller economies that need its approval to borrow, rather than genuine international coordination.

In fact, larger economies such as the United States, Japan, and the European Union can and have used those institutions for leverage, but rarely allow the smaller countries, even collectively, to exercise leverage against them. This was apparent during the previous 1970s–80s episode of petrodollar recycling, when the United States allowed Saudi Arabia to have a larger vote only after conditions were set so that the United States would retain its veto power. It is highly unlikely that major creditor nations in this phase of the cycle, including China as well as oil exporters, can change the rules of the game substantially at those international financial institutions.

Rediscovering the Intent of Sovereign Wealth Funds

Sovereign Wealth Funds came into existence decades ago, for example in Singapore and Kuwait, as stabilization mechanisms: saving during the fat years to allow crucial investment and consumption expenditures to continue during the lean years. Their latest incarnation in the new millennium has also been viewed as a source of financial freedom to pursue the creditor nations' own financial, economic, and even political objectives instead of remaining hostage to the rules of the international financial system, generally dictated by the United States.

Unfortunately, Sovereign Wealth Funds were seduced by the same speculative bubble mentality that had captured most major participants in the global financial system. Thus, many of their strategies were in fact pro-cyclical rather than counter-cyclical, as their *raison d'être* would mandate. In this regard, a survey of SWF investments suggested that Middle-East countries' SWF investments had focused disproportionately on private equity deals in neighboring Middle-East countries, oil and gas investments in other regions such as Scandinavia, financial sector firms, and utilities, all of which were integral parts of the inflating bubble.[33]

In order to invest counter-cyclically, oil-exporting countries' Sovereign Wealth Funds should invest in oil and gas production capacity and alternative energy development during periods of low oil prices. This may seem counterintuitive from the point of view of short-term return, because investment in productive capacity reduces expectations of future prices, and therefore delays recovery. However, the benefits of this investment in the long term should be obvious: It takes place at the lowest cost point, when steel, cranes, and other resources are not overpriced because of regional private construction booms, it provides substitutes for bank financing which dries up during the downswing of the cycle, and it helps to attenuate the upswings in oil prices and eventual recession in later years.[34] Now, rather than 2003–8, is the time for SWFs to invest in Norwegian oil and gas development, as well as development of alternative fuels.

During the boom years, such as we observed during 2003–8, oil-exporting countries' SWFs should have also invested counter-cyclically. One way to invest in this way would be to build their own stockpiles of crude and refined oil products during the lean times, and then to sell those stockpiles when prices rise. This strategy would be particularly effective in cycle attenuation and the prevention of speculation-driven cycle amplification if the United States continues to refuse selling from the SPR for economic reasons. Similarly, SWFs can invest counter-cyclically by buying other commodities, including precious metals, during the lean years and selling them during the boom years, again to prevent speculators from amplifying the cycle, and at the same time making a profit by buying low and selling high.

Benefits and Risks of Model-Based Counter-cyclical Investment

Timing investments to ensure that they act counter-cyclically requires the study of market forces with full understanding of their cyclical comovements, especially in the extreme, where past correlation may be a very poor measure of the degree of interdependence. Therefore, instead of determining whether oil is underpriced (buy signal) or overpriced (sell signal) based on Dollar-price targets of crude barrels, one could use gold prices or other basket-based prices to determine which commodity is overpriced in real terms.

For example, if we assume that prices of approximately $60 per barrel of crude and $1,000 per ounce of gold are "normal," deviation of the barrel price from 0.06 ounces of gold should prompt the SWF to buy gold if the price is higher and to buy oil if the price is lower – a simplistic long-term profitable strategy based on Figure 1.2, which suggests strong mean-reversion in the gold-price of oil. A full model of the real economy can be developed easily to examine relative prices, making proper adjustments for periods of pro-cyclical and counter-cyclical movements of various monetary prices.

The main challenge to incentivize fund managers to target long-term as op-posed to short-term returns should not be present in the case of Sovereign Wealth Funds, which should by definition serve the long-term interests of their nation states, hedging those countries' current and future exposure to various risks. In other words, if the Saudi SWF invests in a manner that loses money in the long term in scenarios where oil prices rise precipitously and remain high, the man-agers of the fund should be rewarded for their shrewd investments if they can prove that they would have earned substantial profits in scenarios where oil prices drop quickly and stay low. Therein lies the problem, of course, because model-based pricing and performance measurement are open to manipulation, even if, or should one say especially if, independent consulting firms and rating agencies are used as neutral arbiters.

Managing Geopolitical Conflicts

The explanation of roots of geopolitical conflicts and the various parties' objectives therein are perhaps the two areas where honest observers are forced to be most cynical. The perpetuation of conflict, including the 60-year old Arab-Israeli conflict, as well as many other interconnected conflicts in the Middle East, is heavily predicated on myopia and selective amnesia. When the disputes are predicated on political, legal, or even religious claims to land and resources, there are always competing claims, with each party conveniently recognizing its own claim and ignoring the others'. When the misgivings and claims of injustice are economic in nature, as we have shown bin Laden's oil-price-based grievances to be in Chapter 3, protagonists often choose the point in the global cycle that best suits their argument (e.g., the highest oil prices in bin Laden's rhetoric, the lowest in "independence from imported oil" rhetoric), thus contributing further to myopic conflicts and short-term zero-sum-game mentalities.

Going forward, the worst part of selective amnesia, which contributes to significantly dangerous myopia, is the various parties' forgetfulness of their failed past strategies. In the Israeli-Palestinian conflict, this selective amnesia has prompted Palestinian negotiators sequentially to demand previously offered deals that are no longer feasible or on the table, perpetually rejecting what may be the best feasible alternative at each round.[35] Equally harmful selective amnesia and myopia has prompted one Israeli administration after the next to adopt the myth that Palestinians "only understand the language of violence," a statement of racial nature superseded only by historical falsehood, as decade after decade has shown that violence is the language least understood.

Similar serial amnesia has contributed to serial conflicts and arms races in the Middle East, especially after the Iranian revolution in 1979 and the first major surge of petrodollars. The devastating eight years of the Iran-Iraq war, followed by the invasion of Kuwait, the first Iraq war, and eventually the second Iraq war, appear only to have contributed to increased geopolitical risk as the arms race has become increasingly nuclear.[36] Increased physical presence of U.S. forces in the Gulf, and increased Iranian and Arab nuclear ambitions (ostensibly for peaceful power generation, which nobody believes) serve short-term petrodollar-recycling purposes but ultimately contribute further to heightened regional risks that may amplify the cycle to catastrophic proportions.

Breaking the Vicious Circle of Violence

There are no solutions in mutual recriminations and revisionist histories to deny, belittle, or trump the victimhood of others, and history has taught us that violence breeds only violence. As Mahatma Gandhi said prophetically: "An eye for an eye makes the whole world blind."[37] In the Israeli-Palestinian conflict, taking birth-rate differentials into account, two eyes for an eye, and other disproportionate responses (barring outright genocide that constitutes blindness of the worst kind), have much the same effect. National-identity fantasies of outlasting "the other" may sustain an intolerable lifestyle for the masses in Palestinian refugee camps and the nervous lifestyle for Israeli settlers in occupied land, but rarely produce the desired exclusivist homeland for either.

The Israeli-Palestinian conflict is a generally viewed in the Middle East as a microcosm of the larger Western-presence-induced conflict in the region. The origins of this conflict are obviously entangled in the colonial past under the British mandate, and parallels continued to be drawn as recently as in the portrayals of Iraqi insurgents against U.S. occupation in the popular Arab media. Similar sentiments underlie Iranian demands that Americans acknowledge their wrongful actions in the mid-twentieth century, not only by President Ahmadinejad but also by Supreme Leader Ali Khamenei, who continued to stress not only past American-Iranian conflicts, but also the current Israeli-Palestinian conflict. Likewise, Al-Qaʿida officials have moved back and forth with great facility between grievances related to Israeli occupation of Palestinian land, American occupation of Iraqi land, and oil-price dynamics.

Avoiding Counterproductive Strategies

As we have argued throughout the book, it is a mistake to ignore the interconnections between geopolitical, energy economic, and financial market factors, with the war-or-terror geopolitical oil-price premium contributing to the very complex dynamics that we have discussed. Cynically, some local powers may act to attenuate the cycle in oil prices by contributing to the geopolitical premium during the downswing of the cycle. However, such activities would be extremely short-sighted because higher oil prices during the downswing of the global business cycle would deepen the recession further and potentially disrupt the entire global financial and trade system. Conversely, cynical views that one can attenuate the oil-price cycle when prices rise by taking military control of a large-reserve country such as Iraq, possibly to turn the spigot and force prices down, have proven to be disastrously flawed.

Therefore, managing the geopolitical component of the super cycle must be a central component of the overall strategic plan to ameliorate the cycle, and it must receive equal attention to avoid wrong solutions based on myopia and serial amnesia. In this regard, the interconnection between Middle-East geopolitics and other aspects of the cycle should not be overly simplified. For example, the invasion of Iraq in 2003 has contributed to the increase in oil prices not only by failing to increase Iraqi oil production and sales, but also indirectly by alienating

Saudi Arabia and therefore preventing this swing producer from helping to ameliorate the cycle. This decline in good will for the Bush administration has also translated into less cooperation in petrodollar recycling, which cooperation could have helped unwind credit markets more gradually, to the benefit of all parties.

Understanding this interconnectedness of Middle-East geopolitics, energy market dynamics, and global finance may serve as a catalyst for viewing the game of Middle-East geopolitics as positive-sum. In other words, all parties to various regional disputes and all other parties who are affected indirectly through the dynamics of energy and financial markets need to recognize the long-term global gains from resolving those disputes. No major countries can afford to free-ride on efforts to resolve the crisis, and short-term profiteering from perpetuating the conflicts – regardless of the ideological rhetoric employed to justify it – should be seen by all in light of its long-term destructive effects of amplifying the global cycles. With such understanding, a grand bargain can be reached with the proper combination of pressure to abandon short-sighted goals and compensation for long-term sacrifices to enhance global welfare.

Conclusion

Very little that we have reviewed in this book will come as a surprise to the informed reader. Moreover, by the time that this book is printed and made available to readers, many of the "latest development" discussions would have long become old news. In today's world, an op-ed piece in the *Wall Street Journal* or the *Financial Times* is already outdated by the afternoon, as hundreds of widely read blogs would have superseded it with later news and several iterations of blogosphere analysis thereof. Those daily and higher-frequency outlets will also contain many very good technical ideas about how to address various issues in the short and long terms. The only advantage that a book-length argument retains in this world is the ability to bring together many seemingly unrelated trends into a coherent framework, especially if the categorical-data points are so few (two phases of the cycle) as to preclude any credible quantitative analysis of the type favored by academic-journal outlets.

We hope that we have made a compelling argument that energy policy, the regulation of financial markets and institutions, and international relations as they pertain to Middle East geopolitics are so closely intertwined that it makes little sense to contemplate any of the three without contemplating the other two simultaneously. Understanding the three intertwined cycles over the past two phases does not provide a perfect guide for what we should expect, but it does provide some guide.

In this regard, it is noteworthy that world reached a turning point around 2003 precisely because of credible stories that "this time was [very] different." The United States invaded Iraq based on (fatally flawed) assumptions that it would help to modulate oil markets and Middle East geopolitics. "Peak oil" theorists prophesied that the world is running out of oil, even as Ahmed Zaki Yamani made the famous quote that "the Stone Age did not end for lack of stone, and the Oil Age will end long before the world runs out of oil."[38] In the meantime, Nobel laureate Robert Lucas was declaring at the American Economic Association that we had learned how to avoid economic depression.

Sheikh Yamani's prophetic statement is almost tautologically true: as the world begins to run out of oil really, the price of each successive barrel will rise so dramatically as to reduce demand, ensuring that the world never runs out of oil. So, while the *The Economist* magazine was correct in suggesting that some things had changed fundamentally since the first oil shock, some other things obviously had not changed, and the second phase of the cycle has mimicked the first in many respects. We have argued in this book that many of those driving forces for perpetuating and potentially amplifying the cycle are still in place. Many of the changes that have taken place, we have argued, have made the downswings of the cycle potentially catastrophic, hence suggesting that we should try to ameliorate the cycle to the extent possible.

As we put the finishing touches on the book, numerous technical solutions abound for energy and financial-market policies, using the lessons that we have learned from the Great Depression, and which convinced Lucas that we will never repeat the same mistakes of the 1930s. Most of those policies have a good chance of success, provided that all parties agree to cooperate on their implementation and avoid engaging in short-term beggar-thy-neighbor behavior. In the meantime, there is a dearth of solutions proposed to resolve geopolitical tensions in the Middle East. Indeed, with the vacuum that the U.S. invasion of Iraq has created, the ascendancy of Iran as a regional superpower has intensified geopolitical risks, spawning further turmoil in other parts of the Middle East and Central Asia, home to most of the world's proven reserves of oil and gas.

Therefore, at the risk of seeming to avoid the responsibility of making explicit and detailed policy prescriptions based on our analysis of energy and financial markets, we have to emphasize the political dimension for two reasons: The first is that Middle-East geopolitics, which require a concerted political efforts by most nations to avoid escalation of violence and instability, are umbilically connected to those two markets. The second is that even purely technical solutions to energy, money, and capital markets require a high degree of coordination to avoid systemic failure. Unfortunately, the era that made Bretton Woods, the Plaza and Louvre Accords, and Bretton Woods II possible seems to have run its course. Technical solutions by their very nature will involve asymmetric interregional and intertemporal distribution of gains and losses. We hope that this book has provided an understanding of the interconnectedness of risk factors to facilitate an equitable and sustainable bargain.

Notes

Chapter 1

1 Paul Krugman wrote in the *New York Times* on January 4, 2009, implicitly reprimanding Robert Lucas for saying in his 2003 presidential address to the American Economic Association that the "central problem of depression-prevention has been solved, for all practical purposes, and has in fact been solved for many decades."

2 "The Doomsayers Who Got It Right: More Bad News in Store for 2009? Last Year's Cassandras Are Still Gloomy," *Wall Street Journal,* January 2, 2009.

3 Department of State, *Bulletin* 70, no. 1806, 14 February 1974, p. 109 – cited in Spiro (1999, p. 26).

4 Testimony of the Chief Reservoir Engineer of Socal before the Church Committee, cited in Achnacarry, P. "The Petroleum Crisis, Saudi Arabia and U.S. Foreign Policy," *Energy Information Service* 3, 14 April 1981, p. 3, suggests that technical problems in the Shedgum section of the Ghawar field was a significant cause of supply disruptions.

5 Bronson (2006).

6 Hotelling (1931, pp. 171–200).

7 Amuzegar (2001, p. 49).

8 Slater and Phillips (2007, p. C.1).

9 Spiro (1999, pp. 1–19).

10 Lawrence (2005).

11 Clark (2005).

12 Amuzegar (2001).

13 This is a standard component of the "resource curse", see Gylfason (2001).

14 Ebrahim-Zadeh (2003, pp. 50–1); Sachs and Warner (2001).

15 Karl (1997); Chaudhry (1997).

16 Auty (1993).

17 Humphreys, Sachs, and Stiglitz (2007).

18 Humphreys, Sachs, and Stiglitz (2007, p. 15).

19 Al-Ahram Center for Political and Strategic Studies (2007, p. 113).

20 Phillips (2006).

21 Pollack (2004).

22 Eichengreen (2008, Chapter 2).

23 Treasury Secretary O'Neal was sacked shortly after stating in public that supporting a strong Dollar was not necessarily the administration's policy.

24 Minsky (2008) and Kindleberger and Aliber (2005).

25 El-Gamal and Jaffe (2008).
26 Karmin (2008, p. 100).

Chapter 2

1 Yergin (1993) remains the best resource on the history of oil.
2 Between 1960 and 1970, free world oil demand had grown by 21 million barrels per day. In the period from 1957 to 1963, surplus capacity in the United States (prorated by the state commissions) had totaled 4 million barrels a day. By 1970, at best a million barrels a day remained. By March 1971, prorating ended and United States oil imports began to soar to 6 million barrels a day in 1973, up from just over 2 million in the late 1960s. See Yergin (1993, p. 567).
3 Ibid., p. 586.
4 Trying to defend OPEC's target price of $34 per barrel, Saudi Arabia paid an extremely high price, as its sales dropped from 10 million b/d in 1980 to 2.3 million b/d in 1984. By 1983, OPEC was forced to cut its price to $29 a barrel – amid rising production from the North Sea and poor demand as the world remained in recession.
5 Amuzegar (2001) and Sachs et al.
6 Veblen (2001).
7 Ibn Khaldun (2004).
8 Coll (2004).
9 Eichengreen (2008).
10 This possibility was explained clearly by John Stuart Mill and highlighted by Frederich von Hayek in his critique of Keynesianism, cf. Hayek (1995). We shall return to this point in Chapters 7 and 8, especially in light of the currently renewed declarations that "we're all Keynesian now."
11 By June 1985, Saudi exports to the United States had dropped to a mere 26,000 b/d, as refiners avoided high official priced oil.
12 A very useful and detailed chronology of oil-price related events is available at http://www.eia.doe.gov/emeu/cabs/AOMC/Overview.html.
13 OPEC *Annual Statistics Bulletin*, available at http://www.opec.org, provides quota figures, and actual production figures are available at http://www.eia.doe.gov/emeu/international/oilproduction.html, accessed August 28, 2009. See also Dahl (2004, Table 6-2, pp. 149–150).
14 Moore (2004).
15 Citation here.
16 For example, the percentage of the population under the age of 15 in 2004 was 30.4% in Algeria, 33.9% in Egypt, 37.6% in Jordan, 24.5% in Kuwait, 29.1% in Lebanon, 31.5% in Morocco, 37.8% in Saudi Arabia, and 38.4% in Syria. Those ratios are not expected to decline significantly by 2015. http://hdr.undp.org/hdr2006/statistics/indicators/44.html, accessed on July 3, 2007.
17 Moreover, ACPSS identified "poverty and marginalization" of educated Egyptian youth as a "time bomb," cf. Al-Ahram Center for Political and Strategic Studies (2006a, pp. 345–58).
18 On August 19, 1967, Law 97 was passed, giving INOC the rights to develop the massive Rumaila field. Progress in this regard began in 1968, when the Soviet Union agreed to provide $140 million in technical assistance toward the development of Iraq's national oil industry.
19 In the late 1980s, OPEC countries planned capacity expansions from 27.6 million b/d in 1990 to 32.95 million b/d by 1995. However, capacity had reached only 29 million b/d by early 1997. Cf. O'Sullivan (2003). Sanctions prevented Iran, Libya,

and Iraq, in particular, from achieving their production targets. Iran's production dropped significantly from its prerevolution level of 7 million b/d. Sanctions, corruption, and oil-field mismanagement have cut Iran's capacity to approximately 4 million b/d. Similarly, Libya's oil-output capacity has never recovered to its 1970 peak of 4 million b/d in 1970, and Iraq's production has never returned to its peak before Saddam Hussein came to power in 1979.

20 As a group, the current members of OPEC have seen their sustainable capacity fall from over 39 million b/d in 1979 to roughly 32 million b/d.

21 Simmons (2006).

22 A recent study of 80 firms over the years 2002–4 reported that, on average, government-owned NOCs that sold petroleum products at subsidized prices suffered 35% efficiency losses relative to comparable privately held firms, cf. Hartley and Medlock (2006).

23 During the 1985 oil price collapse, OPEC was estimated to possess approximately 15 million b/d of excess capacity, equal to 25 percent of world oil demand at the time, with sixty percent of that spare capacity held in Saudi Arabia. On the eve of Iraq's invasion of Kuwait, OPEC's spare capacity began to decrease in the late 1980s, reaching 5.5 million b/d, roughly 8 percent of global demand at the time.

24 Tripp (2000, p. 214). See also Pollack (2004).

25 Foreign currency reserves fell from $30 billion in 1980 to $3 billion in 1983. In the same year, 1983, Iraq's debt had reached $25 billion (ibid., p. 235). More accurate data on Iraq's economy and finances under Ba'thist rule are not available, because they were treated as state secrets, (ibid. p. 214).

26 Frieden (2006, Chapters 16–18).

27 Quoted by IMF staff in a section entitled "Debt and Transition (1981–1989)" at http://www.imf.org/external/np/exr/center/mm/eng/mm_dt_01.htm, accessed on July 4, 2007.

Chapter 3

1 For instance, oil demand outside the Soviet bloc grew by 21 million barrels a day (b/d) between 1960 and 1970. Similarly, global oil demand grew by 12 million b/d between 1996 and 2006, cf. Yergin (1993).

2 In the earlier episode, the United States surplus capacity of 4 million b/d in the 1960s had virtually vanished by 1973, and OPEC's spare capacity was cut in half – from 3-to-4 million b/d to 1.5 million b/d. OPEC spare capacity has returned close to 1.5 million b/d, representing less than 2 percent of total world demand.

3 Venezuelan production rose from 2.6 million b/d in 1990 to 3.5 million b/d in 1997 and was slated to reach 7 million b/d by 2010.

4 Bird, David, "Saudis Not About to Concede Any Markets," October 16, 1997, Dow Jones & Co.; "Saudis Subdue Doubters by Plowing Ahead with Crude Production," *The Oil Daily*, January 8, 1998. Also, see discussion on this subject in Rapporteur's Report, Harvard University Oil and Security Executive Session, May 14. 2003, Environment and Natural Resources Program, Belfer Center for Science and International Affairs.

5 For data, see the PIW/OMI database at www.energyintel.com.

6 The Royal Institute of International Affairs. 1996. "Northeast Asian Energy in a Global Context," p. 11. London.

7 Asian oil demand, which had increased 4.5 percent during 1996-7, fell by 1.9 percent during 1997–8 – from 18.53 million b/d to 18.18 million b/d.

8 PIW March 30, 1998, Vol. 37, No. 13, page 1.

9 PIW September 14, 1998, Vol. 37, No. 37, page 1.
10 See "OPEC Adds Micro-Control to Tight Supply Strategy," *Petroleum Intelligence Weekly* (April 3, 2000, p. 1).
11 *Oil Daily*, November 30, 2004, "OPEC Talks Dollar, Market Ahead of Meeting."
12 Slater and Phillips (2007, p. C.1).
13 Gately and Huntington (2002), Gately (2002, 2004).
14 "Saudis Call for Global Oil Price Summit," *International Oil Daily*, June 10, 2008
15 As stated by U.S. Secretary of Energy Samuel W. Bodman at the Jeddah summit. Worth, R. and J. Mouawad, "Agreements are Elusive at Oil Talks in Saudi Arabia," *New York Times*, June 23, 2008.
16 Authors' interview with regional Middle-East leaders.
17 Wrote Al-Obaid in late 2006, "If Iran responds to UN-imposed sanctions by cutting its oil exports – which its foreign minister implicitly threatened to do this month when he said that the Ôfirst consequences of these sanctions would be an increase in the price of oil to around $200 per barrel' – the impact won't be as severe as many think. In fact, the Kingdom has largely succeeded in achieving this goal (to be able to replace Iranian exports)." See http://www.Saudi -us-relations.org. Later, Al-Obaid wrote in a controversial November 29, 2006, *Washington Post* op ed: "(King) Abdullah may decide to strangle Iranian funding of the militias through oil policy. If Saudi Arabia boosted production and cut the price of oil in half, the kingdom could still finance its current spending. But it would be devastating to Iran, which is facing economic difficulties even with today's high prices. The result would be to limit Tehran's ability to continue funneling hundreds of millions each year to Shiite militias in Iraq and elsewhere."
18 Dahl (2004).
19 It should be noted that there are several, not entirely consistent, estimates of oil reserves. The estimates used here are from World Oil. The *Oil and Gas Journal* estimates include some 174.8 billion barrels of bitumen from Alberta's oil sands. Including those reserves puts Canada in second place after Saudi Arabia. The IEA's estimates put Russia in second place with 14.3% of the world's oil reserves.
20 Crystal (1995).
21 Jaffe, Victor, and Hayes (2006).
22 MEED, August 1995.
23 *International Oil Daily*, March 14, 2007, "Qatar Finding Reservoir Concerns in Giant North Field."
24 *Petroleum Economist*, "World Gas: Iran – The Struggle to Market," May 1, 2007.
25 "Iran Asks: Why Export Gas?" *World Gas Intelligence*, September 7, 2005.
26 "Iran Accuses Qatar of Overproducing Gas," *Energy Compass*, Friday, April 30, 2004, available at www.energyintel.com
27 Baker Institute Report, available at http://bakerinstitute.org/Pubs/report_22.pdf.
28 *Petroleum Intelligence Weekly*, "Gas OPEC May Have Real Clout After All" Monday August 6, 2007.
29 For discussion of the Gulf Arab pricing policies to keep pricing artificially low, see F. Gregory Gause, "Iraq's Decision to Go to War," *Middle East Journal*, Vol. 56, No. 1, Winter 2002 and Freedman and Karsh (1993) as well as the *Washington Post*, January 15, 1991, which described Iraq's dissatisfaction with the Gulf Arab policy of keeping oil prices low. Also, Quandt (1981).
30 Coll (2004).
31 Al-Azdi, Abu-Jandal, *Osama bin Laden: Renewer of History and Conquerer of the Americans* (in Arabic), Minbar Al-Tawhid wa Al-Jihad (electronic), retrieved at

http://www.tawhed.ws/a?i=9 accessed on August 16, 2007. See also Al-Ahram Center for Political and Strategic Studies (2006a, pp. 243–4).

32 Al-Ahram Center for Political and Strategic Studies (2006a, p. 254).

33 Ibid., p. 242.

34 Lawrence (2005, p. 272).

35 Daly, J. "Saudi Oil Facilities: Al-Qa'ida's Next Target?" *Terrorism Monitor*, Middle East Institute 4(4), February 2006 as published on http://www.Saudi -us-relations.org/articles/2006/ioi/060224-daly-Saudi -target.html.

36 http://anonymouse.org/cgi-bin/anon-www.cgi/http:tawhed.ws/r?i=4364.

37 Retrieved electronically at http://www.islamonline.net/servlet/Satellite?pagename=IslamOnline-Arabic-Ask_Scholar/FatwaA/FatwaA&cid=1122528617906 accessed on August 16, 2007.

38 http://www.islamonline.net posted nearly 60 solicited fatwas on the issue of boycotting Western products, and numerous other articles on the subject, including the ones discussed here.

39 Pulizzi, Henry, "Bush Plays Down Tensions with Russia," *Wall Street Journal*, June 1, 2007.

40 Al-Ahram Center for Political and Strategic Studies (2006a, pp. 19–24).

41 ACPSS (2006a).

42 Bookstaber (2007).

43 International Monetary Fund (2008).

Chapter 4

1 El-Erian (2008, p. 22).

2 Bank for International Settlements Triennial Central Bank Survey, December 2007, Foreign Exchange and Derivatives Market Activity in 2007, available at: http://www.bis.org/publ/rpfxf07t.pdf, Table C.5, p. 21.

3 Bookstaber (2007, pp. 10–22).

4 Galbraith, John Kenneth, *Atlantic Monthly*, January 1987, available at http://www.theatlantic.com/doc/198701/galbraith.

5 Soros (2008).

6 Morris (2008, p. 51).

7 Kodres and Pristsker (2002), Allen and Gale (2000), and Dornbush, Park, and Glaessens (2000).

8 Johnson (2007, p. 57).

9 International Monetary Fund (2008).

10 Weisman, S. "Sovereign Wealth Funds Resist IMF Attempt to Draft Code of Conduct," *International Herald Tribune*, February 9, 2008.

11 El-Erian (2008, pp. 91–2).

12 For a survey, see Dungey, Fry, Gonzalez-Hermosillo, and Martin (2008).

13 Bae, Karolyi, and Stulz (2003).

14 Chan-Lau, Mathieson, and Yao (2004).

15 This analysis was conducted by Ibrahim Ergen, whose research assistance is greatly appreciated, using the framework of Poon, Rockinger, and Tawn (2004, pp. 581–610). We generalized the Poon et. al. methodology by considering extreme comovement between one index and portfolios of two other indices. Other approaches that focus on simultaneous comovements in multiple indices are being investigated by more than one research team, but no results were available at the time of writing.

16 In particular, following Poon et al., op. cit., we use the measures

$$\chi = \lim_{q \uparrow 1} P(q) = \lim_{q \uparrow 1} \frac{\Pr\{F(T) > q, F(S) > q\}}{\Pr\{F(S) > q\}}$$

$$\bar{\chi} = \lim_{s \uparrow \infty} \frac{2 \log \Pr\{S > s\}}{\log \Pr\{S > s, T > s\}} - 1$$

If the estimated $\chi = 0$, then we conclude that the two series are asymptotically independent, as $q \uparrow \infty$. In other words, we would conclude that extremely large losses in one series are not generally accompanied by extremely large losses in the other. If we fail to reject that $\chi = 0$, then we measure the amount of dependence by $\bar{\chi}$. Otherwise, if we fail to reject that $\bar{\chi} = 1$, then we conclude that $\chi > 0$ and the two series are asymptotically dependent, meaning that extreme losses in one series, no matter how large, are very likely to be accompanied by equally extremely large losses in the other. The type and degree of asymptotic extreme dependence in this case is measured by the estimated value of χ.

In this regard, the estimates χ and $\bar{\chi}$ and their estimated standard errors are obtained by noting that the minimum of two standard Frechet random variables is itself unit Frechet (this is the driving insight behind the approach of Poon et al.), yielding the following estimates:

$$\hat{\bar{\chi}} = \frac{2}{n_u} \left(\sum_{i=1}^{n_u} \log(z_{(i)}/u) \right) - 1; \quad \text{var}(\hat{\bar{\chi}}) = (\hat{\bar{\chi}} + 1)^2 / n_u$$

$$\hat{\chi} = \frac{u n_u}{n}; \quad \text{var}(\hat{\chi}) = \frac{u^2 n_u (n - n_u)}{n^3}$$

The suggested procedure of Poon et al. is first to estimate $\bar{\chi}$ and to test if it is equal to 1. If we reject that $\bar{\chi} = 1$, then we essentially accept that $\chi = 0$ and use the estimated $\bar{\chi}$ to measure extremal (but nonasymptotic) dependence. Otherwise, if we fail to reject that $\bar{\chi} = 1$, then we estimate $\chi > 0$ as our measure of asymptotic extreme dependence.

17 In particular, we also estimate a model for the returns to follow an AR(1) process with GARCH(1,1) conditional variance process:

$$r_t = \beta_1 + \beta_2 r_{t-1} + \sigma_t Z_t, \quad \text{with} \quad Z_t \overset{i.i.d.}{\sim} N(0,1), \quad \text{and}$$

$$\sigma_t^2 = \gamma + \delta U_{t-1}^2 + \lambda \sigma_{t-1}^2.$$

18 Lecture by chief IEA economist Fatih Birol delivered at the Offshore Technology Conference, Houston, May 6, 2008, available at http://www.otcnet.org/2008 under "Technical Session Tuesday morning."

19 Currently, most natural gas is transported by pipeline, but increasingly, more natural gas is being carried worldwide in the form of liquefied natural gas (LNG), a commodity where natural gas is refrigerated into liquid form, allowing easier transport by vessels across oceans. Between 1990 and 2000, LNG liquefaction export capacity worldwide increased by 85 percent and is projected to rise by another 144 percent to 300 million tons by 2012, cf. Jensen (2003, p. 9).

20 See Hartley and Medlock (2006) for more detail.

21 This globalizations phenomenon is discussed broadly in Jaffe, Victor, and Hayes (2006).

22 The two countries with the largest gas reserves, Russia and Iran, have roughly 45 percent of world natural gas reserves while the two countries with the largest oil reserves, Saudi Arabia and Iraq, have just 36 percent of world oil reserves. The top five-country concentration ratio for the two fuels is roughly the same at 62 percent.

23 "Russia and Qatar Discuss LNG Swaps," *International Oil Daily*, July 27, 2007.

24 "Qatar, Russia Mull Mega-Swap," *Energy Compass*, July 27, 2007; "Russia, Algeria Split," *World Gas Intelligence*, December 12, 2007; "Gazprom, Sonatrach Eye Asset Swaps," *World Gas Intelligence*, January 24, 2007.

25 Judy Dempsey, "Gazprom and Eni Plan Gas Pipeline in Libya," *New York Times*, April 9, 2008; "Gazprom Taps Nigeria for Gas Openings," *International Oil Daily*, January 8, 2008.

26 Fawzi, Aloulou, "Qatar LNG 2010 and the UD Gas Market: Setting a New Global Cost Benchmark", US Department of Energy, Energy Information Administration, Washington, DC, July 2004.

27 Fawzi, ibid.

28 Jaffe and Soligo (2006).

29 Ibid.

30 Iraq has a vast potential; Iraq holds 110 trillion cubic feet (Tcf) of proven natural gas reserves, as well as approximately 160 Tcf in probable reserves.

31 Saudi Arabia has proven natural gas reserves estimated at 237 Tcf. Approximately 60 percent of Saudi Arabia's proven natural gas reserves consist of associated gas, mainly from the onshore Ghawar field and the offshore Safaniya and Zuluf fields.

32 The U.S. Geological Survey has suggested, in agreement with Aramco's statement, that Saudi Arabia has at least 530 Tcf of undiscovered reserves of nonassociated gas.

33 The Rubʿ Al-Khali alone is believed to contain natural gas reserves as high as 300 Tcf. C.f. "Saudi Arabia Country Analysis Brief," August 2005, Energy Intelligence Agency, U.S. Department of Energy.

34 The Dorra field is estimated to hold recoverable reserves of between 7 and 13 Tcf of gas and is located offshore near the Khafji oil field in the Neutral Zone.

35 He said that "it is estimated that by the end of 2010–2015, gas exports could reach 248 bncm/y, both as LNG and through pipelines." Cf. "World Gas: Iran – The Struggle to Market," *Petroleum Economist*, May 1, 2007.

36 Dan Brumberg, BIPP NOC study.

37 "Iran Asks: Why Export Gas?" *World Gas Intelligence*, September 7, 2005.

38 Brumberg, Elass, Jaffe, and Medlock (2008).

39 Parasiliti (2001).

40 Kechichian (1999, pp. 232–53).

41 Zahlan (2001).

42 John Partin, History and Research Office, USSOCCOM, Special Operation Forces in Operation Earnest Will, Prime Chance I, April 1998, pp. 5–7; also, Al-Alkim (2001).

43 O'Sullivan (2003, p. 3).

44 Earlier sanctions included an import ban on Iran and the freezing of $12 billion in Iranian assets in November 1979 following the Iranian seizure of the U.S. embassy in Tehran. A month later in that same year, Iraq and Libya were put on the State Department's list of state sponsors of terrorism and the U.S. issued a ban of exports of dual-use technologies to the two countries.

45 For a survey of the debilitated state of Iraq's oil industry ahead of the U.S. invasion, see the oil supplement to Guiding Principles for a Post-War Iraq published by the James A. Baker III Institute for Public Policy, www.bakerinstitute.org.

46 O'Sullivan (2003) provides a good survey of the effects of various sanctions. In the late 1980s, OPEC had planned capacity expansions to a total of 32.95 million barrels

a day targeted for 1995. However, by early 1997, OPEC capacity had reached only 29 million barrels a day. Iran, Libya and Iraq had all failed to achieve production targets because of international sanctions policy. Iran had aimed to reach 4 million b/d, Libya 1.6 million b/d, and Iraq 4.5in million barrels a day, but were constrained at 3.8 million b/d, 1.4 million b/d, and 1.2 million b/d, respectively. See "Political, Economic, Social, Cultural, and Religious Trends in the Middle East and the Gulf and Their Impact on Energy Supply, Security and Pricing," Baker Institute seminar report available at http://www.rice.edu/energy/publications/docs/TrendsinMiddleEast_FactorsAffectSupplyOilMiddleEast.pdf.

47 Jaffe (2004).
48 Paradoxically, the same mantra of "independence from Middle-East oil" resonated also in the rhetoric of President Obama, who had opposed the invasion of Iraq.
49 "Defeating the Oil Weapon," 2002, available at http:agriculture.senate.govHearingsOilWeapon.pdf
50 Cohen, A. "Energy Security at Risk," May 23, 2003, available in the press room at www.heritage.orgpresscommentaryed052703a.cfm
51 For discussion of the Gulf Arab pricing policies to keep pricing artificially low, see F. Gregory Gause, "Iraq's Decision to Go to War" *Middle East Journal*, Winter 2002 (Volume 56, No. 1) and Freedman and Karsh (1993) as well as the *Washington Post*, January 15, 1991, which described Iraq's dissatisfaction with the Gulf Arab policy of keeping oil prices low. Also, Quandt (1981).
52 Report is available at http://people-press.org/.
53 A copy of the report is available at www.bakerinstitute.org.
54 Schmitt, E. "After effects of the Pullout: US to Withdraw All Combat Units from Saudi Arabia," *New York Times*, April 30, 2003, p. 1; O'Neill, S., J. Bradley, and D. Rennie, "Pullout May Make Life Easier for Saudi Regime," *The Telegraph*, May 1, 2003.
55 Krepinevich, A. "How to Win in Iraq," *Foreign Affairs*, vol. 84, no. 5, September/October 2005, pp. 87–104.
56 Kessler, G. "Saudi s Tie al Qa'ida to Attacks," *Washington Post*, May 14, 2003, p 1.
57 Discussed on the online service Gulf 2000 at Columbia University. Several publications, including the U.K.'s Sunday newspaper, the *Observer* and the on-line intelligence group, Stratfor.com, also reported that anti-government demonstrations occurred across the Kingdom in the Spring and summer of 2002 and into 2003.
58 Bush State of the Union address, www.whitehouse.gov/news/releases/2002/01/20020129-11.html
59 Hoge, W. and E. Sciolino, "Security Council Adds Sanctions against Iran," *New York Times*, March 4, 2008.
60 CNN, "Iran Warns U.S. on Oil Shipments," June 4, 2006, http:www.cnn.com2006WORLDmeast0604us.Iran.
61 See "Saudi Aramco: National Flagship with International Responsibilities," at http:www.rice.eduenergy.
62 Wright, R. "Iranian Boats May Not Have Made Radio Threat, Pentagon Says," *Washington Post*, January 11, 2008.

Chapter 5

1 Karmin (2008, p. 100).
2 The reference of choice, which most IMF recruits were advised to study, was Corden (1977).
3 Karmin (2008, p. 123).

4 Ibid., p. 125.
5 See Taylor (1999).
6 Dooley, Folkerts-Landau and Garber (2003, 2004).
7 Roubini and Setser (2005).
8 El-Erian (2008, p. 110).
9 Roubini and Setser (2005).
10 http://news.bbc.co.uk/2/hi/business/7288940.stm
11 See Andersen and Gruen (1995, pp. 279–319).
12 Fischer (1993, pp. 485–512).
13 Kindleberger and Aliber (2005, p. 64).
14 Soros (2008, pp. 81–2).
15 Soros (2008, pp. 92–3).
16 Minsky (2008).
17 Shiller (2000).
18 Minsky (1982, pp. 25–9).
19 Minsky (2008, pp. 219–45).
20 " 'Greenspan Put' May Be Encouraging Complacency," *Financial Times*, December 8, 2000.
21 Goldman Sachs analyst Arjun N. Murti first argued that oil prices would top $100 a barrel in March 2008 and then again in May when he issued a report that predicted that oil prices would top $200 and stay above $100 into 2011 based on rising demand. His widely touted forecast joined the ranks of famed oil shares raider T. Boone Pickens and investment advisor Matthew Simmons, who were all predicting an extended bull market in oil. Louise Story, "An Oracle of Oil Predicts $200-a-barrel Crude: *New York Times*, May 21, 2008 (www.nytimes.com/2008/05/21/business/21oil.html).
22 There was a surge in publications on the "peak oil" hypothesis circa 2004–5, as prices began to soar. See, for example, Deffeyes (2004), Roberts (2004), and Simmons (2005).
23 Deffeyes (2004), Colin Campbell (1998), and others are on the record as predicting world oil production would peak as early as 2005. World oil production rates continue to rise.
24 Campbell and Laherrere (1998). Campbell, like other Peak Oil theorists, argued that 90 percent of existing oil production was coming from fields discovered more than 20 years ago, with 70 percent coming from fields over 30 years old, leading the world to use up "its geological endowment of oil at a prodigious rate" as discovery rates for new fields fail to keep pace with soaring demand.
25 With a spin that was not just limited to geologic considerations but also geopolitical and economic factors, it became fashionable within the global oil industry to assert that world oil supply would plateau at 100 million barrels a day (b/d) while demand would rage far above this level based on miraculous and unrestrainable economic growth in Asia and the developing world. This magical 100 million b/d limit, repeated by oil company chairmen in public fora and in various publications including the U.S. National Petroleum Council's report "Facing the Hard Truths about Energy," sent oil market traders and commentators alike into a frenzy that pressed the price of oil ever higher. Cf. "Perspective: The 100 Million Barrel World," *Energy Compass*, December 21, 2007, Energy Intelligence Group, New York.
26 Simon (1995, p. 165).
27 Akins (1972).
28 Klare (2002) noted: "No highly industrialized society can survive at present without substantial supplies of oil, and so any significant threat to the continued availability of

this resource will prove a cause of crisis, and, in extreme cases, provoke the use of military force."

29 El-Hefnawy, N. "The Impending Oil Shock," *Survival*, June 2008.

30 El-Gamal and Jaffe (2008).

31 This was true especially in key oil commodities such as heavy fuel oil and naphtha whose use was less tied to inventory demand linked to stockpiling ahead of the Beijing Olympics. Chinese fuel oil demand in the first half of 2008 was 13.5 percent lower than the year earlier, according to estimates. China's naphtha imports fell 75 percent in the first five months of 2008. *Oil Daily*, August 1, 2008, and July 3, 2008. For the months ahead of the Beijing Olympics, Chinese oil demand was averaging 6.7 percent growth year on year, but slipped to little more than 167,000 b/d of oil more in November 2008 versus a year earlier or about 2 percent based on weakening demand for Chinese export products and the closing of more than 70,000 Chinese export-oriented factories. See "Global Oil Demand: Everybody Hurts," *Oil Market Intelligence*, December 2008.

32 As the recession took hold in the U.S., oil demand had fallen more than 9 percent to 18.66 million b/d in November 2008, down 1.87 million b/d from November 2007. With 533,000 American jobs lost in November 2008 alone (the highest level since the 1973 oil crisis), U.S. oil demand was forecast to fall by at least a further 2 percent or more in 2009.

Chapter 6

1 Eichengreen (2004, pp. 7–11).

2 Hiskett (1932).

3 Yergin (1993, pp. 493–5).

4 Block (1977).

5 Also, Clark (2005, p. 19).

6 Eichengreen (2004, pp. 13–20).

7 Kissinger (1982, pp. 915–6).

8 Ole Gunnar Austvik, "Oil Prices and the Dollar Dilemma," *OPEC Review*, No. 4, December 1987.

9 El-Beblawi (1980, pp. 305–311).

10 Bronson (2006).

11 Kissinger (1999, p. 667). Kissinger added, "A century earlier, the consuming nations would have responded by seizing the oil fields. From time to time, as will be seen, the United States threatened to do just that but never received any support from other industrialized democracies."

12 Ibid., p. 677.

13 Ibid.

14 Bronson (2006, pp. 125–32).

15 Ibid., p. 126.

16 Salaman (2004).

17 William Dowell, "Saddam Turns His Back on Greenbacks," *Time*, November 13, 2000.

18 Charles Recknagel, "Baghdad Moves to Euro," Radio Free Europe, November 1, 2000.

19 Hill, P. "OPEC Faces Dollar Headaches; Iran, Venezuela Seek Action," *Washington Times*, November 17, 2007, quoting Saudi Foreign Minister Prince Saud al-Faisal.

20 "OPEC to Study the Effect of Weak U.S. Dollar on Oil Prices," Associated Press, November 18, 2007.

21 "As Financing Difficulties Mount, Iran Attempts to Circumvent U.S. Pressure," *Middle East Economic Survey*, Vol. LI, No. 6, February 11, 2008.
22 "Iran Uses Euro Open Credit Lines to Buy Fuel-Source," Reuters, January 15, 2008.
23 "Iran Stops Conducting Oil Transactions in U.S. Dollars," Associated Press, April 30, 2008.
24 Somini Sengupta and Heather Timmons, "Visit by Iranian Leader Offers Bonus for India," *International Herald Tribune*, April 30, 2008, p. 5.
25 Williams, P. "OPEC Chief Muses about Gradually Switching Oil Pricing to Euros," *Middle East Economic Digest*, February 8, 2008.
26 "Saudi Arabia Rules Out Oil Pricing in Euros," *Middle East Economic Survey*, Vol LI, No. 9, March 3, 2008.
27 Higgins, Klitgaard, and Lerman (2006).
28 These estimates do not include Middle-East monies channeled to the U.S. through third party countries such as Britain.
29 Dooley, Folkerts-Landau, and Garber (2004b, p. 5).
30 Dooley, Folkerts-Landau, and Garber (2004c, 2004b).
31 Ibid.
32 Eichengreen (2004).
33 Ibid.
34 Summers (2004).
35 Barro and Sal-i-Martin (1992).
36 Neuhaus (2006).
37 See Durlauf and Quah (1999) for a survey of early studies in this direction.
38 Fischer (2003).
39 UNDP (2005).
40 For instance, Saudi Arabia's real per capita GDP was approximately double that of Thailand, and yet both countries had identical values of the Human Development Index; ibid., p. 24.
41 Cooper (2008).
42 Eichengreen (2004).
43 UNDP (2005, p. 116).
44 Ibid., p. 119.
45 Ibid., p. 121.
46 Authors' interviews: Amy's source.
47 Keith Johnson posting at http://blogs.wsj.com/environmentalcapital/2008/12/01/team-obama-new-national-security-adviser-jim-jones-puts-energy-first/.
48 Report available at http://www.humanrightsfirst.info/pdf/080311-cah-investing-in-tragedy-report.pdf, referenced in *Business Week* article by M. Herbst, "Oil for China, Guns for Darfur," March 14, 2008.
49 Douglas, Nelson, and Schwartz (2006).
50 Lei and Xuejun (2007).
51 Phillips (2006).
52 Jones (2008).
53 Kindleberger (1993), Eichengreen (2008, p. 7).
54 Ibid.
55 Ibid, Chapter 2.
56 Interview with Witteveen cited by Spiro (1999, p. 98).
57 Spiro (1999, p. 100).
58 El-Beblawi (1980).

59 El-Erian (2008, p. 110).

Chapter 7

1 Chari, Christiano, and Kehoe (2008).
2 Minsky (2008, p. 5).
3 Amuzegar (2001, p. 49).
4 Cummins, C. "Dubai Faces Hit as Property Boom Fades," *Wall Street Journal*, November 13, 2008.
5 For a thorough review of the historical, legal, and economic content of Islamic finance, see El-Gamal (2006).
6 Ibid.
7 A hedge-fund managers marketing an "Islamic hedge fund" in the Middle East told one of the authors that he saw it as his duty to help "relieve the liquidity constipation" in the region.
8 See for instance Sachs and Warner (2001) and the references therein.
9 Some of the presentations at the conference, organized by Energy Intelligence, are available at the conference website: http://www.energyintel.com/om/program.asp?Year=2008.
10 For such results, see, for instance, Ely and Välimäki (2002) and the references therein.
11 Spiro (1999, pp. 98–102).
12 Jaffe (2004).
13 Medlock and Soligo (2001).
14 Medlock and Soligo (2002).
15 Cambridge Energy Research Associates (2006).
16 International Energy Agency (2008).
17 Ibid., p. 98.
18 U.S. Department of Energy Forecast of 2006, Energy Information Administration, http://tonto.eia.doe.gov.
19 Medlock, K. and A. Jaffe, U.S. Energy Policy and Transportation, Baker Institute Working Paper Series, The Global Energy Market: Comprehensive Strategies to Meet Geopolitical and Financial Risks –The G8, Energy Security and Global Climate Issues, available at www.rice.edu/energy
20 See Bohi and Toman (1996, pp. 14–5 and 44–5).
21 International Energy Agency (2006).
22 "Big Oil has a problem," stated the *Wall Street Journal* in a 2007 article, "Big Oil's Latest Roadblock: Governments Reduce Access to Aid National Champions amid Scramble for Supply," *Wall Street Journal*, September 24, 2007, p. C10.
23 A. Jaffe and R. Soligo, The International Oil Companies, Baker Institute Working Paper Series, The Role of National Oil Companies on International Energy Markets, available at www.rice.edu/energy.
24 A. Jaffe and R. Soligo, "Militarization of Energy – Geopolitical Threats to the Global Energy System," Baker Institute Working Paper Series, The Global Energy Market: Comprehensive Strategies to Meet Geopolitical and Financial Risks, May 2008; online at www.rice.edu/energy/publications.
25 Ibid.
26 P. Hartley, S. Eller and K. Medlock, "Empirical Evidence on the Operational Efficiency of National Oil Companies," Baker Institute Working Paper Series, The Changing Role of National Oil Companies in International Energy Markets, Available at www.rice.edu/energy.
27 A recent report of CIBC World Markets calculated that "soaring rates of consumption

in Russia, in Mexico and in member states of the Organization of Petroleum Exporting Counties would reduce crude oil exports by as much as 2.5 million barrels a day by the end of the decade." Krause, C. "Oil-Rich Nations Use More Energy, Cutting Exports," *New York Times*, December 9, 2007.

28 See case study on Indonesia in the Baker Institute study The Emerging Role of National Oil Companies on International Energy Markets, available at www.rice.edu/energy.

29 International Energy Agency (2008, p. 172).

30 Ibid., p. 159.

31 CERA (2006).

32 Report available at www.mckinsey.com/clientservices/ccsi/greenhousegas.asp

33 Pollin, Garrett-Peltier, Heintz, and Scharber (2008).

34 *Wall Street Journal*, "The Wizards of Oil: As Prices Fall, So Do the Ambitions of Vladimir, Hugo, and Mahmoud," *Wall Street Journal* Review and Outlook, December 30, 2008.

35 Osborn, A. "Russia Firm Cuts Gas to Ukraine, But EU Hit Is Cushioned," *Wall Street Journal*, January 2, 2009.

36 Hardy, R. "Migrants Demand Labor Rights in the Gulf," BBC News Channel, February 27, 2008, http://news.bbc.co.uk./1/hi/world/middle_east/7266610.stm.

37 Kenyon, P. "Economic Crisis Dampens Gulf Building Boom," http://www.npr.org/templates/story/story.php?storyId=2100740.

38 In the case of Venezuela, President Hugo Chavez in February 2008 threatened to cut off oil exports to the United States if ExxonMobil pursued its legal battle to attach Venezuelan assets in the West as collateral payment for upstream oil field stake nationalized in Venezuela by Caracas last year. Similarly, Iran said it would cut its oil exports to the West if a U.S.-led coalition imposed sanctions on it in response to its alleged plans to develop nuclear weapons. Iranian Supreme Leader Ayatollah Ali Khamenei in June 2006 warned the U.S. that Washington "should know that the slightest misbehavior on your part would endanger the entire region's energy security.... You are not capable of guaranteeing energy security in the region."

39 MacFarquhar, N. "Tide of Arab Opinion Turns to Support for Hizbullah," *New York Times*, July 8, 2006.

40 So argues Geoffrey Kemp in his monograph "U.S. and Iran: The Nuclear Dilemma: Next Steps," available at www.nixoncenter.org.

41 "Iran Warns U.S. on Oil Shipments." CNN website. June 4, 2006. http://www.cnn.com/2006/WORLD/meast/06/04us.Iran/ Also, for more details of the risks of the Iran nuclear standoff to the Straits, see Brito and Jaffe (2005).

42 Broad, W. and D. Sanger, "With Eye on Iran, Rivals Also Want Nuclear Power," *The New York Times*, April 15, 2007.

43 "Gulf Nuclear Plans Face Big Hurdles, Says IAEA," Reuters, January 28, 2008.

44 "Saudi King Says Iran Putting Region in Danger," Reuters, January 27, 2007.

45 Nasr and Tayeyh (2008).

46 Stearns, Scott, "Bush in Saudi Arabia for Nuclear Deal," May 16, 2008. Voice of America Website http://voanews.com/english/2008-05-16-voa23.cfm.

47 Greenspan, S. "Why We Keep Falling for Financial Scams," *Wall Street Journal*, January 3, 2009.

48 Krugman, P. "The Madoff Economy," *New York Times*, December 19, 2008.

49 Ibid.

50 Phillips (2006).

51 Blodget, H. "Why Wall Street Always Blows It," *Atlantic Monthly* 302(5), December 2008.

52 Smith, Suchanek, and Williams (1988).
53 Lei, Noussair, and Plott (2004).
54 Hayek (1995).
55 Ibid, pp. 247–55.
56 *Wall Street Journal*, "We're All Keynesian Now," *Wall Street Journal* Review and Outlook, January 18, 2008.
57 Hamilton (1983).
58 Federer (1996).
59 See Krugman, P. "A Return of that 70s Show," *New York Times*, June 2, 2008. Krugman was arguing at the time that this was a fundamental difference between the inflationary environment following the oil price shocks of the 1970s and the lack thereof during the oil price surge between 2003 and 2008.
60 *OECD Economic Outlook*, July 1981; Stobaugh and Yergin (1979).
61 Nordhaus (1980) found that only 11.4 percent of the increase in inflation and 10.5 percent of the increase in the unemployment rate were attributable to oil price increases. Instead, he cites other factors including economic policies of the day as responsible for the negative economic effects. Brown, Oppedahl, and Yucel (1996) further argued that an expansionary monetary policy could have mitigated some of the recessionary effects of high oil prices.
62 Yergin and Hillenbrand (1982). In this context, Bohi and Toman (1996) defined energy security as "the concept of maintaining stable supply of energy at a reasonable price in order to avoid the macroeconomic dislocations associated with unexpected disruptions in supply or increases in price." Energy policy, therefore, should aim to avoid "the loss of economic welfare that might occur as a result of a change in the price or availability of energy."
63 Gately (1984).
64 Jaffe (2004).
65 "Oil Markets Braced for a Choppy 2009," *Petroleum Intelligence Weekly*, January 5, 2009.

Chapter 8

1 China's Central Bankers have become increasingly vocal, especially before the G20 summit in London, April 2009, about the need for an alternative to Dollars. Russians have echoed the same sentiments, supporting essentially the Chinese proposal of using IMF Special Drawing Rights (SDRs) as a substitute for the Dollar as global reserve currency.
2 Gambroni and Newfarmer (2009).
3 Note, however, that anecdotal evidence also suggests that FDI protectionism remains a possibility, cf. Sauvant, K. "Watch Out for the Rise of Protectionism in FDI," *Financial Times*, March 14, 2009.
4 Minsky (2008, Part 5).
5 The term "libertarian paternalism" was coined by Sunstein and Thaler (2003) and Thaler and Sunstein (2003).
6 Akerlof and Shiller (2009) draw very telling parallels between the 1920s boom and eventual crash that contributed to the Great Depression and more recent bubbles and crashes.
7 Becker, G. and K. Murphy, "Do Not Let The 'Cure' Destroy Capitalism," *Financial Times*, March 19, 2009.
8 Deaton (2006).
9 Already, in early 2009, reports of reduced investment in fuel production capacity

suggest that the next phase of the cycle may be more extreme, cf. Crooks, E. "Threat to Oil Investment from Falling Price of Crude," *Financial Times*, January 13, 2009.

10 Chinese central bankers' proposals of creating an alternative international reserve currency through International Monetary Fund Special Drawing Rights are highly contingent upon drastic realignment of power within the International Monetary Fund as well as in the global financial system, as we shall discuss later, cf. Anderlini, J. "China Urges Switch from Dollar as Reserve Currency," *Financial Times*, March 24, 2009.

11 For instance, see Secretary Geithner's statement on regulatory overhaul of the international financial system, at http://www.house.gov/apps/list/hearing/financialsvcs_dem/geithner032609.pdf.

12 Javier Blas and Ed Crooks, "Drive on Biofuels Risks Oil Price Surge," *Financial Times*, June 5, 2007.

13 Jad Mouawad, "OPEC Blames 'Mismanaged' U.S. Economy for Soaring Oil Prices," *International Herald Tribune*, March 6, 2008.

14 For instance, see Hickman et al. (1987); Federer (1996); Mork et al. (1994); Lee et al. (1995, pp. 39–56).

15 Jaffe, A., W. Gao, and K. Medlock, "The Effects of Oil Price Volatility on Technical Change," Baker Institute working paper, 1999.

16 According to U.S. Energy Information Administration (EIA) statistics, U.S. oil demand averaged 19.2 million barrels a day (b/d) in December 2008, down 1.5 million b/d from December 2007.

17 By January 2009, China's demand was down 2.1 percent relative to the previous year.

18 High inventories have been weighing on the price of U.S. benchmark West Texas Intermediate crude oil. OECD days-forward oil cover in storage (a statistic watched closely in the oil trading community) is a full four days higher than last year and U.S. crude oil stocks rose by 50 million barrels in just four months (from October 2008 to January 2009).

19 Mork et al. (1994).

20 Yergin and Hillenbrand (1982).

21 Miyagiwa, K. and Ohno, Y. "Oil and Strategic Development of Substitute Technology," Baker Institute Working Paper Series, 2000, available at www.bakerinstitute.org.

22 Medlock and Hartley (2004).

23 President Obama has pitched creating a "green economy" as a means to U.S. economic recovery and has pledged to find a way to invest $150 billion over 10 years to develop alternative energy, which the administration claims will create 5 million new U.S. jobs, cf. "Stimulus Bill Pushes Renewable Energy" Reuters, January 16, 2009.

24 About 19 percent of all electricity generated in the United States derives from the combustion of natural gas, which is up from only about 10 percent in 1986, when natural gas prices were fully decontrolled. In fact, due largely to efficiency and environmental considerations, natural gas accounts for 90 percent of all newly installed megawatts of capacity in the United States since 1995. Nuclear power represents 20 percent of U.S. electricity supply, while renewable energy – mainly from hydroelectric sources – constitutes 8 percent of supply.

25 Although a major stock release was not activated immediately after Iraq's invasion in 1990, political coordination among IEA member countries and prolific oil producers such as Saudi Arabia, the UAE, and Venezuela and public announcements about the readiness of the IEA system all helped cap oil prices in the aftermath of Iraq's invasion of Kuwait. The United States worked to build a broad effort to replace the roughly 4

million b/d of Kuwait and Iraqi exports lost from the global oil supply system. Supplementing a request made in person by then U.S. Defense Secretary Richard Cheney to allow U.S. troops in Saudi Arabia to repel the Iraqi invasion, U.S. President George H. W. Bush sent a letter to Saudi King Fahd requesting that the kingdom increase its production to a maximum level to ensure that the impact of Iraq's invasion was ameliorated, increasing the chances of a diplomatic coalition against Iraq's government. King Fahd granted the request and Saudi Aramco began investigating how much oil was needed on the market and how quickly it could expand its output potential to meet this demand.

Bringing in international service companies to work double-man-hour, round-the-clock shifts, Saudi Aramco announced plans to boost production. It had been believed in the last 1980s that Saudi Aramco had sustainable capacity of over 8 million barrels a day, were it to demothball its shut-in fields, but instead the demothballing process showed the kingdom would have to do more work than expected to boost its output. Within three months of the official announcement that Saudi Arabia would be boosting output, its production was raised by 2 million b/d to 7.3 million b/d, c.f. "Capacity Ample to Replace Loss if Producers Move," *Petroleum Intelligence Weekly*, August 13, 1990, p. 1. Oil prices, which had hit over $40 in the immediate aftermath of Iraq's invasion of Kuwait, fell back to normal pre-invasion levels.

26 Jickling, M. and L. Cunningham, "CRS Report for Congress: Speculation and Energy Prices: Legislative Responses," June 30, 2008, Congressional Research Service Order Code RL34555.

27 Many economists continued to debate whether the spike in oil prices in the first half of 2008 was caused by market fundamentals, à la "peak oil," or speculative bubble dynamics, cf. Hamilton (2008).

28 U.S. Government Accountability Office, "Trends in Energy Derivatives Markets Raise Questions about CFTC Oversight," GAO 08-25, October 2007.

29 Benoit, B., Q. Peel, and C. Bryant, "Merkel Warns on Stimulus," *Financial Times*, March 28, 2009.

30 Spiro (1999) details in Chapters 4 and 5 how U.S. policy makers actively sabotaged the IMF's attempts to convince Saudi Arabia and Kuwait to recycle petrodollars through low-interest loans to the IMF.

31 In June 2006, then Chancellor of the Exchequer Brown spoke at a conference organized by the Muslim Council of Britain and expressed his view that London is "well placed to become a gateway for Islamic trade and finance," cf. http://news.bbc.co.uk/2/hi/business/5074068.stm.

32 First news of a Saudi Sovereign Wealth Fund broke in April 2008, cf. England, A. "Cautious Saudi Steps into Arena of Wealth Funds," *Financial Times*, April 29, 2008.

33 Chhaochharia and Laeven (2008).

34 Indeed, some private corporations, such as Devon Energy and Anadarko Petroleum were able to make substantial profits by investing in capacity expansion during the low-oil-price years of the early to mid-1990s.

35 Abba Eban famously summarized this myopia and serial amnesia in his statement that "the Arabs never miss an opportunity to miss an opportunity," cf. *The Jerusalem Post*, November 18, 2002.

36 Most recently, the United States has agreed to provide nuclear technology to the oil-rich Emirate of Abu Dhabi, ostensibly for energy-diversification purposes, but quite clearly as a way to create parity with Iranian nuclear ambitions, cf. Solomon, J. and M. Coker, "Oil-Rich Arab State Pushes Nuclear Bid with U.S. Help," *Wall Street Journal*, April 2, 2009.

37 http://www.quotationspage.com/quote/30302.html.
38 *Economist*, October 23, 2003.

Bibliography

Al-Ahram Center for Political and Strategic Studies. (2006a). *Directory of Islamist Movements Worldwide* (in Arabic) (Cairo: Ahram Center for Political and Strategic Studies).

Al-Ahram Center for Political and Strategic Studies. (2006b). *Strategic Economic Trends Report* (in Arabic) (Cairo: Ahram Center for Political and Strategic Studies).

Al-Ahram Center for Political and Strategic Studies. (2007). *Strategic Economic Trends Report* (in Arabic). (Cairo: Al-Ahram Center for Political and Strategic Studies).

Akerlof, G. and R. Shiller. (2009). *Animal Spirits: How Human Psychology Drives the Economy, and Why It Matters for Global Capitalism* (Princeton, NJ: Princeton University Press).

Akins, J. (1972). "The Oil Crisis: This Time the Wolf Is Here," *Foreign Affairs* 51:462.

Al-Alkim, H. (2001). "The Arabian Gulf at the New Millennium: Security Challenges," in Kechichian, J. (ed.) *Iran, Iraq, and the Arab Gulf States* (New York: Palgrave).

Allen, F. and D. Gale. (2000). "Financial Contagion," *Journal of Political Economy* 108(1).

Amuzegar, J. (2001). *Managing the Oil Wealth: OPEC's Windfalls and Pitfalls* (London: I.B. Tauris).

Andersen, P. and D. Gruen. (1995). "Macroeconomic Policies and Growth," in Andersen, P. J. Dwyer, and D. Gruen (eds.) *Productivity and Growth* (Sydney: Reserve Bank of Australia).

Auty, R. (1993). *Sustaining Development in Mineral Economies: The Resource Curse Thesis* (London: Routledge).

Bae, K, G. Karolyi, and R. Stulz. (2003). "A New Approach to Measuring Financial Contagion," *Review of Financial Studies* 16(3), Fall.

Barro, R. and X. Sal-i-Martin. (1992). "Convergence," *Journal of Political Economy* 100(2).

Block, F. (1977). *The Origins of International Economic Disorder: A Study of the United States International Monetary Policy from World War II to the Present* (Berkeley: University of California Press)

Bohi, D. and M. Toman (1996). *The Economics of Energy Security* (Boston, MA: Kluwer Academic Publishers).

Bookstaber, R. (2007). *A Demon of Our Own Design* (New Jersey: John Wiley & Sons).

Brito, D. and A. Jaffe. (2005). "Reducing Vulnerability of Persian Gulf Oil" in Sokolski, H. and P. Clawson (eds.) *Getting Ready for a Nuclear Ready Iran* (U.S. Army War College Strategic Studies Institute).

Bronson, R. (2006). *Thicker than Oil* (New York: Oxford University Press).

Brown, S., D. Oppedahl, and M. Yucel. (1996). "Oil Prices and Aggregate Economic Activity: A Study of Eight OECD Countries," Working Paper 96-13, Federal Reserve

Bank of Dallas, October.

Brumberg, D., J. Elass, A. Jaffe, and K. Medlock. (2008). "Iran, Energy and Geopolitics," Baker Institute for Public Policy Working Paper Series: The Global Energy Market: Comprehensive Strategies to Meet Geopolitical and Financial Risks, available at www.rice.edu/energy/publications/WorkingPapers/globalenergymkt.html, May, accessed on August 28, 2009.

Cambridge Energy Research Associates. (2006). *Dawn of a New Age: Global Energy Scenarios for Strategic Decision Making* (Cambridge, MA: CERA).

Campbell, C. and J. Laherrere. (1998) "The End of Cheap Oil," *Scientific American*, March.

Chan-Lau, J., D. Mathieson, and J. Yao. (2004). "Extreme Contagion in Equity Markets," *IMF Staff Papers* 51(2).

Chari, V., L. Christiano, and P. Kehoe. (2008). "Facts and Myths about the Financial Crisis of 2008," Minneapolis Federal Reserve Bank Working Paper #666, October.

Chaudhry, K. (1997). *The Price of Wealth: Economies and Institutions in the Middle East* (Ithaca: Cornell University Press).

Chhaochharia, V. and L. Laeven. (2008). "Sovereign Wealth Funds: Their Investment Strategies and Performance," CEPR Discussion Paper No. DP6959. Available at SSRN: http://ssrn.com/abstract=1308030

Clark, W. (2005). *Petrodollar Warfare* (Gabriola Island, Canada: New Society)

Coll, S. (2004). *Ghost Wars: The Secret History of the CIA, Afghanistan, and Bin Laden, from the Soviet Invasion to September 10, 2001* (London: Penguin).

Cooper, R. (2008). "Global Imbalances: Globalization, Demography, and Sustainability," *Journal of Economic Perspectives* 22(3).

Corden, W. M. (1977). *Economic Policy, Exchange Rates, and the International System* (Chicago: University of Chicago Press).

Crystal, J. (1995). *Oil and Politics in the Gulf: Rulers and Merchants in Kuwait and Qatar* (New York: Cambridge University Press).

Dahl, C. (2004). *International Energy Markets: Understanding Pricing, Policies, and Profits* (Tulsa, OK: Penn Well).

Deaton, A. (2006). "Measuring Poverty," in Banerjee, A., R. Bénabou, and D. Mookherjee (eds.), *Understanding Poverty* (Oxford: Oxford University Press).

Deffeyes, K. (2005). *Beyond Oil: The View from Hubbert's Peak* (New York: Hill and Wang).

Dooley, M., D. Folkerts-Landau and P. Garber. (2003). "An Essay on the Revived Bretton Woods System," NBER working paper # 9971.

Dooley, M., D. Folkerts-Landau, and P. Garber. (2004). "The Revived Bretton Woods System: Alive and Well," Deutsche Bank, December.

Dooley, M., D. Folkerts-Landau, and P. Garber. (2004b). "Direct Investment, Rising Real Wages, and the Absorption of Excess Labor in the Periphery," NBER working paper 10626, July.

Dooley, M., D. Folkerts-Landau, and P. Garber. (2004c) "The Revived Bretton Woods System: The Effects of Periphery Intervention and Reserve Management on Interest Rates and Exchange Rates in Center Countries," NBER WP #10332, March.

Dornbush, R., Y. Park, and S. Glaessens. (2000). "Contagion: Understanding How It Spreads," *The World Bank Research Observer* 15(2), August.

Douglas, J., M. Nelson, and K. Schwartz. (2006). "Fueling the Dragon's Flame: How China's Energy Demands Affect Its Relationships in the Middle East," report to U.S.-China Economic and Security Review Commission, September 14, 2006. Available at http://www.uscc.gov/researchpapers/2006/China_ME_FINAL.pdf

Dungey, M., R. Fry, B. Gonzalez-Hermosillo, and V. Martin. (2008). "Empirical Modeling of Contagion: A Review of Methodologies," IMF working paper WP/04/78.

Durlauf, S. and D. Quah. (1999). "The New Empirics of Economics Growth," in Taylor, J. and M. Woodward (eds.), *Handbook of Macroeconomics* 1A, Chapter 4 (Amsterdam: North Holland).

Ebrahim-Zadeh, C. (2003). "Back to Basics: Dutch Disease. Too Much Wealth Managed Unwisely," *Finance and Development*, 40(1).

Eichengreen, B. (2004). "Global Imbalances and the Lessons of Bretton Woods," NBER working paper 10497, May.

Eichengreen, B. (2008). *Globalizing Capital: A History of the International Monetary System* 2nd Edition (Princeton, NJ: Princeton University Press).

El-Beblawi, H. (1980). "Dollar Crisis, Oil Prices, and Foreign Exchange Risks: The Case for Basket Currencies as Numeraire," *International Journal of Middle East Studies* 11.

El-Erian, M. (2008). *When Markets Collide: Investment Strategies for the Age of Global Economic Change* (New York: McGraw-Hill).

El-Gamal, M. (2006). *Islamic Finance: Law, Economics, and Practice* (New York: Cambridge University Press).

El-Gamal, M. and A. Jaffe. (2008). "Energy, Financial Contagion, and the Dollar," Baker Institute for Public Policy Working Paper Series: The Global Energy Market: Comprehensive Strategies to Meet Geopolitical and Financial Risks, online at http://www.rice.edu/nationalmedia/multimedia/contagion.pdf, May.

Ely, J., and J. Välimäki. (2002). "A Robust Folk Theorem for the Prisoner's Dilemma," *Journal of Economic Theory* 102(1).

Ferderer, P. (1996). "Oil Price Volatility and the Macroeconomy," *Journal of Macroeconomics* Winter.

Fischer, S. (1993). "The Role of Macroeconomic Factors in Growth," *Journal of Monetary Economics* 32(3).

Fischer, S. (2003). "Globalization and Its Challenges," *American Economic Review* 93(2).

Freedman, L. and E. Karsh (1993). *The Gulf Conflict 1990–1991* (Princeton, NJ: Princeton University Press).

Frieden, J. (2006). *Global Capitalism: Its Fall and Rise in the Twentieth Century* (New York: W. W. Norton).

Gambroni, E. and R. Newfarmer. (2009). "Trade Protection: Incipient but Worrisome Trends," World Bank Trade Note 37, at http://siteresources.worldbank.org/NEWS/Resources/Trade_Note_37.pdf

Gately, D. (1984). "A Ten Year Retrospective: OPEC and the World Oil Market," *Journal of Economic Literature* 22(3).

Gately, D. and H. Huntington (2002). "The Asymmetric Effects of Changes in Price and Income on Energy and Oil Demand," *Energy Journal* 23(1).

Gately, D. (2002). "How Plausible Is the Current Consensus Projection of Oil Below $25 and Persian Gulf Oil Capacity and Output Doubling by 2020?" *Energy Journal* 22 (4).

Gately, D. (2004). "OPEC's Incentives for Faster Output Growth," *Energy Journal* 25.

Gylfason, T. (2001). "Natural Resources, Education, and Economic Development," *European Economic Review*, 45(4–6), pp. 847–59.

Hamilton, J. (1983). "Oil and the Macroeconomy Since World War II," *Journal of Political Economy* 91(2).

Hamilton, J. (2008). "Understanding Oil Prices," NBER Working Paper No. w14492, November.

Hartley, P. and K. Medlock. (2006). "Political and Economic Influences on the Future World Market for Natural Gas," in Jaffe, A., D. Victor and M. Hayes (eds.) *The Geopolitics of Natural Gas* (New York: Cambridge University Press).

Hayek, F. (1995). *Contra Keynes and Cambridge: Essays, Correspondence*, Caldwell, B. (ed.)

(Chicago: Chicago University Press).

Hickman, B., H. Huntington, and J. Sweeney. (1987). *Macroeconomic Impacts of Energy Shocks* (New York: North Holland).

Higgins, M., T. Klitgaard, and R. Lerman. (2006). "Current Issues in Economics and Finance," *Federal Reserve Bank of New York: Current Issues* 12 (9).

Hiskett, W. (1932). *The Tyranny of Gold: A Way to Escape* (London: William and Norgate, Ltd.).

Hotelling, H. (1931). "The Economics of Exhaustible Resources," *Journal of Political Economy* 39(2), pp. 171–200.

Humphreys, M., J. Sachs, and J. Stiglitz (eds.). (2007). *Escaping the Resource Curse* (New York: Columbia University Press).

Ibn Khaldun. (2004). *Al-Muqaddimah: An Introduction to History* (Princeton, NJ: Princeton University Press).

International Energy Agency. (2006). *World Energy Outlook 2006* (Paris: IEA).

International Energy Agency. (2008). *World Energy Outlook 2008* (Paris: IEA).

International Monetary Fund. (2008). "Sovereign Wealth Funds – A Work Agenda," February 29.

Jaffe, A. (2004). "Geopolitics of Oil," in Cleveland, C. (ed.) *Encyclopedia of Energy* (San Diego, CA: Elsevier Publishers).

Jaffe, A., D. Victor and M. Hayes (eds.). (2006). *The Geopolitics of Natural Gas* (New York: Cambridge University Press).

Jaffe, A. and R. Soligo. (2006). "Market Structure in the New Gas Economy: Is Cartelization Possible?" Jaffe, A., D. Victor and M. Hayes (eds.). (2006). *The Geopolitics of Natural Gas* (New York: Cambridge University Press).

Jensen, J. (2003) "The LNG Revolution," *Energy Journal* 24(2).

Johnson, S. (2007). "The Rise of Sovereign Wealth Funds," *Finance and Development* September.

Jones, A. (2008). "Inflation Under the Roman Empire," *The Economic History Review* 5(3).

Karl, T. (1997). *The Paradox of Plenty: Oil Booms and Petro-States* (Berkeley: University of California Press).

Karmin, C. (2008). *Biography of the Dollar* (New York: Crown Business).

Kechichian, J. (1999). "Trends in Saudi National Security," *Middle East Journal* 53(2).

Kindleberger, C. (1993). *A financial history of western Europe* (Oxford: Oxford University Press).

Kindleberger, C. and R. Aliber. (2005). *Manias, Panics, and Crashes: A History of Financial Crises*, Fifth Edition (New York: John Wiley & Sons).

Kissinger, H. (1982). *Years of Upheaval* (Boston: Little Brown).

Kissinger, H. (1999). *Years of Renewal* (New York: Simon and Schuster).

Klare, M. (2002). *Resource Wars: The New Landscape of Global Conflict* (New York: Holt).

Kodres, L., and M. Pristsker. (2002). "A Rational Expectations Model of Financial Contagion," *Journal of Finance* LVII (2).

Lawrence, B. (2005). *Messages to the World: The Statements of Osama bin Laden* (New York: Verso).

Lee, K., N. Shawn, and R. Ratti. (1995). "Oil Shocks and the macroeconomy: The Role of Price variability," *Energy Journal* 16(4).

Lei, V., C. Noussair, and C. Plott. (2004). "Nonspeculative Bubbles in Experimental Asset Markets: Lack of Common Knowledge of Rationality vs. Actual Irrationality," *Econometrica* 69(4).

Lei, W., and L. Xuejun. (2007). "China or the United States: Which Threatens Energy Security?" *OPEC Review* 31(3).

Medlock, K. and P. Hartley. (2004). "The Role of Nuclear Power in Enhancing Japan's Energy Security," James A. Baker III Institute for Public Policy Working Paper, March. At: http://www.ruf.rice.edu/~econ/faculty/Hartley/TEPCO_FINAL.pdf

Medlock, K. and R. Soligo. (2001). "Economic Development and End-Use Energy Demand," *The Energy Journal* 22(2).

Medlock, K. and R. Soligo. (2002). "Automobile Ownership and Economic Development – Forecasting Motor Vehicle Stocks to 2015," *The Journal of Transport Economics and Policy* Spring.

Minsky, H. (1982). *Can "It" Happen Again: Essays on Instability and Finance* (New York: M. E. Sharpe).

Minsky, H. (2008). *Stabilizing an Unstable Economy* (New York: McGraw-Hill).

Moore, P. (2004). *Doing Business in the Middle East: Politics and Economic Crisis in Jordan and Kuwait* (New York: Cambridge University Press).

Mork, K., H. Mysen, and O. Olson. (1994). "Macroeconomic Responses to Oil Price Increases and Decreases in Seven OECD Countries," *Energy Journal* 4.

Morris, C. (2008). *The Trillion Dollar Meltdown: Easy Money, High Rollers, and the Great Credit Crash* (New York: Public Affairs).

Nasr, V. and R. Tayeyh. (2008). "The Costs of Containing Iran," *Foreign Affairs* 87(1).

Nordhaus, W. (1980). "Oil and Economic Performance in Industrial Countries," Brookings Papers on Economic Activity, Vol. 2.

Neuhaus, M. (2006). *The Impact of FDI on Economic Growth: An Analysis for the Transition Countries of Central and Eastern Europe* (Heidelberg: Physica-Verlag).

O'Sullivan, M. (2003). *Shrewd Sanctions: Statecraft and State Sponsors of Terrorism* (Washington, DC: The Brookings Institution Press).

Parasiliti, A. (2001). "The Military in Iraqi Politics," in Kechichian, J. (ed.) *Iran, Iraq, and the Arab Gulf States* (New York: Palgrave).

Phillips, K. (2006). *American Theocracy: The Perils and Politics of Radical Religion, Oil, and Borrowed Money in the 21*st *Century.* (New York: Penguin).

Pollack, K. (2004). *The Persian Puzzle* (New York: Random House).

Pollin, R., H. Garrett-Peltier, J. Heintz, and H. Scharber. (2008). "Green Recovery: A Program to Create Good Jobs and Start Building a Low-Carbon Economy," Center for American Progress, September. Available at www.americanprogress.org or www.peri.umass.edu

Poon, S.H., M. Rockinger, and J. Tawn. (2004). "Extreme-Value Dependence in Financial Markets: Diagnostics, Models, and Financial Implications," *Review of Financial Studies* 17.

Quandt, W. (1981). *Saudi Arabia in the 1980s: Foreign Policy, Security and Oil* (Washington, DC: The Brookings Institution).

Roberts, P. (2004). *The End of Oil: On the Edge of a Perilous New World* (Boston: Houghton Mifflin Company).

Roubini, N. and B. Setser. (2005). "Will the Bretton Woods 2 Regime Unravel Soon? The Risk of a Hard Landing in 2005–2006," New York University and Oxford University, February.

Sachs, J. and A. Warner. (2001). "The Curse of Natural Resources," *European Economic Review*, 45(4-6), pp. 827–38.

Salman, R. (2004). "The US Dollar and Oil Pricing Revisited," *Middle East Economic Survey* XLVII(1).

Shiller, R. (2000). *Irrational Exuberance* (Princeton, NJ: Princeton University Press).

Simmons, M. (2006). *Twilight in the Desert: The Coming Saudi Oil Shock and the World Economy* (New York: John Wiley & Sons).

Simon, J. (1995). *The Ultimate Resource 2* (Princeton, NJ: Princeton University Press).

Slater, J. and M. Phillips. (2007). "Will Weakness in Dollar Bust Some Couples?", *Wall*

Street Journal, May 22.

Smith, V., G. Suchanek, and A. Williams. (1988). "Bubbles, Crashes, and Endogenous Expectations in Experimental Spot Asset Markets" *Econometrica* 56(5).

Soros, G. (2008). *The New Paradigm for Financial Markets: The Credit Crisis of 2008 and What It Means* (New York: Public Affairs).

Spiro, D. (1999). *The Hidden Hand of American Hegemony: Petrodollar Recycling and International Markets* (Ithaca, New York: Cornell University Press).

Stobaugh, P. and D. Yergin. eds. (1979). *Energy future: Report of the Energy Project at the Harvard Business School* (New York: Random House).

Summers, L. (2004). "The U.S. Current Account Deficit and the Global Economy," Lecture at the Per Jacobson Foundation, Washington, DC, October 3.

Sunstein, C. and R. Thaler. (2003) "Libertarian Paternalism Is Not an Oxymoron," *The University of Chicago Law Review* 70(4).

Taylor, J. (1999). *Monetary Policy Rules* (Chicago: University of Chicago Press and NBER).

Thaler, R. and C. Sustein. (2003). "Libertarian Paternalism," *American Economic Review* 93(2).

Tripp, C. (2000). *A History of Iraq* (New York: Cambridge University Press).

UNDP. (2005). *Human Development Report 2005: International Cooperation at a Crossroads – Aid, Trade, and Security in an Unequal World* (New York: UNDP).

Veblen, T. (2001). *The Theory of the Leisure Class* (New York: Modern Library Classical).

Yergin, D. (1993). *The Prize: The Epic Quest for Oil, Money, and Power* (New York: Free Press).

Yergin, D. and M. Hillenbrand. (1982). *Global Insecurity* (Boston: Houghton Mifflin Company).

Zahlan, R. (2001). "The Impact of U.S. Policy on the Stability of the Gulf States: A Historian's View," in Kechichian, J. (ed.) *Iran, Iraq, and the Arab Gulf States* (New York: Palgrave).

Index